A GUIDE TO
CIVIL WAR MAPS
IN
THE NATIONAL ARCHIVES

A GUIDE TO
CIVIL WAR MAPS
∽ IN ∾
THE NATIONAL ARCHIVES

THE NATIONAL ARCHIVES

NATIONAL ARCHIVES AND RECORDS ADMINISTRATION

WASHINGTON, D.C. 1986

Cover: Map of the Battlefield of Antietam, prepared by Lieut. Wm. H. Willcox (RG 77: G 443, vol. 9, p. 10).

ISBN 0-911333-36-3
PUBLISHED FOR THE
NATIONAL ARCHIVES AND RECORDS ADMINISTRATION
BY THE
NATIONAL ARCHIVES TRUST FUND BOARD

Library of Congress Cataloging-in-Publication Data

A Guide to Civil War maps in the National Archives.

    Includes index.
    1. United States—History—Civil War, 1861-1865—
Maps—Bibliography—Catalogs. 2. United States.
National Archives—Catalogs. I. United States.
National Archives and Records Administration.
Z1242.G85 1986 [468.9] 016.911'73   86-5132
ISBN 0-911333-36-3

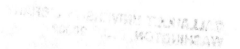

FOREWORD

The National Archives and Records Administration is responsible for administering the permanently valuable records of the Federal Government. These archival holdings, now amounting to more than 1.3 million cubic feet, date from the days of the Continental Congress and include the basic records of the legislative, judicial, and executive branches of the Federal Government. The Presidential libraries of Herbert Hoover, Franklin D. Roosevelt, Harry S Truman, Dwight D. Eisenhower, John F. Kennedy, Lyndon B. Johnson, and Gerald R. Ford contain the papers of those Presidents and many of their associates in office. NARA is also responsible for the presidential papers of Richard M. Nixon, which are stored in the Washington, D.C., area, and of Jimmy Carter, which are stored in Atlanta, Ga. These research resources document significant events in our Nation's history, but most of them are preserved for their continuing practical use in the ordinary processes of government and for the research use of scholars, students, and other individual researchers.

To make its records better known and easier to use, the National Archives publishes many guides and other finding aids. This guide is the second edition of *Civil War Maps in the National Archives*, which was first published in 1964 for the centennial of the Civil War. One of the objectives of the national Civil War Centennial Commission was to promote the publication of books and the collection of sources, which will stand as a permanent memorial of this commission." The National Archives, by revising *Civil War Maps in the National Archives*, continues to meet that objective.

PREFACE TO THE SECOND EDITION

When it was first published in 1964, *Civil War Maps in the National Archives* reflected the scholarly and popular interest in the Civil War during its centennial. This second edition of *Civil War Maps* underscores that continuing interest in the war.'

Three significant changes have been made in this new edition. It includes maps from Record Group 109, War Department Collection of Confederate Records, that were not included in the first edition. File numbers of individual maps have been inserted (in parentheses) within paragraphs that describe maps filed as part of Record Group 77, Records of the Office of the Chief of Engineers; these allow the staff of the National Archives to identify and locate specific maps more quickly. More illustrations have been included to show the type and variety of maps available.

Many National Archives staff members worked on this publication. The 1964 edition was prepared by Charlotte N. Ashby, Franklin W. Burch, Thomas A. Devan, and Laura E. Kelsay under the direction of A. Philip Muntz. Herman R. Friis provided advice and assistance.

This second edition was prepared by William H. Cunliffe, William J. Heynen, John Dwyer, and Charles Taylor. Mary C. Ryan, John H. Hedges, Camille Cormier, Michael Honey, and Kevin Hardwick helped with the research and revisions. Shelby G. Bale and Constance Potter edited the manuscript, and Richard B. Smith guided it through production.

CONTENTS

LIST OF ILLUSTRATIONS

INTRODUCTION

Civil War Maps in the National Archives lists the approximately 8,000 Civil War maps, charts, and plans in the Cartographic and Architectural Branch of the National Archives, the largest single body of cartographic records pertaining to the American Civil War.

The records described in this guide are maps, plans, and charts containing information relating directly to Civil War operations and installations. Most of the material described dates from the war and was produced for use by the military forces or to accompany official reports. Many of the maps that are contemporary with the war do not deal specifically with military operations, but do provide information concerning the areas directly affected by the conflict. A number of postwar maps contain military information, usually prepared for historical purposes or in connection with official investigations of Civil War operations.

Almost all of the Civil War maps in the National Archives are Federal maps, prepared by or for the Union forces or other agencies of the Federal Government. A few are commercially published maps that were acquired for use and annotated by personnel in Federal military or civilian offices. The Confederate maps described in this guide were, for the most part, captured by Union officers. Maps that are filed with Civil War correspondence, reports, and similar documents are not included here.

Like all the other records in the National Archives, the maps and related materials described are assigned to record groups. These usually consist of the records of a single Federal agency, typically at the bureau level, and its predecessors. The record groups described in this guide are listed in the table of contents as well as enumerated alphabetically and numerically on pages 3–71. More than half the maps described are from Record Group 77, Records of the Office of the Chief of Engineers, which includes the records of the Corps of Topographical Engineers and the Corps of Engineers, the organizations responsible for most of the military mapping accomplished during the war. Some of the other record groups containing Civil War maps are Records of the Coast and Geodetic Survey, Record Group 23; Records of the Office of the Quartermaster General, Record Group 92; Records of the Adjutant General's Office, 1780s-1917, Record Group 94; and Records of U.S. Army Continental Commands, 1821-1920, Record Group 393.

These maps are useful for many types of research. By using these maps, historians can document the actions of military units and organizations throughout the war or in a particular battle. Local historians can use the maps to trace old roads and boundaries, and many of the maps show the topography of an area or how a river flowed in the 1860s. Other maps show who owned the property at the site of a battle—information that can be useful to genealogists.

All of the maps described are permanently on file and are available for examination at the Cartographic and Architectural Branch. Reproductions may be ordered for a fee. Available reproductions include electrostatic copies, photocopies, and color slides. Prices depend on the type of reproduction used and the size of the original map. To obtain the latest information about prices and availability of reproductions, contact the Cartographic and Architectural Branch, National Archives and Records Administration, Washington, DC 20408.

HOW TO USE THIS PUBLICATION

Civil War Maps is divided into two parts. Part I is a general guide to the approximately 8,000 Civil War maps in the Cartographic and Architectural Branch. Part II describes selected maps in more detail. The special introductions to parts I and II describe the arrangement of entries and provide additional information.

Index. Locations of Civil War battles and campaigns, such as Atlanta and Vicksburg, appear in several widely scattered entries because Civil War maps can be found in several different record groups. For this reason, researchers should consult the index before beginning a search for particular information.

The index refers to places shown on the maps as well as people responsible for the creation of the maps. The index refers to entry numbers, *not* page numbers.

Entry numbers, found at the beginning of each entry, are indicated by the designation "1.00" for part I and "2.00" for part II. For example: "1.35. Operations at Blakely" is the 35th entry in part I; "2.130. Map of the Country between Vicksburg and Meridian, Miss." is the 130th entry in part II.

Map file numbers appear in both parts I and II. In part I, the numbers appear in parentheses. For example: operations of the Union forces under Gen. John Pope (Q 86-1 through Q 86-3). In part II, the map file number is at the end of the entry and always begins with "RG," which is the abbreviation for Record Group. For example, RG 77: Dr. 139-12; or RG 77: S 4-2; or RG 77: US 231.

These map file numbers indicate the location of the maps in the National Archives and are necessary to find the map or make a copy of it. In part I, only those map file numbers most useful for retrieving maps in Record Group 77 by the staff of the National Archives are shown. When ordering a map reproduction by mail, please use the map file number as shown in the text; if no map file number is shown, use the entry number ("1._____") and the staff will consult additional indexes to locate the map.

PART I

Maps are described in this part by government hierarchy and thereunder by National Archives record group. Under a record group, map descriptions are arranged in numbered entries on the basis of the area, subject, or, occasionally, origin of the maps. The spellings of names are those found on the maps. When place names vary from map to map, the modern spelling is used.

Congress

Records of the U.S. Senate. RG 46

Maps relating to the Civil War in this record group consist of manuscript and annotated maps forwarded to the Senate from the War Department and maps published for Congress at the special request of the Senate.

1.1. Maps Submitted to the Military Committee of the Senate. 1865. 16 items.

Manuscript and annotated maps, numbered from 1 to 22 with some gaps, submitted to the Military Committee of the Senate, 38th Congress, and signed Richard Delafield, General and Chief Engineer, U.S. Army, February 1865. Among these are published maps of the United States annotated to show the limits of the loyal States in 1861, the area controlled by U.S. forces, November 1864 (see entry 2.3), and boundaries of Federal military departments and divisions in 1865 (see entry 2.4). The remaining maps are published, some with annotations, and cover the military departments in the South, the operations against Richmond and Petersburg, the Atlanta campaign, the siege of Vicksburg, the activities at Fort Fisher, N.C., and the defenses of Washington, D.C.

1.2. Gettysburg, Pa. 1880. 4 items.

Maps, published by order of the Senate, of the field of operations of Gregg's (Union) and Stuart's (Confederate) cavalries at Gettysburg, July 2 and 3, 1863, surveyed by Frank O. Maxson, Civil Engineer, under the direction of John B. Bachelder. These maps are numbered 4 (6 p.m. to 8 p.m., July 2), 10 (4 a.m. to 11 a.m., July 3), 11 (11 a.m. to 2 p.m., July 3), and 12 (2 p.m. to 5 p.m., July 3).

Records of the U.S. House of Representatives. RG 233

The following maps were published in House documents.

1.3. Mobile Bay, Ala., and Nashville, Tenn. 1866. 2 items.

Published maps of the siege operations at Spanish Fort, Mobile Bay, April 8 and 9, 1865, and the battlefields in front of Nashville, December 15 and 16, 1864. These maps, which appeared in the report of the Chief Engineer of the Army, published as part of *H. Ex. Doc.* 1, 39 Cong., 2 sess., show troop positions and Union and Confederate defenses.

1.4. Chickamauga, Ga., and Chattanooga, Tenn. 1901. 1 vol.

An Atlas of the Battlefields of Chickamauga, Chattanooga and Vicinity, compiled by the Chickamauga and Chattanooga National Park Commission and republished, with additional position maps, by order of Congress as *H. Doc.* 514, 56 Cong., 2 sess. The atlas consists of 14 published maps showing troop positions in successive stages of the battle at Chickamauga, movements from Chickamauga to Rossville and Chattanooga, and plans of the engagements at Wauhatchie and Brown's Ferry, Orchard Knob, Lookout Mountain, and Missionary Ridge.

DEPARTMENT OF THE TREASURY

General Records of the Department of the Treasury. RG 56

During and after the Civil War, special agents of the Department of the Treasury were concerned with enforcing restrictions on commerce in the Confederate States, with the collection of abandoned and captured property in these States, and with carrying out the regulations for the welfare and employment of freedmen.

1.5. Land and Property Maps. 1860-74. 12 items.

Manuscript, published, and annotated maps of land districts along the Mississippi River in Arkansas, Louisiana, and Mississippi, prepared or used by special agents of the Treasury Department and showing plantations—some still occupied by owners, some abandoned by owners, and some leased by the Treasury Department; miscellaneous maps of parts of Louisiana along the Mississippi River; and General Land Office published maps of Louisiana and Florida.

1.6. Government Farms for Freedmen. N.d. 2 items.

Maps showing the locations of Government farms for freedmen in Virginia and North Carolina.

Records of the Internal Revenue Service. RG 58

Under an act of August 5, 1861, direct tax commissions were created to levy and collect Federal taxes in the Confederate States; subsequent acts passed during the Civil War and Reconstruction era further regulated their activities. The records of the Direct Tax Commission for the District of South Carolina were transferred with the functions of the discontinued Commission to the Collector of Internal Revenue at Charleston, S.C., in 1870.

1.7. South Carolina Parish and City Maps and Survey Notes. 1862-67. 70 items.

Manuscript, annotated, and published maps and related records used by the Commission in establishing the amount of taxes to be levied. These consist of maps of the Parish of St. Helena and the cities of Beaufort and Port Royal showing information about property owners, school farms, and the sales of land. Among these is a large-scale map of the Parish of St. Helena prepared at the direction of the Commission and showing the rectangular land subdivision carried out under the provisions of the acts of June 7 and July 17, 1862, and February 6, 1863, relating to the collection of direct taxes and the confiscation of land and the acts of March 3, 1865, and July 16, 1866, creating and extending the Bureau of Refugees, Freedmen, and Abandoned Lands. Other records consist of 29 field survey notebooks of surveys of the sea islands in the Parishes of St. Helena and St. Luke and of a survey of Port Royal.

DEPARTMENT OF WAR

Records of the Adjutant General's Office, 1780s–1917.
RG 94

The War Records Office, which was established for the purpose of publishing the official records of the Civil War, was merged with the Records and Pension Office of the War Department in 1899, and in 1904 the latter agency became a part of the Adjutant General's Office. The entries below describe records of the War Records Office, which was responsible for preparing the 128-volume work entitled *The War of the Rebellion: A Compilation of the Official Records of the Union and Confederate Armies*, 1881-1901. The compilation of this work was first authorized in 1864, and in 1874 provision was made for an atlas to accompany the textual volumes. The *Atlas to Accompany the Official Records of the Union and Confederate Armies* was published between 1891 and 1895 as a series of separate folios. In 1903 the atlas was issued in two bound volumes as *H. Misc. Doc.* 261, 52 Cong., 1 sess.

The cartographic records of the War Records Office consist of three series: the published atlas; maps used in compiling the atlas; and other maps related to the atlas.

1.8. The Published Atlas. 1891-95, 1903. 5 inches.

Retained as record copies are several of the separately published folios, 1891-95, and the bound, two-volume atlas, 1903. The atlas contains 175 plates, most of which are composed of several small maps illustrating campaigns, battles, skirmishes, and routes of campaigns followed by the opposing forces. Also included are 26 sheets entitled "General Topographic Map," which cover most of the southeastern and south-central United States and show drainage and relief features, railroads, and place names. Another group of maps shows the boundaries of Union and Confederate territorial commands for given dates. Other illustrations include plans and views of forts and defended areas; pictures of uniforms, flags, and badges; and construction drawings of defensive and offensive equipment. Nearly every item in the atlas contains a reference to related textual material. The atlas also contains an index to names of commanding officers and senior and assistant Engineer officers responsible for preparing individual maps and an index to areas and campaigns represented.

1.9. Maps Used in Compiling the Atlas. 1861-89. 800 items.

An incomplete collection of manuscript, annotated, and published maps, most of which were reproduced with only editorial changes or otherwise used in compiling some of the maps appearing on plates 1 through 150 of the published atlas. Among these are manuscript maps sent in with official records or reports of Union officers; manuscript maps sent in from personal collections of former Union and Confederate officers or from collections in local archives or historical societies; published maps with additions or corrections made by Union or Confederate officers; and published maps, many with editorial changes, compiled by Government agencies and commercial firms during and after the war.

The records in this collection consist primarily of battlefield maps, maps of local terrain, plans of Union and Confederate defenses, maps showing campaign routes, and a few views of defensive works (see entries 2.222, 2.237, 2.243, and 2.257). Most of them are stamped "Union" or "Confederate" to indicate their source and with a plate number corresponding to the plate numbers in the published atlas. Many also have correspondence numbers relating to textual documents. Arranged by plate number. The comprehensive index appearing in the published atlas serves as an index to this collection.

1.10. Other Maps Related to the Atlas. 1890, 1896. 2 items.

A blueprint of a copy of a map of Richmond, Va., and vicinity, originally compiled under the direction of the Chief Engineer of the Department of Northern Virginia, C.S.A., 1862, and copied in the War Records Office in 1890, showing roads, drainage features, buildings, names of residents, and swampy areas; and a manuscript map of the assault on Kennesaw Mountain, Ga., June 27, 1864, showing Confederate and Union positions plotted from postwar reports by participants, originally compiled by F. B. James, formerly a captain in the 52d Ohio Volunteer Infantry, and received in the War Records Office in 1896.

Records of U.S. Army Continental Commands, 1821–1920. RG 393

Before the Civil War began, the United States was divided into geographical areas to facilitate peacetime operations of the Army. As the war progressed, the organization of military territorial commands became increasingly complex, and frequent changes in their boundaries were necessary. By 1863 the usual organization of territorial commands consisted of geographic divisions, each division divided into two or more departments, and the departments usually subdivided into districts. Also, there were departments that were not assigned to divisions. Maps showing the boundaries of these territorial commands during the war may be found among the records of the U.S. Senate, the records of the Office of the Chief of Engineers, and in the *Atlas to Accompany the Official Records of the Union and Confederate Armies*, a record copy of which is among the records of the Adjutant General's Office. An 1881 publication of the Adjutant General's Office entitled *Notes Illustrating the Military Geography of the United States*, compiled by Raphael P. Thian, contains information on the establishment and composition of territorial commands of the United States to 1881 and on the assignment of commanding officers to them.

During the Civil War, troop commands, usually armies or army corps, were assigned to operate within military departments, and the chief of the military department was usually the commanding general of the troop command. The major mapping activity of these commands was the preparation of maps of local areas for the use of commanders and other officers. Of special significance are the photographic reproductions of maps printed in the field by Capt. Wm. Margedant's "Quick Method for Field Map Printing." The records of a military unit often include maps compiled after the war to illustrate wartime campaigns of the commanding officer even though he was not connected with the unit during the war.

The cartographic records described below as part of Record Group 393 are published maps. Many manuscript maps compiled under the direction of Civil War Army commands are to be found in the Civil Works and Fortifications Map Files of the Office of the Chief of Engineers, Record Group 77. Since the first edition of this guide was published in 1964, certain maps have been reassigned to Record Group 77. These reassignments are noted.

The records are arranged and described below according to command. Records of armies assigned to territorial commands are described with the records of the corresponding territorial command since there is little distinction as to the final responsibility for the maps.

MILITARY DIVISIONS

MILITARY DIVISION OF THE GULF

The Military Division of the Gulf, composed of the Military Departments of the Mississippi, Louisiana, Texas, and Florida, was established June 27, 1865, and encompassed much of the area occupied by the former Military Department of the Gulf. Gen. Philip H. Sheridan was appointed commanding officer of this division, and the maps illustrate his campaigns in Virginia.

1.11. Sheridan's Campaigns in Virginia. 1865. 6 items.
Maps identified as Engineer's Office, Military Division of the Gulf. Maps 3 through 6 and an unnumbered map. No. 3 is a map of the battlefield of Dinwiddie Court House, March 31, 1865, showing troop positions (now filed as Div. Gulf-1); No. 4 is a map of the battlefield of Five Forks, April 1, 1865, showing troop positions (now filed as Div. Gulf-2); No. 5 is a map of the Upper Potomac from McCoy's Ferry to Conrad's Ferry showing operations of the Army of the Shenandoah commanded by Sheridan and indicating the different routes into the Shenandoah Valley and points of encounter with the Confederate forces in August and September 1864 (now filed as Div. Gulf-3); No. 6 is a map of central Virginia showing Sheridan's campaigns, 1864-65 (reassigned to RG 77: G 317-1); and a second version of No. 6 also shows the line of Gen. R. E. Lee's retreat (reassigned to RG 77: G 317-2). The unnumbered one is a map of the battlefield of Cedar Creek, October 19, 1864, and of the cavalry fight at Tomsbrook, October 9, 1864, showing troop positions at both engagements (reassigned to RG 77: WDMC 62-Va.).

MILITARY DIVISION OF THE MISSISSIPPI

The Division of the Mississippi was established October 16, 1863, to include the Departments of the Cumberland, Ohio, and Tennessee. The maps described in entry 1.12 were prepared in the division during the war. The map described in entry 1.13 was prepared after the war to illustrate the activities of Gen. W. T. Sherman, who was in command of the division shortly before it was disbanded in 1866.

1.12. Georgia and Tennessee. 1864. 4 items.
Maps of middle and western Tennessee showing roads (reassigned to RG 77: T 81); a map showing the area of

army movements around Chattanooga, Tenn., prepared to accompany a report by Gen. U. S. Grant; and a map showing the advance upon and operations around Atlanta, Ga.

1.13. Sherman's Campaigns in the Southeastern States. 1865. 1 item.

A map of the area from Memphis east to Atlanta and north to Washington, showing the marches of Union forces under the command of Sherman, 1863-65 (reassigned to RG 77: US 254 1/2).

MILITARY DIVISION OF THE MISSOURI

The Military Division of the Missouri was originally organized in January 1865 and disbanded in June 1865; it was reorganized in August 1866 and in existence until 1890. The maps of this division that pertain to the Civil War were made after the war; one illustrates activities of Sheridan, who commanded the division.

1.14. Battlefield of Chickamauga, Ga. 1879. 1 item (reassigned to RG 77: N 174).

1.15. Sheridan's Campaigns in Virginia. 1882. 1 item.

A reprinting, with modifications, of map No. 6 described in entry 1.11, showing Sheridan's campaigns in Virginia, 1864-65.

MILITARY DIVISION OF THE TENNESSEE

The Military Division of the Tennessee was established June 27, 1865, and disbanded in August 1866. The one Civil War map of this division illustrates activities of the Army of the Cumberland, which operated in the area later assigned to the division.

1.16. Campaigns of the Army of the Cumberland in the Southeastern States. N.d. 1 item.

A map showing routes of the Army of the Cumberland by colored symbols. The route of Jefferson Davis' flight is also shown.

MILITARY DEPARTMENTS AND ARMIES

MILITARY DEPARTMENT AND ARMY OF THE CUMBERLAND

The Department of the Cumberland was originally organized on August 15, 1861, to include the States of Kentucky and Tennessee. As the war progressed the department included only the eastern parts of Tennessee and those parts of northern Alabama and Georgia occu-

pied by Union forces. The Army of the Cumberland was assigned to the department. The department was disbanded on June 27, 1865.

Most of the cartographic records of the department and of the army were compiled under the direction of Capt. William E. Merrill or Capt. Nathaniel Michler, both of whom served as Chief Engineer of the department and of the army.

1.17. Kentucky and Tennessee. 1862-65. 48 items.

Maps of middle and eastern Tennessee and parts of adjoining States, dated 1862 and 1865 (reassigned to RG 77: WDMC 44-Tenn.; T 84-3); a series of maps covering the Chattanooga region (see entry 2.182); a map of Chattanooga and its approaches, and a map showing Confederate fortifications near the city (reassigned to RG 77: T 57); an information map of the area between Cottonport, Tenn., and Dalton, Ga. (see entry 2.185); maps of battlefields including Chaplin Hills (reassigned to RG 77: T 27) and Logan's Cross Roads, Ky. (reassigned to RG 77: T 50), and Franklin (reassigned to RG 77: T 89-1), Stones River, and Nashville, Tenn. (reassigned to RG 77: T 86-4); a city plan of Murfreesboro (reassigned to RG 77: T 47), and maps of the vicinities of Columbia (reassigned to RG 77: T 51), Decherd (reassigned to RG 77: T 117), Hillsboro (reassigned to RG 77: T 56-B), Jasper (reassigned to RG 77: T 102), Kingston (reassigned to RG 77: T 54), Murfreesboro, Nashville (reassigned to RG 77: T 34), Shelbyville (reassigned to RG 77: T 32), Tullahoma (reassigned to RG 77: T 39 and T 105), and Winchester, Tenn. (reassigned to RG 77: T 58), some of which were printed in the field by Captain Margedant's "Quick Method"; and topographic sketches of the country adjacent to turnpikes between Franklin and Columbia (reassigned to RG 77: T 80), Nashville and Gallatin (reassigned to RG 77: T 48), and Gallatin and Hartsville (reassigned to RG 77: T 40), Tenn.

1.18. Alabama and Georgia. 1863-65. 20 items.

A map of the Tennessee River through northern Alabama showing adjacent parts of Tennessee, Mississippi, and Georgia, 1865 (see entry 2.25); maps of parts of northern Georgia, some of which were printed on cloth in the field (see entries 2.53 and 2.66) and some of which were apparently printed by Margedant's "Quick Method" (see entry 2.73); a map of part of Murray County (reassigned to RG 77: N 40), and maps showing land survey lines in parts of Cobb, DeKalb and Fulton Counties (reassigned to RG 77: N 51; N 52; N 54), Ga., two of them with notes asking that the topographical engineers return them "with all the Information they are able to obtain"; a map of the battlefield of Chickamauga (reassigned to RG 77: N 56); maps of Selma, Ala. (reassigned to RG 77: Dr. 121-4), and Atlanta and vicinity (reassigned to RG 77: N 39) and Rome and vicinity (reassigned to RG 77: N 38), Ga., showing street patterns, defenses, and access roads; and a street plan of Atlanta (see entry 2.54).

MILITARY DEPARTMENT OF THE GULF

The Department of the Gulf was organized February 23, 1862, to include those parts of the States bordering the Gulf of Mexico occupied by Union forces. As the war progressed, the territory controlled by the department expanded. The department was disbanded June 27, 1865, and the Military Division of the Gulf was organized to administer the areas formerly in the department.

The cartographic records of this department consist of an incomplete set of maps numbered 1 through 54 with many gaps and several unnumbered maps. For the most part, these consist of maps of varying scales of the territory under the control of the department.

1.19. Alabama, Arkansas, Florida, Georgia, Louisiana, Mississippi, Tennessee, and Texas. 1863-65. 40 items.

A map of the Department of the Gulf in 1864; maps of States, groups of States, and parts of States composing the department (see entries 2.84 and 2.202); maps of the gulf coast, particularly in the vicinity of Mobile, Ala., Pensacola, Fla. (see entry 2.50), and the mouth of the Mississippi River; a map of a reconnaissance of the Mississippi River between Rodney, Miss., and Sargent's Bend below Vicksburg (reassigned to RG 77: M 119); maps showing defenses of Port Hudson, La.; maps showing defenses of Brazos Island, Tex. (reassigned to RG 77: Dr. 148-39 and Dr. 148-42); plans of Baton Rouge (reassigned to RG 77: M 110-2) and New Orleans, La., the one of Baton Rouge showing the site occupied by the Union garrison and the one of New Orleans showing defenses and approaches to the city (see entry 2.93); a plan of the siege operations at Fort Morgan, Ala. (see entry 2.23); maps showing the field of operation on the Bayou Teche and the battlefields of Fort Bisland and Irish Bend, La. (reassigned to RG 77: M 111); and a map of the Red River near Alexandria, La., showing the falls, with inset plans of the dams constructed to permit Admiral Porter's fleet to repass the falls (reassigned to RG 77: Dr. 133-81-B).

1.20. Manassas Battlefield, Va. 1864. 1 item.

A copy of a map of the battlefield of Manassas, July 21, 1861, compiled by the Army of the Potomac and published by the Department of the Gulf in 1864. The original map had an inscription stating that it was presented to the city of New Orleans by Gen. G. T. Beauregard (reassigned to RG 77: G 136).

ARMY OF THE JAMES

1.21. The Richmond-Petersburg Area, Va. 1865. 1 item.

A map showing the positions of entrenched lines occupied by Union forces.

MIDDLE DEPARTMENT

The Middle Department was established March 22, 1862, to include New Jersey, Pennsylvania, Delaware, the eastern parts of Maryland and Virginia, and Baltimore and vicinity, Md. The department underwent several changes during the war years, and at the end of the war included Pennsylvania, Delaware, West Virginia, parts of northern and eastern Maryland, and the eastern shore area of Virginia.

1.22. Baltimore City and County, Md. 1862-63. 2 items.

A map of the city showing defenses and military hospitals, 1862 (reassigned to RG 77: Dr. 135-8; duplicate filed as F 77); and a military map of the county showing forts, camps, roads, and names of residents, 1863 (see entry 2.105).

DEPARTMENT OF THE MISSISSIPPI

The Department of the Mississippi was originally organized March 11, 1862, to include the States of Kansas, Missouri, Iowa, Wisconsin, Illinois, Indiana, and Arkansas; parts of Michigan, Ohio, Kentucky, and Tennessee; and the Colorado, the Nebraska, and the Indian Territories. It was disbanded on September 9, 1862, and reorganized in November 1864 to include the State of Mississippi and Tennessee west of the Tennessee River. The maps of this department were prepared under the direction of the department as it existed in 1862.

1.23. Kentucky, Mississippi, Missouri, and Tennessee. 1862. 6 items.

A map of the country between Monterey, Tenn., and Corinth, Miss., showing entrenchments and routes of the Union forces in the advance upon Corinth in May 1862 (reassigned to RG 77: Dr. 138-10; duplicate filed as US 222-2); maps showing the defenses of Columbus, Ky. (reassigned to RG 77: T 60), and of Island No. 10 in the Mississippi River and the adjacent Kentucky shore (reassigned to RG 77: Dr. 132-9A; G 443, vol. 9, p. 8); a military map of St. Louis and vicinity showing defenses (reassigned to RG 77: Q 93); and two slightly differing maps of the battlefield of Shiloh, Tenn.

DEPARTMENT AND ARMY OF THE OHIO

The Department of the Ohio was organized originally on May 3, 1861, to include the States of Ohio, Indiana, and Illinois. It was disbanded on March 11, 1862, and reorganized August 19, 1862. The later organization included at various times the States of Ohio, Michigan, Indiana, Illinois, Wisconsin, Kentucky, and Tennessee. The department was permanently disbanded January 1, 1865.

1.24. Kentucky, Mississippi, and Tennessee. 1862-65. 5 items.

A large-scale military map of Kentucky and Tennessee (reassigned to RG 77: T 68-2); a map showing the route of the Army of the Ohio from Shiloh, Tenn., to Corinth, Miss., in 1862 (reassigned to RG 77: US 223); sketches of Decherd, Tenn. (reassigned to RG 77: T 30), and Corinth (reassigned to RG 77: S 13); and a map of the battlefield of Shiloh showing positions of General Buell's command.

ARMY OF THE POTOMAC

The Army of the Potomac operated in the Department of the Potomac, which was organized August 17, 1861, to include Virginia, Maryland, Delaware, and the District of Columbia. The maps compiled under the direction of this army constitute the largest volume of Civil War maps in this record group. Included are maps compiled by Coast Survey personnel assigned to the army. Most of these items are photographic reproductions of reconnaissance sketches compiled for the use of the army in the field.

1.25. Virginia, Maryland, West Virginia, and the District of Columbia. 1861-65. 160 items.

Maps mainly covering central and southeastern Virginia including a large-scale, detailed map of Virginia from Loudoun County south to King George County and west to Fauquier County with adjacent parts of the District of Columbia and Montgomery, Charles, and Prince Georges Counties, Md., showing roads, towns, names of rural residents, and the forts encircling Washington; a map of Harpers Ferry and vicinity, W. Va., showing defenses (reassigned to RG 77: US 491-20); a map showing roads into the District of Columbia (reassigned to RG 77: F 74); and a series of large-scale, detailed maps of Virginia covering the area from Leesburg to Petersburg from surveys by Nathaniel Michler (reassigned to RG 77: G 211). Maps of Frederick (reassigned to RG 77: F 68), Washington (reassigned to RG 77: F 67), and parts of Montgomery Counties, Md., the one of Montgomery County showing the approaches to Washington, D.C. (see entry 2.110). Maps of Loudoun, Frederick (reassigned to RG 77: G 93), and Rockbridge Counties (reassigned to RG 77: G 75-1), Va., and Jefferson (reassigned to RG 77: G 67) and Berkeley Counties, W. Va. Maps illustrating the Peninsular Campaign in Virginia, including maps of the area from Yorktown to Harrison's Landing, a map showing

positions of the siege of Yorktown, and a map showing the Confederate defenses of Yorktown (reassigned to RG 77: G 86). Maps of the battlefields of Antietam, Md. (reassigned to RG 77: X 6-18), and Todd's Tavern (reassigned to RG 77: G 185), North Anna (reassigned to RG 77: G 181), and Spotsylvania Court House (reassigned to RG 77: G 183), Va., showing troop positions and defenses. A plan of the siege of Petersburg, Va.

DEPARTMENT OF THE SOUTH

This department was created March 15, 1862, to include that part of the coasts of South Carolina, Georgia, and Florida held by Union forces. The department was disbanded June 27, 1865.

1.26. Georgia and South Carolina. 1862-65. 3 items.

A map showing the positions of the Union batteries in the reduction of Fort Pulaski, Ga., April 1862 (reassigned to RG 77: Dr. 129-14); and maps submitted to accompany a report of Maj. Gen. Q. A. Gillmore, Commanding the Department of the South, showing the defenses of Charleston, S.C., the works erected by Union forces in 1863 and 1864 (reassigned to RG 77: Dr. 64-53), and the condition of Fort Sumter at the time of its capture by Union forces in February 1865 (reassigned to RG 77: I 58-11; duplicate filed as Dr. 66-86½).

MILITARY DEPARTMENT OF THE TENNESSEE

The Department of the Tennessee was established November 10, 1862, and disbanded November 28, 1864. It included parts of Kentucky and Tennessee west of the Tennessee River, Forts Henry and Donelson, Tenn., northern Mississippi, and Cairo and vicinity, Ill.

1.27. Mississippi and Tennessee. 1862-63. 4 items.

A map of Vicksburg, Miss., showing defenses and positions in the siege of the city (see entry 2.126); a map showing positions of Forts Henry and Donelson, and plans of the forts (reassigned to RG 77: Dr. 147-4 through Dr. 147-7); and a topographic map of Memphis, Tenn., and vicinity (see entry 2.195).

MILITARY DEPARTMENT OF WEST VIRGINIA

The Department of West Virginia was established June 24, 1863, and included parts of West Virginia south of Ohio County, adjacent counties in Ohio and Maryland, and part of Virginia near Harpers Ferry. It was disbanded June 27, 1865.

1.28. West Virginia. 1863-64. 3 items.

A map of part of West Virginia and adjacent States showing topography and roads (see entry 2.258); a map of the Shenandoah and Upper Potomac region (see entry 2.251); and a map showing routes of the three expeditions

commanded by Gen. W. W. Averell (reassigned to RG 77: 2903 Portfolio).

Records of the Office of the Chief of Engineers. RG 77

When the Civil War began, the engineering duties of the War Department were divided between the Corps of Engineers and the Corps of Topographical Engineers. In 1861 and 1862, most officers of both corps were withdrawn from their regular work on rivers and harbors, surveys of the Great Lakes, defenses, explorations, and boundaries and were assigned to emergency military work in Washington or with armies and departments in the field. It was found that Engineer activities in the field were not facilitated by the division of work between the two corps. By an act "to promote the efficiency of the Corps of Engineers," approved March 3, 1863, the Corps

of Topographical Engineers was abolished and merged with the Corps of Engineers. In 1866 the designation "Chief Engineer" was changed to "Chief of Engineers."

During the war, Engineer officers and their staffs produced several thousand maps and plans that are now preserved as part of the records of the Office of the Chief of Engineers in three files: the Civil Works (Headquarters) Map File, the Fortifications Map File, and the War Department Map Collection. For descriptive purposes in this guide, the maps have been grouped by State and thereunder by the file to which they belong. Maps of areas within more than one State are described under the

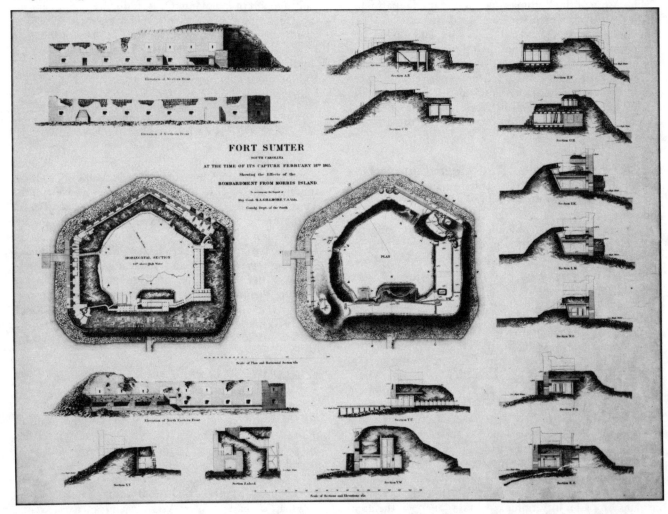

Condition of Fort Sumter at the time of its capture by Union forces, Feb. 18, 1865. RG 77: I 58-11. See entry 1.26.

United States, except those for the Upper Potomac and Shenandoah Valleys, which are described under Virginia. Standard construction drawings from the Fortifications Map File, which do not pertain to any specific locality, are described in entry 1.33.

Finding aids include unpublished map registers, a card catalog, and detailed lists of maps and plans of fortifications.

Civil Works (Headquarters) Map File

This file was created in the Office of the Chief of Engineers after the Civil War. In addition to Civil War maps, it consists of maps of surveys and explorations made before 1860, many of which had been collected by the Topographical Bureau, and postwar maps of Western surveys and explorations and of river and harbor surveys. The maps were arranged in a geographic and subject matter classification system. Later the file grew principally by the addition of maps and plans of Engineer civil works projects.

Included in this file are about 2,900 Civil War maps. Maps in the "Z" file were principally captured from the Confederates or received from Engineer officers after the war.

For descriptive purposes, maps from this file are grouped into entries showing general origin, subject matter, or area under the United States or the appropriate State. Recurring entries under many of the States are for maps showing general information, field reconnaissances and surveys, local defenses, battlefields, operations, routes of armies, and general campaigns. Also described are maps of military departments, maps compiled and published by the Bureau of Topographical Engineers and the Engineer Bureau, captured Confederate maps, and maps resulting from investigations into the conduct of military operations. The individual items of the following three portfolios have been described under the appropriate entries: a collection by Maj. Gen. J. G. Barnard, who at the close of the war was Chief Engineer of the Armies in the Field; a manuscript group entitled "Rebel Campaign maps in Virginia, Maryland & Penn. . . . 1865"; and a manuscript group entitled "Copies of Confederate Maps from originals loaned to the War Depart. by the Southern Historical Society in 1878."

Fortifications Map File

This file was created in the Office of the Chief of Engineers for maps and plans of fortifications. Most of the items relate to the permanent coastal fortifications of the United States, but there are also items for temporary defenses and defended areas, Confederate defenses (some of which were captured and occupied by Union troops), and a few other items whose relation to fortifications is not obvious. Most maps and plans relating to permanent fortifications were made by Engineer officers and their staffs who were assigned to the installations, whereas those relating to temporary defenses and defended areas were usually made by personnel under the direction of officers of military divisions and departments or armies in the field.

The file consists of about 15,000 items; of these about 2,200 are Civil War maps and plans, most of them manuscript.

During the war the permanent fortifications, some of which were held by the Confederates, were manned for defense and also were used as training centers, troop depots, and prisons. The entire body of records relating to a permanent fort, for example, one established early in the 1800's and maintained throughout the century, shows in great detail its construction and armament, and there may be several hundred items. The relatively few maps and plans made during the war for permanent fortifications pertain primarily to the expansion and modification of defense facilities and to armament and damage. Some permanent fortifications in strategic areas are noted as having maps and plans dated before the war, but these maps and plans are not described or included in the item count.

The temporary defenses and defended areas were principally in the northeast, Great Lakes area, and Border States. The records for these areas include maps showing topography and lines of defenses; plans of installations; details of forts, batteries, redoubts, blockhouses, gates, barbettes, and casemates; and lists of the number and the kinds of armaments.

War Department Map Collection

This collection, known earlier as the General Staff Map Collection, originated about 1895 in the Military Information Division of the Adjutant General's Office. It was a general depository for maps received from military organizations, military attaches, other official sources, and private individuals. The maps are filed by area. Here, maps relating to the Civil War are described in separate entries under the appropriate State.

UNITED STATES

CIVIL WORKS MAP FILE

1.29. General Information. 13 items.

Historical Sketch of the Rebellion, showing the limit of loyal States in July 1861, the territory controlled by Union forces in July 1863, and the territory gained from July 1863 to January 1864, published by the Coast Survey and having a few annotations and corrections (US 247); maps, principally of the Southern States, published in 1862 and 1863 and annotated from information compiled under the direction of Col. J. N. Macomb to show the gauges of southern railroads (US 485; G 443, vol. 7, p. 15); a railroad map of the Southeastern States compiled under the direction of Brig. Gen. W. F. Smith in 1863 (US 257); and other manuscript and annotated maps covering most of the Southern States and showing roads, railroads, towns, villages, and other general information (US 217-5; US 220; US 240; US 248; US 260; US 279). A photoprocessed map of the United States compiled in the Bureau of Engineers in 1865 showing forts, arsenals, camps, railroads, and routes, with annotations added in the Office of the Chief of Engineers in 1871 showing new military installations, public works, areas examined and surveyed, and distances from Washington, D.C. (Z 467).

1.30. Military Departments. 28 items.

A manuscript map of a part of the Military Department of the Cumberland (covering middle and eastern Kentucky and Tennessee and small parts of adjoining States) compiled in the Bureau of Topographical Engineers in 1861 (T 18); manuscript (see entry 2.6) and published maps of parts of the Military Departments of the Cumberland, the South, and the Gulf (covering parts of Florida, Alabama, and Georgia) compiled in 1863 (US 215-2; Pub. 1863, No. 5); manuscript (US 209) (see entry 2.7) and photoprocessed (Pub. 1862, No. 6) maps of parts of the Military Departments of the Missouri and the Ohio (covering parts of Kentucky, Tennessee, Missouri, and Arkansas) compiled in the Bureau of Topographical Engineers in 1862; photoprocessed and engraved maps of the eastern part of the Military Department of North Carolina (including part of Virginia) compiled in the Engineer Bureau in 1862 (Pub. 1862, No. 2, and Pub. 1862, No. 3); manuscript map (US 244) (see entry 2.8) of the Military Department of the South (covering South Carolina and parts of North Carolina and Georgia) compiled in 1864, and 1865 published editions— one of which contains insets of Fort Fisher (Pub. 1865, No. 6); published maps of parts of the Military Departments of Virginia, Washington, the Middle, and the Susquehanna prepared in the Engineer Department in 1863 (US 203½); a published map of western Georgia with adjoining parts of Tennessee and Alabama, being part of the Department of the Cumberland, compiled in the Engineer Bureau in January 1863 (N 207); manuscript and published maps of parts of Virginia and North Carolina compiled and printed in the Engineer Bureau in 1864 (Pub. 1864, No. 2); various forms of the maps of the Military Department of Southeastern Virginia and Fort Monroe (G 112; G 115; Pub. 1862, No. 4); manuscript (US 203) (see entry 2.9) and photoprocessed (Pub. 1861, No. 2) maps of parts of the Military Departments of Washington, Annapolis, Pennsylvania, and Northeastern Virginia compiled in the Bureau of Topographical Engineers in 1861; a published map of that part of the Military Department of Washington embracing the lower counties of Maryland, prepared in the Engineer Bureau in 1865 (Pub. 1865, No. 10); and a photoprocessed copy of an 1864 map of the

Military Department of New Mexico (covering the Territories of Arizona and New Mexico) annotated in 1866 to show new military posts (W 83-2). Other department maps for North Carolina and Virginia are described in entries 1.95 and 1.136.

1.31. Campaigns of the Armies of the Cumberland and the Ohio. 7 items.

Maps compiled by Edward Ruger under the orders of Maj. Gen. George H. Thomas, consisting of a manuscript map showing the lines of operations of the Armies of the Cumberland and the Ohio while commanded by Brig. Gen. Robert Anderson, Brig. Gen. W. T. Sherman, and Maj. Gen. D. C. Buell, with a printed description of the operations and inset maps of the battlefield of Logan's Cross Roads and the Confederate position at Mill Springs, Ky., January 19, 1862, the battlefield of Perryville, Ky., October 8, 1862, the field of Shiloh, Tenn., April 6 and 7, 1862, the operations at Cumberland Gap, Tenn., 1862, and the country between Monterey, Tenn., and Corinth, Miss., showing the lines of entrenchments and the routes taken in the advance on Corinth in May 1862 (US 291); an unfinished manuscript map and an annotated lithographed map of the country between Monterey and Corinth (US 222-1; US 222-2); a manuscript map showing the campaigns of the Army of the Cumberland under the command of Maj. Gen. W. S. Rosecrans, including a printed description of the operations and inset maps of the battlefields of Stones River, Tenn., December 31, 1862, to January 2, 1863, and Chickamauga, Ga., September 19 and 20, 1863 (US 288); a manuscript map showing the campaigns of the Army of the Cumberland with printed descriptions and other details (US 275-1) (see entry 2.10); and a printed base map (US 275) and a reduced lithographed copy (US 275-5) overprinted to show the lines of march of the various campaigns, annotated with a note explaining the alterations from the original map and to show the route of the Confederate marches in Kentucky under Generals Bragg and Kirby Smith in the fall of 1862, used in the proceedings of the military commission that investigated the operations under Buell.

1.32. Campaigns of the Army of the Tennessee and the Armies under the Command of General Sherman. 286 items.

A manuscript map showing the routes taken by the Army of the Tennessee from Chattanooga to Atlanta, May to July 1864, under the command of Maj. Gen. J. B. McPherson and Maj. Gen. O. O. Howard and also showing Union and Confederate works in the vicinities of Marietta, Atlanta, and Jonesboro, made under the direction of Capt. C. B. Reese and compiled and drawn by Capt. L. Helmle (US 278-1); eight unfinished maps of surveys along the route (US 278-3 through US 278-10); maps showing the route of march from Atlanta to Savannah (US 278-2; N 58); a composite map from Coast

Survey sources with lines added illustrating the march of the army under the command of Sherman from Atlanta to Savannah and to Goldsboro (US 256); manuscript maps showing the routes of march of the 14th, 15th, 17th, and 20th Corps from Savannah to Goldsboro and Raleigh, January to April 1865, and from Goldsboro and Raleigh to Washington, April 10 to May 20, 1865, as surveyed and drawn under the direction of Brig. Gen. O. M. Poe (US 258; US 259); manuscript campaign maps in book form showing the routes of the divisions of the 20th Corps from Savannah to Goldsboro, January 17 to March 24, 1865, including maps of the battlefields of Averysboro and Bentonsville (US 280) (see entry 2.143); a manuscript map showing the routes of march of the Army of the Tennessee under the command of Howard during the winter campaign in the Carolinas, surveyed and compiled under the direction of Col. C. B. Reese (US 277); approximately 270 manuscript sketches showing the routes of the 15th and 17th Corps in the winter campaign of 1865 in the Carolinas, the route of the 15th and 17th Corps from Goldsboro to Raleigh and to Washington, and the routes of the 14th and 20th Corps from Raleigh to Alexandria, with several odometer surveys of the general route of the various corps (Z 12-1 through Z 12-233); and a published map showing the routes from Atlanta to Goldsboro (Pub. 1865, No. 2).

FORTIFICATIONS MAP FILE

1.33. General Information Maps and Standard Construction Drawings. About 200 items.

A published map of the United States annotated to show military departments in August 1863, and a map showing the route of the United States Military Railroad from a point near Waynesboro, Ky., to Knoxville, Tenn.

Plans of batteries, blockhouses, barracks, and other buildings used in fortifications or along defense lines; plans of guns, torpedo boats and torpedoes, and some ironclad boats or floating batteries; plans for constructing pontoon bridges; plans of wagons; plans of engineer equipment; and plans of miscellaneous equipment used in defense lines. These drawings are "standard" for use in military construction and do not apply to any particular area or installation. Plans of specific fortifications are described under separate States.

ALABAMA

CIVIL WORKS MAP FILE

1.34. General Information. 4 items.

A detailed manuscript map of part of the State from 32° N. latitude to the Tennessee line, drawn by William Claypool and noted on reverse "under Genl. Wilson," and showing topography, drainage pattern, places, roads, and railroads (Z 3); a manuscript map showing the area on either side of the Tennessee River around Decatur and railroad connections, ferries, roads, and other general information in Limestone and Morgan Counties (J 36); part of La Tourette's map of the State of Alabama and West Florida, revised and published in 1856 and annotated to show railroads, additional places, and roads in the southern half of the State (J 39); and a manuscript map of townships 9-22 N., Rs. 5-24 E., St. Stephens Meridian, showing rivers and streams, county boundaries, roads, towns, and post offices (Z 290). For regional and other related maps, see also entries 1.29, 1.30, 1.48, 1.79, and 1.112.

1.35. Operations at Blakely. 2 items.

A published map of the assault at Blakely showing the line of Confederate works captured by the Army of West Mississippi on April 9, 1865, and the line of Union positions and works (Pub. 1865, No. 4); and a manuscript map relating to the assault (J 34) (see entry 2.15).

1.36. Local Defenses and Reconnaissances. 14 items.

A manuscript sketch of a reconnaissance near Cedar Bluff on the Coosa River by H. Spaerke in 1864 showing roads, places, and the headquarters of the Armies of the Ohio and the Tennessee (Z 105); manuscript maps of surveys in the vicinities of Decatur (Z 73) and Huntsville (Z 63); published maps of the defenses of Mobile—one showing three lines of entrenchments erected 1862-64, the batteries and obstructions in Mobile Bay, and lines of works around Blakely and Spanish Fort, and the other map showing the lines of Confederate defenses after occupation by Union forces under Maj. Gen. E. R. S. Canby (US 491); an annotated photoprocessed copy of a map of Mobile and vicinity (J 62-2) (see entry 2.19); a group of manuscript maps, including a large-scale map of the approaches to the city of Mobile, accompanying the February 6, 1866, report of Bvt. Col. W. E. Merrill and prepared under the direction of Capt. P. C. Hains in November 1864, with later additions showing the conditions of the harbor and the obstructions to navigation, and four sketch maps showing obstructions at the mouth of the Mobile and Spanish Rivers (J 33½-1 through J 33½-5); a copy of a Confederate map of the Mobile vicinity (J 41); and manuscript maps of Stevenson and vicinity prepared under the direction of Merrill by Maj. James R. Willett from surveys made by P. M. Radford in 1864 and January 1865, showing fortifications, roads and railroads, houses, abandoned plantations, and a ferry across the Tennessee River, with notes on water levels and types of timber (J 31).

FORTIFICATIONS MAP FILE

1.37. Alabama Fortifications. 86 items.

Two copies of a map of Blakely (Dr. 121-17) and vicinity showing the Confederate line of works captured by the Army of the West Mississippi on April 9, 1865, and the position and approaches of the Union forces. A map of Bridgeport and vicinity (Dr. 147-A 57) showing defenses, 1865. A topographic map of Decatur and vicinity (Dr. 121-14) showing defenses and the site of a pontoon bridge over the Tennessee River, 1864. A map showing the line of defenses erected by Maj. Gen. G. Granger's Expeditionary Corps in August 1864 around Fort Gaines, including a list of the number of guns located at each battery (see entry 2.16). A map of Huntsville and vicinity (Dr. 121-13) showing defenses, 1864. Maps of the city of Mobile and vicinity showing Confederate defenses and defense lines occupied by Union forces (see entries 2.20 and 2.22); and 67 plans of individual redoubts, forts, and batteries composing the line of defenses, some of which were prepared by members of the Confederate Army and recopied by Union forces, as follows: Forts Jeb Stuart, Mouton, and Sidney Johnston and Batteries Buchanan, Gladden or Pinto, McIntosh, and Missouri, 1864-65. Maps of Mobile Bay and vicinity showing the adjacent shoreline and defenses (see entry 2.18), and a map of the siege operations at Spanish Fort showing lines of Union and Confederate works, 1863-65 (see entry 2.21). A map of Stevenson and vicinity showing defenses erected by Union forces (see entry 2.24), plans of blockhouses located on the line of defenses, and plans of Redoubts Harker and Mitchell, 1864-65.

ARKANSAS

CIVIL WORKS MAP FILE

1.38. General Information. 11 items.

A manuscript map showing roads in the area between the Arkansas and the St. Francis Rivers and extending west from the Mississippi River to Little Rock, with the notation "Maj. Gen. Sherman with the compliments of Rear Admiral Porter:" (Q 124); a map from the Engineer Office, Department of Arkansas, printed on tracing cloth and showing towns and roads in the area west of the White River between De Valls Bluff and the Arkansas Post (Q 113); and manuscript maps of the southwestern corner of the State showing roads and ferries across the Red River (Z 54-10), of Desha (Z 48-11), Drew (Z 48-10), Dallas (Z 48-1), and Ouashita (Z 48-2 through Z 48-9) Counties (see entry 2.28), of the vicinity of Dooleys Ferry (Z 280) (see entry 2.29), of roads and adjacent terrain between Pea Ridge and Fayetteville (Z 174), and of roads in the Camden area (Z 35-1; Z 35-2).

1.39. Battlefields and Defenses. 15 items.

Maps and plans of the battlefield of Pea Ridge including battlefield surveys by H. A. Ulffers and 1st Lt. A. Hoeppner (Q 87-1; Q 87-2) and a manuscript map showing the Union and Confederate lines (Q 109) (see entry 2.36), with a manuscript copy prepared for publication (Q 109) and a copy of the edition published in 1876 (Pub. 1876, No. 3); a manuscript map of the battlefield of Prairie Grove, December 7, 1862 (Q 463) (see entry 2.37); a copy of a plan of the fortifications and fort at Arkansas Post (Z 189) (see entry 2.31); a map of De Valls Bluff and vicinity (Z 327) (see entry 2.30); maps of Helena and vicinity showing the location of Fort Curtis and batteries (Z 361-1; Z 361-2); a manuscript sketch showing Little Rock and vicinity, including roads (Z 59); a large-scale map showing Little Rock streets, the U.S. Arsenal, St. John's College (used as a general hospital), and the line of fortifications around the city (Z 320); a map of the north side of the Arkansas River opposite Little Rock showing the railroad station, depots, the pontoon bridge, and the line of fortifications (Z 354); a manuscript map of the field of operations of the Expeditionary Army commanded by Maj. Gen. Frederick Steele in 1863, showing fortifications in the vicinity of Little Rock and at De Valls Bluff (Z 219); a manuscript map of Fort Smith showing its fortifications and noted as official by Lieutenant MacKenzie (Z 294-1); and a similar map showing new fortifications at Fort Smith (Z 294½-2).

FORTIFICATIONS MAP FILE

1.40. Arkansas Fortifications. 33 items.

A map of the District of Arkansas showing roads, prepared by the Department of the Trans-Mississippi, 1864 (see entry 2.26). A map showing Major General Steele's route from Little Rock to Camden and return, 1864 (see entry 2.27). A map of Arkansas Post and vicinity showing lines of defenses and routes of march with an inset plan of Fort Hindman as it was when surrendered to Union forces in January 1863, and a larger scale, detailed plan of the fort. A map of Arkadelphia and vicinity (Dr. 123-17) showing fords over the Ouachita River, defenses of the city, and headquarters of Generals Holmes and Price. A map of Camden and vicinity (Dr. 123-5-1) showing lines of defenses, 1864. Maps of Fort Smith and vicinity showing lines of field defenses, plans of the four forts composing the defenses, and plans of the drawbridges, blockhouses, and magazines used in the construction of the forts, 1865. Maps of Helena and vicinity showing defenses (see entry 2.32), one showing works that were started but never completed; and plans of Fort Curtis and of the well and powder magazine at the fort, 1865. A map of Little Rock and vicinity showing defenses (see entry 2.33), a map of the north shore of the Arkansas River across from Little Rock showing the railroad line and depot and the position of a pontoon bridge crossing the river (see entry 2.34), and a map showing the approaches to the city, 1863-64 (see entry 2.35).

CONNECTICUT

FORTIFICATIONS MAP FILE

1.41. Connecticut. 26 items.

A volume of field notes and sketches relating to the condition of coastal defenses and proposed locations for additional defenses, 1863. A plat of the Government lands at Fort Griswold; plans of the battery, including one for a proposed modification; and an armament sheet for 1865. Plans for the restoration of Fort Hale, 1863-65, and an armament sheet for 1865. A contoured map of New Haven and vicinity, and a plan of the proposed defensive works at Oyster Point, 1863-65. A plan of the proposed defensive works at Saybrook Point, 1863. Plans of batteries and modifications of batteries, and an armament sheet for Fort Trumbull, 1863-65.

Forts Griswold, Hale, and Trumbull were permanent fortifications.

DELAWARE

FORTIFICATIONS MAP FILE

1.42. Delaware Fortifications. 18 items.

Plans of Fort Delaware, a permanent fortification, dated 1862-65, consisting of plans of improvements to the barracks, a cross section of the counterscarp, plans of the sluiceway and dock, and an armament sheet for 1865. Plans of the proposed Fort Dupont and the battery that preceded the fort, 1863-65. Fort Dupont later became a permanent fortification.

DISTRICT OF COLUMBIA AND VICINITY

CIVIL WORKS MAP FILE

1.43. General Information. 10 items.

A manuscript topographic map of the District of Columbia as surveyed by A. Boschke, 1856-59, and three annotated copies of the 1861 published edition—one of which was issued to Major Woodbury by Maj. J. N. Macomb on September 21, 1861 (F 69-1 through F 69-4); a published copy of Boschke's 1857 map of the city of Washington annotated to show wards (F 42); a map of Georgetown traced in July 1863 from the 1830 engraved map by William Bussard (F 81-1); two manuscript copies of maps of the topography adjoining the northeast and southeast sides of the District as surveyed in 1863 by Coast Survey parties under orders of Col. J. N. Macomb (F 86-1; F 86-2); a photoprocessed copy of a Coast Survey map showing the topography adjoining the northwest side of the District and along the left bank of the Potomac River to Great Falls, with wooded areas and roads shown in color (F 83-3); and a composite map made of photoprocessed copies of Coast Survey maps of the country along the right bank of the Potomac above Georgetown and the left bank from Chain Bridge to Great Falls, with roads shown in color (F 100-5).

1.44. Defenses of Washington. 79 items.

A composite map of the District and vicinity made from photoprocessed copies of maps of surveys by parties of the Coast Survey acting under the orders of Lt. J. N. Macomb and from an annotated photoprocessed copy of part of the 1861 Boschke map, with additional fortifications added in manuscript, and sent to Maj. Gen. George B. McClellan by the Coast Survey Office on March 15, 1862 (Z 238); three maps of the District and vicinity made from published copies of the Boschke map with manuscript additions for adjacent areas in Virginia and Maryland and annotated to show the line of fortifications around Washington and Alexandria, (US 265-A; US 265-B; Z 445) (see entry 2.38); a manuscript map showing the triangulation of the principal defenses of the District (F 118) (see entry 2.39); a manuscript sketch of the Anacostia River from Navy Yard Bridge to Bladensburg, August 28, 1861, showing soundings taken at low water, a narrow strip of country along the river banks, a battery and fort (apparently Fort Lincoln), and a powder magazine (F 98-3); manuscript and photoprocessed copies of maps of topographic surveys of the country along the right bank of the Potomac River from below Alexandria to Chain Bridge by Coast Survey parties in 1861-62 showing camps and fortifications for the defense of Washington, some of which were annotated and sent to General Barnard on August 10 and September 1, 1862 (F 100-1 through F 100-4); a published copy of E. G. Arnold's 1862 topographic map of the District and vicinity with additional forts, batteries, and redoubts added in manuscript (F 102); a manuscript map in 10 sheets, some of which are incomplete, of Washington and vicinity (see entry 2.41) with an index map, and numerous manuscript sheets used in compiling the map (F 99-1 through F 99-65), including unfinished compilation sheets showing the defenses of Washington (F 104-A; F 104-B); and a large manuscript map received from General Alexander in 1866 showing fortifications south of the Potomac and in the vicinity of Alexandria (F 103).

A published map entitled "Extract of Military Map of N.E. Virginia Showing Forts and Roads, Engineer Bureau . . . 1865," including the District of Columbia and adjacent parts of Maryland, showing the line of fortifications around Washington and Alexandria (Pub. 1865, No. 3); a revised copy prepared for a new edition (G 450-3); and the 1911 published edition (G 450-5).

FORTIFICATIONS MAP FILE

1.45. District of Columbia Fortifications. 298 items.

Maps of the city of Washington, including adjacent parts of Virginia and Maryland, showing lines of defenses, locations of forts, batteries, and redoubts defending the city, and the approaches to the city, one of which shows the defenses as proposed by Professor Mahan in 1861 and another of which is a detailed map in 11 sheets of the outskirts of the city prepared to accompany General Barnard's report on the defenses of Washington (see entry 2.39). Miscellaneous topographic maps of parts of the city showing defense lines and rifle pits in detail. Plans of the defenses of the bridges and roads approaching the city. A volume of sketches and related text describing signal stations. Tables prepared by the Coast Survey on the latitude, longitude, and distances of the principal forts, batteries, and other trigonometrical points and on the heights of the fortifications and other trigonometrical points above the mean tidal level of the Potomac River. Tabular statements on the armament and capacity of the forts and other defenses. Plans of bombproof blockhouses

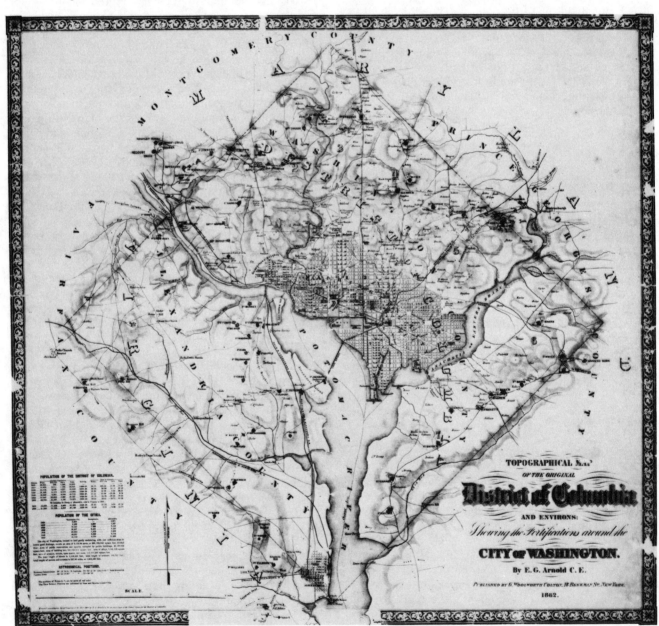

Published copy of E. G. Arnold's 1862 topographic map of the District of Columbia and vicinity with additional forts, batteries, and redoubts added in manuscript. RG 77: F 102. See entry 1.44.

used on the line of defenses. A map of the Anacostia River (Dr. 127-7) showing soundings, bridges, a powder magazine, and the camp of the California regiment.

Detailed plans, including original plans and changes and modifications, of the individual defenses of Washington including Forts Baker, Bayard, Bunker Hill, Carroll, Chaplin, Circle, DeRussy, Dupont, Gaines, Greble, Kearny, Lincoln, Mahan, Reno, Ricketts, Saratoga, Slemmer, Slocum, Snyder, Stanton, Stevens (formerly called Massachusetts), Thayer, Totten, Wagner, and the fort on Kennedy's Hill and Batteries Cameron, Carroll, DeRussy, Kemble, Martin Scott, Morris, Parrott, Pennsylvania (later Fort Reno), Smeade, Vermont, and the battery to the right of Rock Creek; and plans of unnamed batteries, usually those forming a part of one of the larger forts.

For forts, batteries, and redoubts defending the city but located in Maryland or Virginia, see entries 1.75 and 1.151, respectively.

FLORIDA

CIVIL WORKS MAP FILE

1.46. Local Defenses. 11 items.

An 1864 manuscript Coast Survey map of Jacksonville (L 108-1) (see entry 2.49) and two manuscript plans showing names of streets, block and lot numbers, and buildings (L 108-2; L 108-3); manuscript map of the channels and shoals near Fort Jefferson (L-98) (see entry 2.47); a manuscript copy of a Coast Survey map showing roads and the line of defense around Palatka as surveyed in March 1864 at the request of Brig. Gen. T. Seymour (L 100-1), undated manuscript maps of the town and its defenses (one approved by Capt. Charles R. Suter, Chief Engineer) (L 100-2), and an annotated plat of the town (L 109); a manuscript map of Pensacola and vicinity prepared by order of Maj. Gen. N. P. Banks in 1864 and compiled from maps and information obtained by C. D. Elliot, Assistant Engineer, showing the drainage pattern, ferries, roads and trails, forts, tracts of land and their owners, Confederate crossing of the Escambia River, the Confederate battery on Santa Rosa Sound spiked on October 6, 1862, the camp of the expedition on Santa Rosa Island, and the positions of a steamer and two sloops at the entrance to Choctawhatchee Bay (Z 359); a manuscript map of St. Augustine and vicinity (L 107) (see entry 2.51); and a topographic map of Warrington and vicinity (Z 353) (see entry 2.52). For regional and other related maps, see also entries 1.29, 1.30, and 1.34.

FORTIFICATIONS MAP FILE

1.47. Florida Fortifications. 80 items.

A plan of the partly built lunette on Bird Key, 1861, and plans with cross sections of the fort to be constructed on the Key. A map of Jacksonville and vicinity (Dr. 128-129) showing lines of defenses, roads, and railroads.

Plans of the permanent Forts Barrancas, Clinch, Jefferson, Pickens, and Taylor dating before the war, and maps and plans relating to these forts during the war as follows: a plan of the earthworks and an armament sheet for Fort Barrancas, 1865; plans of the modifications to Fort Clinch and plans of barracks, offices, sanitary facilities, and gun platforms, 1863-65; plans of Fort Pickens including a plan for strengthening the magazine doors at the fort, a plan of the 15-inch gun platform in the central bastion, an armament sheet for 1863, and maps showing the positions and supposed strength of enemy batteries near the fort and the positions and strength of the sand batteries defending the fort, 1863-65 (see entry 2.48); and maps, plans, and an armament sheet, dated 1865, for Fort Taylor including plans showing the distribution of armament and plans of the gun embrasures, 1861-65.

GEORGIA

CIVIL WORKS MAP FILE

1.48. General Information. 39 items.

An unfinished manuscript map of part of the State north of 33° N. latitude drawn by Charles Schott (Z 7); rough manuscript maps covering part of northern Georgia (Z 18-1 through Z 18-8; Z 21-1 through Z 21-9); copies of Confederate maps of parts of northwestern Georgia (US 393-21; N 207); unfinished, large-scale manuscript maps covering part of central and eastern Georgia (Z 1½); a manuscript map of the coast of Georgia and Florida from Savannah to St. Augustine compiled in the Bureau of Topographical Engineers in 1862 (N 29), and a photo-processed copy colored to emphasize canals and marshlands (Pub. 1862, No. 5); a large-scale map showing survey routes between Chehaw, Ala., and Marthasville and Covington, Ga. (Rds. 198); and a post route map of Georgia and Alabama with information added in the Census Office to show population by race, agricultural products, and number and kinds of livestock by county (US 266). For regional maps, see also entries 1.29 and 1.30.

1.49. Chickamauga. 23 items.

A small-scale map of the battlefield (N 66) (see entry 2.67); manuscript maps of the battlefield, September 19 and 20, 1863 (N 77-19; N 77-20) (see entries 2.68 and 2.69); lithographed copies of similar maps (some of which have notes stating that the positions shown were not approved by a board convened in 1879 by order of the Adjutant General's Office), a copy with corrections made in accordance with the recommendations of the board, other copies with additions and corrections, and tracings and overlays (N 77-1 through N 77-35); and a manuscript copy of a Confederate map (US 393-24).

1.50. Atlanta Campaign. 146 items.

Manuscript maps illustrating the five epochs of the campaign of 1864 compiled by Edward Ruger (see entries 2.56 through 2.60) and showing topography in detail and the routes of march of the Armies of the Cumberland, the Ohio, and the Tennessee (N 80; N 81; N 82; N 85; N 86); partial tracings of the five maps, manuscript maps compiled for publication, and editions published in 1874-77 (N 98-1; N 97-1; N 101; N 106-1; N 105-2; Pub. 1874, No. 6; Pub. 1875, No. 1; Pub. 1875, No. 2); and a photoprocessed map illustrating the operations from May 5 to September 4, 1864, annotated to show the status of preparation of the maps on May 24, 1875 (N 55).

Among manuscript maps and plotting sheets received from Capt. Edward Ruger (N 213 through N 225), many of which were used as compilation material for the maps previously described, are maps of the vicinity of Forsyth (N 213); Confederate maps of the vicinities of Dalton (N 214-2; N 214-3); surveys by the Department and Army of the Tennessee during the summer and fall of 1864 (N 217; N 222); a Confederate map showing Hardee's and Hood's Corps and Union positions from May 25 to July 9, 1864, north of the Chattahoochee River (N 220) (see entry 2.72); and 75 items including compilation sheets, road reconnaissances in various county districts (some probably of Confederate origin), compilation squares, and related maps (N 221-1 through N 221-75).

Other items include maps prepared under the direction of Bvt. Brig. Gen. O. M. Poe to illustrate the operations of the army under the command of Maj. Gen. W. T. Sherman, one dated September 25, 1866, showing the routes from the seizure of the railroad south of Allatoona Pass to the fall of Atlanta and Union and Confederate lines (N 69), and another illustrating the operations from the Tennessee River to Lovejoy's Station from May 5 to September 4, 1864 (N 124); an unfinished manuscript map of Allatoona Pass and vicinity showing defensive works as they existed at the time of the Confederate attack and the position of the attacking force, compiled in the Office of the Chief of Engineers in 1875 (N 103-1); a manuscript outline of the Union and Confederate lines and fortifications in the Dalton-Reseca area and in the Cassville-Atlanta-Lovejoy's Station area (957 Roll); manuscript map of Dalton and vicinity (Z 72-2) (see entry 2.70), and a map of the area on a smaller scale (Z 72-1); and a manuscript map of the railroad extending north from Dalton to the Georgia and Tennessee State line (Z 92). See also entry 1.32.

1.51. Battle and Siege of Atlanta. 7 items.

A manuscript map illustrating the siege of Atlanta from July 19 to August 26, 1864 (N 68-1) (see entry 2.61); a small map of the Battle of Atlanta drawn by A. Hickenlooper and forwarded by Gen. O. M. Poe (N 107); a manuscript map showing the position of the left wing of the 16th Corps during the engagement near Atlanta on July 22 presented by Gen. O. M. Poe in 1878 (N 109);

a manuscript map illustrating the operations in front of Atlanta from July 19 to August 26, including insets of plans of Union and Confederate defenses (N 102), and a copy of the published edition (Pub. 1875, No. 2); and a manuscript map of Decatur and vicinity, dated October 1864 and signed by Capt. Wm. J. Twinina, A. D. C., Chief Engineer, Army of the Ohio, showing the street pattern, the Georgia Railroad, roads, lines of works, and the headquarters of the Army of the Ohio (N 75).

1.52. March from Atlanta to Savannah. 93 items.

Manuscript maps illustrating the march of Sherman's army from Atlanta to Savannah, November 15 to December 10, 1864, prepared under the direction of Capt. O. M. Poe and showing the routes of the 14th, 15th, 17th, and 20th Corps (956 Roll-1; 956 Roll-2); similar maps dated November 15 to December 21, 1864, showing also Union and Confederate works in the vicinity of Savannah (N 57); a set of 11 maps entitled "Campaign of the 20th Army Corps from Atlanta to Savannah," including notes, showing routes of march from November 15 to December 11 and operations at Savannah from December 12 to 19 (N 59-1) (see entry 2.64); a similar set without notes (N 59-2); a manuscript map showing the routes of the 15th and 17th Corps of the Army of the Tennessee from Atlanta to Savannah (N 58) (see entry 2.62); a manuscript sketch map of the route of the 14th Corps of Sherman's army showing the number of miles covered each day from November 16 to December 9 (Z 28) (see entry 2.63); twenty manuscript sketch maps of the routes of the 15th Corps from White Hall Ruins to Savannah from November 15 to December 9 (Z 9); manuscript sketch maps of the routes of the 17th Corps from Terry's Mill near Atlanta to the Ogeechee River from November 15 to 30 (Z 14-1 through Z 14-43) (see entry 2.65); detailed manuscript maps of Macon and vicinity (N 76-1 through N 76-3) (see entry 2.71), and an annotated published map of the same area (N 76-2). See also entry 1.32.

1.53. Operations and Surveys around Savannah. 8 items.

A compiled manuscript map of Savannah and vicinity illustrating the operations of Sherman's Army (N 70) (see entry 2.74); a manuscript map illustrating the defense of Savannah and operations that resulted in its capture on December 21, 1864, compiled in 1880-81 under the direction of Bvt. Brig. Gen. O. M. Poe (N 121); an unfinished manuscript map of surveys in the vicinity of Savannah showing lines and fortifications, and a copy of a Confederate map with additions from surveys by the Army of the Tennessee (Z 19-1; Z 19-2); a manuscript map dated December 28, 1864, of a survey of the roads between the Ogeechee and Medway Rivers in the vicinity of Fort McAllister (Z 32); a manuscript map of Tybee and vicinity from a Coast Survey sketch and corrected by observations and reconnaissances, showing Fort Pulaski and batteries near the south channel of the Savannah River, Fort Jackson, and other batteries and camps, dated Hilton Head, S.C., January 1, 1862, by Lt. James H. Wilson, Chief Topographical Engineer, Department of the South (N 30); a Coast Survey chart of the Savannah River published in 1855 and revised in February 1862 to show buoys and obstructions, accompanying the April 2, 1866, report of Capt. C. R. Suter (N 78); and a manuscript Coast Survey reconnaissance of the inland passages between Wassaw Sound and the Savannah River, made in January 1865 and accompanying Suter's report, showing the line of works across Whitmarsh Island, fortifications along St. Augustine Creek, and obstructions in the river (N 72).

FORTIFICATIONS MAP FILE

1.54. Georgia Fortifications. 12 items.

A map of Atlanta showing the line of Confederate defenses (see entry 2.55) and a manuscript profile of fortifications at Atlanta. Maps of Savannah showing lines of defenses and Confederate and Union troop entrenchments, some of which include as insets plans of forts and batteries, among these Forts Tattnall, Lee, and Thunderbolt and the fort on Causten's Bluff. A map of a reconnaissance of Wilmington River and St. Augustine Creek showing fortifications (see entry 2.75).

Maps and plans of the permanent Forts Oglethorpe and Pulaski, dated before the war. In addition there is a plan of Fort Oglethorpe, formerly called Jackson, show-

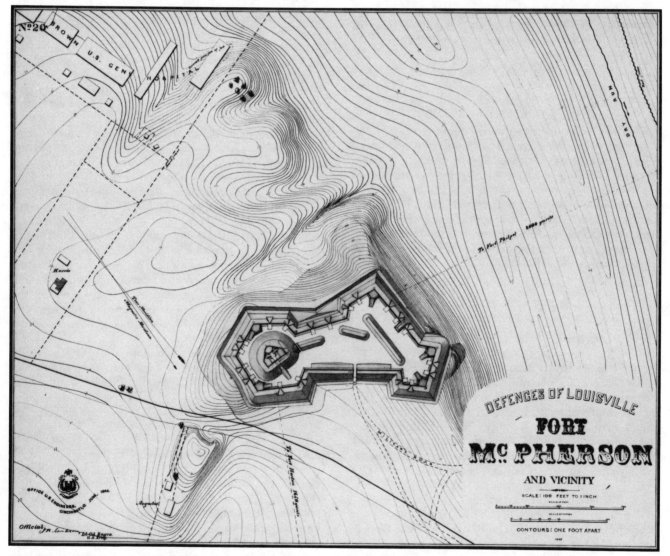

Plan of Fort McPherson, Ky., 1865. RG 77: Dr. 132-46.16. See entry 1.61.

ing alterations made when it was occupied by Confederate forces during the war.

WAR DEPARTMENT MAP COLLECTION

1.55. Northern Georgia and Atlanta. 2 items.
Capt. William Margedant's maps of parts of northern Georgia and the vicinity of Atlanta printed on cloth and annotated to show signal stations and lines.

ILLINOIS

FORTIFICATIONS MAP FILE

1.56. Illinois Fortifications. 1 item.
A map of the Rock Island Military Reservation dated November 18, 1862, showing U.S. lands, barracks, and the location of Fort Armstrong.

KANSAS

CIVIL WORKS MAP FILE

1.57. Fort Scott and Vicinity. 2 items.
A manuscript map sketched by Capt. William Hoelcke from his own surveys and dated Fort Scott, Kans., January 26, 1863, showing roads and footpaths, private houses occupied by Quartermaster, Commissary, and Medical Departments, other private dwellings, old rifle pits and entrenchments, rifle pits and enclosures to be constructed, cuttings made to ford the river, and camps along the river (Q 89); and a finished copy apparently prepared for publication (Z 360).

KENTUCKY

CIVIL WORKS MAP FILE

1.58. General Information. 4 items.
Two copies of a map of Kentucky by Edmund F. Lee, published in 1852 and annotated in 1861 to show geological information (Z 17½-1; Z 17½-2); a manuscript sketch map of western Kentucky (T 107); and a map of the Kentucky River from Three Forks in Owsley County to its confluence with the Ohio River (Z 246). For regional maps, see also entries 1.29, 1.30, 1.111, and 1.112.

1.59. Battlefields. 7 items.
A map of the vicinity of Munfordville showing the action of December 17, 1861, at Rowlett's Station (Z 500) (see entry 2.81); a manuscript copy with a troop position overlay, and the 1877 published edition, of a sketch of the battlefield of Logan's Cross Roads and the Confederate fortified position at Mill Springs, January 19, 1862, drawn under the direction of Capt. N. Michler and Edward Ruger (T 140-1; T 140-2; Pub. 1877, No. 2); and

a manuscript copy with a troop position overlay, and the 1877 published edition, of a map of the battlefield of Perryville, October 8, 1862, compiled by Edward Ruger and Anton Kilp by order of Maj. Gen. George H. Thomas (T 139-1; T 139-2; Pub. 1877, No. 1). See also entry 1.31.

1.60. Local Defenses. 39 items.
Maps of Bowling Green and vicinity compiled under the direction of Capt. N. Michler, showing camps, roads, railroads, and farms, with descriptive notes about the country (T 26-1 through T 26-3); an unfinished sketch of the vicinity of Covington, Ludlow, and Newport dated 1861 (T 12); a manuscript map of the defenses of Cincinnati, Ohio, and Covington and Newport, Ky., with 23 plans of the individual forts, batteries, and magazines accompanying Maj. J. H. Simpson's report of November 27, 1862; an additional manuscript copy and a copy of the edition published in 1877 (P 100; Pub. 1877, No. 4); a photoprocessed map of the vicinity of Lexington dated 1863, annotated to show a bridge across the Kentucky River near Hickman Creek and the partially graded part of a railroad line below Nicholasville (T 23); a manuscript map dated April 21, 1863, of the vicinity of Hickman Creek showing roads, the type of country in the bend of the Kentucky River, and a table of distances from the mouth of Hickman Creek to towns in Kentucky and Tennessee, compiled in the Engineer Office of the District of Central Kentucky by order of Major General Burnside under the direction of Capt. T. B. Brooks (Z 264); maps pertaining to the defense of Louisville including a manuscript map of the area made under the direction of Lt. Col. O. E. Babcock in April 1863 showing the railroads and fortified positions (T 124-1), part of a published map annotated to show fortified positions (T 124-2), and a large-scale manuscript map of the city showing the defenses in detail (T 124-3) (see entry 2.80); a photoprocessed map of Camp Nelson and its defenses annotated to show elevations, locations of works, and a reservoir (T 77); and manuscript maps, one of Paducah and vicinity including camps (Z 206) (see entry 2.82); and one of Smithland and vicinity (Z 175) (see entry 2.83).

FORTIFICATIONS MAP FILE

1.61. Kentucky Fortifications. 105 items.
A map of the Kentucky Central Railroad and valley of the Licking River from Benton Station to Lexington showing all important bridges, with 10 inset maps giving positions of defenses of the bridges, several inset plans of the blockhouses, and a supplemental sheet giving alterations to the blockhouses, 1863 (see entry 2.79). A map of Bowling Green and vicinity (Dr. 32-14) showing approaches and defenses. A map of Camp Burnside, Pulaski County, showing defenses. Maps of Camp Nelson and vicinity (see entries 2.76 and 2.77) showing the defenses across the neck of land between the Kentucky

River and Hickman Creek and proposed defenses across Polly's Bend of the Kentucky River; plans of the camp showing hospitals, barracks, machine shops, and other facilities; a plan of the depot magazine; and plans of Forts Bramlette, Hatch, Jackson, Jones, McKee, Nelson, Pope, Putnam, Studdiford, and Taylor, which composed the defenses of the camp, 1864. A map of Columbus and vicinity (Dr. 132-1; Dr. 132-2) showing defenses and the location of the capstan used to stretch a chain across the Mississippi River, and a plan of the powder magazine at Fort Halleck. Maps of Covington and vicinity showing defenses erected by the Union Army in 1861-63 for the protection of Covington and Newport, Ky., and Cincinnati, Ohio (Dr. 132-5 and 132-13) (see entry 2.78); and plans of the individual forts composing the defenses including Forts Burnside, Mitchell, Whittlesey, and Wright, Batteries Bates, Burbank, Burnett, Carlisle, Coombs, Harrison, Hatch, Holt, Hooper, J. L. Kirby Smith, Kyle, Larz Anderson, McLean, McRae, Perry, Phil Kearney, Shaler, and several unnamed batteries, 1862-64.

Plans of forts defending Cumberland Gap including Forts Foote (formerly Hunter), McClellan (partly located in Virginia), McRae (formerly Mallory), and McCook (formerly Raines), 1862. (For defenses of Cumberland Gap located in Tennessee and Virginia, see entries 1.126 and 1.151.) A map of Frankfort and vicinity (Dr. 132-52) showing lines of defenses, and a plan of Fort Boone, 1864-65. A map of Glasgow and vicinity showing defenses, with an inset plan of Fort Williams, 1863. Maps showing Confederate batteries on Island No. 10 in the Mississippi River and on the adjacent Kentucky shore as captured by Union forces, April 7, 1862. A map of Lexington and vicinity showing lines of defenses, and plans of Forts Clay and Crittenden, 1865. A map of Louisa and vicinity showing lines of defenses, and a plan of Fort Bishop, 1865. Maps of Louisville and vicinity showing defenses and facilities for the use of the military, such as stables and barracks, and the range of fire from the line of forts defending the city; plans of Forts Clark, Elstner, Engle, Hill, Horton, Karnasch, McPherson, Philpot, St. Clair Morton, Saunders, and Southworth and Battery Camp; and miscellaneous plans showing details of platforms and hurdle revetments for embrasures used in the forts, 1863-65.

Defenses erected by Union Army, 1861-63, for the protection of Covington and Newport, Ky., and Cincinnati, Ohio. RG 77: Dr. 132-5. See entry 1.61.

A map of Mount Sterling and vicinity showing lines of defenses with an inset plan of Fort Hutchinson, and a more detailed plan of the fort, 1865. A map of Muldraugh's Hill showing the defenses of the Louisville and Nashville Railroad with inset plans for Forts Boyle and Sands, 1863. A map of Munfordville and vicinity showing defenses of the Louisville and Nashville Railroad bridge and the location of a pontoon bridge, 1863. A plan of Fort Robinson, defending Paris, 1864. A map of Rolling Fork and vicinity showing defenses of the Louisville and Nashville Railroad with an inset plan of Fort Jones, 1863. A map of Shepherdsville and vicinity showing defenses of the Louisville and Nashville Railroad, 1863.

LOUISIANA

CIVIL WORKS MAP FILE

1.62. General Information. 16 items.

A map of Louisiana showing land districts in 1859 and annotated to show roads, railroads, parishes, and additional names (M 129); an unfinished manuscript map covering several townships in the central and northwestern parts of the State sent to the Engineer Bureau in 1866 by Captain Reese (M 129); parts of State maps annotated to show roads in northwestern and southwestern Louisiana (M 95; M 115); an outline map of Madison Parish showing rivers, bayous, and roads (M 127); a manuscript map of the Mississippi Basin prepared under the direction of Capt. P. C. Hains in August 1864 covering the lower southeastern part of Louisiana and part of Mississippi (M 118-2); a map of the State and parts of Mississippi and Texas compiled in 1853 by G. W. R. Bayley, Civil Engineer, and annotated by him to show railroads constructed, being constructed, and projected and the boundaries of the uplands (Z 262); a photoprocessed map of northwestern Louisiana annotated to show roads (Z 211); a manuscript Confederate map of the country north of Logansport and Mansfield showing greatest detail west of the Red River between Bayou Pierre and Soda Lake (Z 272) (see entry 2.85); a manuscript map of the Red River and country to the south and east of Alexandria (Z 330-1) (see entry 2.98) and a more detailed map of the Fort DeRussy area (Z 330-2); a manuscript map of the country between Baton Rouge and the Tickfaw River (Z 323); a manuscript map of part of St. Bernard Parish (Z 335) (see entry 2.100); a manuscript sketch map of the area between the Mississippi River and Barataria and Vermilion Bays (Z 58); a copy of part of La Tourette's 1847 map of Mississippi, with parts of southern Louisiana and southwestern Alabama, annotated to show roads (Z 274); and a map of southwestern Louisiana showing tracts of land, drainage features, marshlands, and a proposed railroad line (Z 325). For regional maps, see also entries 1.29 and 1.79.

1.63. Portfolios of Captured Confederate Maps. 360 items.

A group of manuscript parish maps received from Reese in 1866 generally showing township and private land claim lines, place names, names of landholders, roads, and routes of reconnaissances; maps of the vicinities of Pineville, Alexandria, Natchitoches, and Grand Ecore and of several surveys and road reconnaissances in northwestern Louisiana; a map of southwestern Louisiana; and a sketch of the country between the Atchafalaya and the Mississippi Rivers occupied by Major General Walker's division during part of November and December 1863 (Z 33-1 through Z 33-144).

A group of Land Office township plats of parts of the District North of the Red River and parts of the Northwestern and Southwestern Districts, some of the plats showing wooded and swamp areas, fields and other tracts of land, names of landholders, and roads (which are often marked in red) (Z 36); and three special plats of the Mansfield area showing details of the terrain, the drainage pattern, roads, names of residents, locations of the battles of April 7 and 8, 1864, and other information (Z 34-1 through Z 34-5).

1.64. Bayou Teche Expedition. 11 items.

A sketch of the approach to Tiger Island, April 4, 1863, by Oltmanns, showing the locations of forts and the cities of Brashear and Berwick (M 116-1); a manuscript map showing the position of Union works at Brashear City (Z 276) (see entry 2.91); maps of the battlefield of Fort Bisland and Irish Bend on Bayou Teche, April 13 and 14, 1863, with Union and Confederate forces shown (M 111); a larger scale map of Fort Bisland battlefield (M 112); a manuscript map showing Confederate works along Bayou Teche (Z 33-144); photoprocessed copies of a map of the Atchafalaya Basin prepared by order of Banks in February 1863 with later annotations, some of which show Confederate works above the mouth of Bayou Teche, points of skirmishes along the route between Brashear City and Alexandria on April 16 and 17, and the headquarters of the 19th Corps on April 16 and 20, and May 16, 1863 (M 99; M 99½) (see entry 2.88).

1.65. Red River Campaign. 40 items.

Photoprocessed copies of maps drawn under the direction of the Engineer Department by Theodore von Kamecke and Theodore Kolecki in 1865, including a map of the Red River Valley from the Mississippi River to Shreveport illustrating the campaign under the command of Banks in the spring of 1864 (M 121); individual maps of Fort de Russy captured March 14, the affair at Henderson's Hill on March 21, the cavalry fight at Wilson's Farm on April 7, the repulse of the enemy at Pleasant Grove on April 8, the Confederate attack at Sabine Cross Roads on April 8, the Battle of Pleasant Hill on April 9, the affair at Monett's Bluff on April 23, and the Battle of Mansura on May 16 (M 121-1 through M 121-13); and manuscript and annotated photoprocessed maps showing the route of the army in the spring of 1864 and places of battles (M 103; M 114) (see entry 2.99), troop positions along the road from Pleasant Hill to Mansfield as surveyed on April 7 (M 125-2) (see entry 2.97), the battlefield of Pleasant Hill (M 125-1) (see entry 2.96), the country in the vicinity of Alexandria (M 126-1 through M 126-3) (see entry 2.87), Bailey's Dam on the Red River at the falls near Alexandria as completed May 12 (M 173), roads between Alexandria and Natchitoches and between Grand Ecore and Pleasant Hill, forts near the mouth of the Yellow Bayou, the road from Semmsport to Morganza as surveyed in May by Lt. S. E. McGregory, and reconnaissances in the Red River country in June by Oswald Dietz (M 123-1 through M 123-20).

1.66. Baton Rouge and Port Hudson. 11 items.

A manuscript map showing military works at Baton Rouge as surveyed by Charles Hosmer, Coast Survey (Z 314); a map of Baton Rouge showing old rifle pits and new works at Fort Williams (Z 293); a large-scale plan of Fort Williams (Z 346); a topographic plan of Baton Rouge showing Union and Confederate troop positions for the battle on August 5, 1862, (Z 275) (see entry 2.90); a manuscript drawing of the State House at Baton Rouge (Z 41); a manuscript sketch map (Z 218-2) (see entry 2.89) and a traced copy (Z 218-1) of the area from Baton Rouge to Port Hudson showing positions of the 19th Army Corps on March 14, 1863; a manuscript map of Port Hudson and vicinity prepared in 1864 by order of Banks under the direction of Maj. D. C. Houston, Chief Engineer, Department of the Gulf, and Capt. P. C. Hains, showing Union and Confederate positions and batteries, with a new title bearing the date 1875 pasted over the old title (M 107); profiles of Confederate works at Port Hudson (M 109); and a Confederate plan of Port Hudson and its defenses (Z 33-141).

1.67. Fort Butler and Bayou Lafourche. 7 items.

Manuscript diagrams drawn by B. von Reizenstein in the Office of the Chief Engineer, Department of the Gulf, showing Fort Butler at Donaldsonville and Camp Weitzel on the opposite side of Bayou Lafourche (Z 278; Z 278-3); manuscript plans of Fort Butler, one dated November 25, 1863, showing buildings and with an armament list (Z 278-2 through Z 278-4); and manuscript maps of Bayou Lafourche from Donaldsonville to Lockport surveyed in 1860-61 under the direction of J. K. Duncan, Chief Engineer, Bureau of Public Works, drawn by A. F. Wrotnowski, and annotated to show camping grounds from October 26 to 29, 1862 (Z 352-1 through Z 352-3).

1.68. New Orleans, the Lower Mississippi, and Fort Livingston. 8 items.

A manuscript plan of levee, ward, and drainage district No. 1 constituting St. Bernard and part of Plaquemines Parishes, showing the Mississippi River from New Orleans to its mouth (Z 315); a sketch showing terrain and canals on the right bank of the Mississippi River in New Orleans and vicinity, drawn by J. G. Oltmanns, Coast Survey (Z 342); a large-scale manuscript sketch map of the Mississippi River above and below New Orleans (Z 336); a manuscript map showing canal defenses on the right bank of the Mississippi River in Jefferson Parish (Z 279) (see entry 2.95); a map of Bayou Goula showing plantations, a Confederate camp, and paths, with notes about wagon roads (Z 297); a large-scale manuscript map of the military approaches to New Orleans prepared by order of Maj. Gen. N. P. Banks in July 1863 under the direction of Maj. D. C. Houston, and a reduced photoprocessed copy annotated to show additional roads, canals, and bridges (M 106-1; M 106-2); and a manuscript sketch showing Fort Livingston, quarters, and a lighthouse on Isle Grande Terre near the Grand Pass entrance to Barataria Bay, made to accompany the August 17, 1863, report of Capt. W. J. Long, Assistant Engineer (Z 286).

FORTIFICATIONS MAP FILE

1.69. Louisiana Fortifications. 47 items.

Plans of Fort Williams located at Baton Rouge, 1865; of the fortification located on Bayou St. John, 1864; and of Fort Buchanan located at Berwick Bay, 1864. Maps of Brashear City (Dr. 133-87) showing defense lines, and a plan of the fort located in the city, 1864-65. Plans of Fort Banks located near Carrollton, 1865, and of Fort Butler located near Donaldsonville, 1863-65. A plan of the proposed Fort St. Leon located at English Turn, Mississippi River, 1864. A map of Morganzia and vicinity (Dr. 133-82) showing defense lines, and plans of the field works, 1865. A plan of the defenses of Company Canal located in Jefferson Parish in the vicinity of New Orleans, 1864. A map of New Orleans and vicinity showing positions of troops in September 1862; maps of Camp Parapet and vicinity showing the outline of the camp and its defenses (see entry 2.94); and plans of the main redoubt, the star redoubt, and the Cavalier Battery, 1863-64. Maps of Port Hudson and vicinity showing lines of defenses, and detailed plans of the inner defenses, 1863-65. A plan for building a dam at the falls of the Red River near Alexandria to raise the height of the river in order to permit Admiral Porter's squadron to repass the falls.

Maps and plans dated before the war of the permanent fortifications including Battery Bienvenue; Tower Dupre; Forts Jackson, Livingston, Macomb, and Pike; the Tower at Proctor's Landing; and Fort St. Philip. Armament sheets dated 1865 for Battery Bienvenue; Tower Dupre; and Forts Macomb, Pike, and St. Philip. Plans of Fort Jackson and its batteries; a map showing the limits of fire of Forts Jackson and St. Philip (see entry 2.92); and maps of the Mississippi River in the vicinity of these two forts, 1862-65. A plan of the gateway, bridge, and counterscarp at Fort Livingston, 1863.

MAINE

FORTIFICATIONS MAP FILE

1.70. Maine Fortifications. 130 items.

A map of the Penobscot River area showing railroads and stage routes, 1864. A map of the coasts of Maine and Massachusetts showing temporary works erected in 1863-64. A general plan, with detailed insets, of magazines and gun platforms of the field batteries at Belfast, Castine, Eastport, Machiasport, and Rockland; and separate plans of the batteries at each site showing also the extent of Government-owned land, 1863. A plan of the battery located on Cushing Island, 1864. Maps of Portland and vicinity showing fields of fire of the forts, batteries defending the harbor, and locations for proposed defenses; and plans of proposed batteries, 1862-64. A map of Richmond's Island showing the locations of temporary defenses.

Plans of the permanent Forts Gorges, Knox, McClary, Popham, Preble, and Scammel dated before the war. Plans of the forts dated 1861-65 include plans of existing and proposed batteries and changes or modifications to the batteries, armament sheets for each fort dated 1865, and maps of Fort Popham and vicinity showing additional lands required for barracks.

MARYLAND

CIVIL WORKS MAP FILE

1.71. General Information. 23 items.

Manuscript, annotated, and published maps of western Maryland from about 78° W. longitude to the West Virginia boundary with adjacent parts of Virginia and West Virginia (Z 119; Z 143); a large-scale, unfinished manuscript map of western Maryland (Z 115-1), and a manuscript map of the country along the Maryland and West Virginia boundary (Z 136); manuscript maps copied from an 1840 geological map showing parts of the State between the Potomac River and Chesapeake Bay (F 51-2); manuscript copies of maps of surveys at Lower Cedar Point and Point Lookout by the Coast Survey (F 88; F 53); a lithographed military map of Baltimore County compiled under the direction of Col. W. F. Raynolds in 1863 and annotated to show fortifications around Baltimore (F 87); a photoprocessed copy of a map of part of Montgomery County prepared under the direction of Col. J. N. Macomb in 1861 with minor annotations (F 71); a manuscript map (F 72) (see entry 2.111) and a duplicate tracing (F 72 Tracing) of Montgomery County compiled in the Bureau of Topographical Engineers in September 1862, and a copy printed at the Coast Survey in June 1863 (F 72 Dup.); a manuscript map of the area around Laytonsville and Brookeville showing roads and, apparently, proposed canal routes (G 463-17); manuscript and annotated blueprint copies of Martenet and Bond's map of Montgomery County received by Lt. Col. J. C. Woodruff in 1865 (F 89); a photoprocessed map of part of Washington County, dated September 1862 (F 276-2) (see entry 2.116); manuscript Confederate maps of Howard and Frederick Counties (US 253-4; US 253-4a; US 253-15); a manuscript profile of the Baltimore and Ohio Railroad from Monocacy to Cumberland showing information about the location of bridges, culverts, trestles, and other structures along the route (Z 154-1); a manuscript map showing the Baltimore and Washington and the Annapolis and Elk Ridge Railroads, common roads, and turnpikes drawn from Martenet's maps of Anne Arundel and Prince Georges Counties (Rds. 168); and manuscript maps copied in 1861 and 1862 showing the located line of the Metropolitan Railroad and roads in Frederick, Montgomery, and Washington Counties and the adjacent parts of the District of Columbia (Rds. 169) (see entry 2.109).

1.72. Antietam and South Mountain. 76 items and 1 atlas.

A large-scale map of the Battle of Antietam fought on September 16 and 17, 1862 (F 85) (see entry 2.102); several photoprocessed copies of maps sketched under the direction of Capt. J. C. Duane by Maj. D. C. Houston and annotated to show troop positions and information obtained from officers (F 73-1 through F 73-4; F 73-7); a manuscript map of a part of the battlefield (F 79) (see entry 2.103); a manuscript map and an annotated photoprocessed copy of a reconnaissance of the ground occupied by the 1st Corps under Maj. Gen. Hooker, made under the direction of Houston by Lt. W. A. Roebling and W. S. Long, Civil Engineer (F 73-5; 10547 Roll, No. 4); manuscript map showing the Confederate line of battle on September 16 and 17 and the line of retreat (10547 Roll, No. 3); photoprocessed copies of a base map of Antietam battlefield with annotated troop positions (10547 Roll-5; 10547 Roll-6); a large-scale manuscript map made for the Antietam Battlefield Board (6291 Roll) (see entry 2.104) and a group of photographic reductions of the map annotated by Gen. E. A. Carman to show the position of troops at stated intervals from daybreak until 5:30 p.m. on September 17 (6824 Flat-1 through 6824 Flat-14); five proof sheets of the 1904 edition of the 1899 Antietam Battlefield Board map and two sets of the 1904 edition, one of which is "General Carman's revision, 1908" (6824 Flat-31 through 6824 Flat-61); the 1904 and 1908 editions of the *Atlas of the Battlefield of Antietam* prepared under the direction of the Antietam Battlefield Board from surveys by Lt. Col. E. B. Cope and H. W. Mattern, drawn by Charles H. Ourand in 1899 with troop positions by General E. A. Carman, published under the direction of the Chief of Engineers (Pub. 1904; Pub. 1908); and manuscript and published maps of the battlefield from the surveys by Maj. N. Michler during and after the war (G 204-31; Pub. 1867, No. 15). See also entry 1.137.

A two-sheet manuscript map showing the positions of the Union and Confederate forces at the Battle of South Mountain fought September 14, 1862 (F 91-1; F 91-2) (see entry 2.115), an 1872 published edition of the map (Pub. 1872, No. 1), and a manuscript map of part of the battlefield (F 91-3) (see entry 2.114).

1.73. Cumberland, Pleasant Mills, Hagerstown, and Williamsport. 8 items.

A topographic map of Cumberland and vicinity surveyed under the direction of Lt. J. R. Meigs in 1864 (F 83), and an undated manuscript map of Cumberland (Z 140) (see entry 2.107); a manuscript plan of the Battlefield of Pleasant Mills, near Cumberland, for the engagement of August 1, 1864 (Z 160) (see entry 2.113); four manuscript maps of the vicinity of Hagerstown, Funkstown, Williamsport, and Falling Waters showing positions of Union and Confederate forces (F 97-1 through F 97-4) (see entry 2.117), one of which probably accompanied the October 1, 1863, report of Maj. Gen. G. G. Meade on the Battle of Gettysburg, and a published copy (Pub. 1879, No. 3); and a Confederate manuscript map of the Williamsport area (US 253-13) (see entry 2.118).

1.74. Annapolis Junction. 2 items.

Manuscript maps of the camp of instruction at Annapolis Junction and the surrounding area (F 82; F 75) (see entry 2.101).

FORTIFICATIONS MAP FILE

1.75. Maryland Fortifications. 107 items.

Topographic maps of parts of Maryland near Broad Creek and Oxon Hill copied from the Archives of the Coast and Geodetic Survey, 1863 (Dr. 135-10; Dr. 55-26½). Maps of Baltimore County (Dr. 135-13) showing the inner and outer lines of defenses for the city of Baltimore, and plans of the forts and batteries composing these defenses, including Fort Washington, 1863-64. A map of Montgomery County (Dr. 135-11) annotated to show the route traveled by a pontoon train commanded by Gen. H. W. Benham from Washington to Edward's Ferry and return, 1862, and plans of Forts Alexander, Franklin, Mansfield, Ripley, and Sumner and Redoubts Cross, Kirby, and Davis (see entry 2.108), which were included in the temporary defenses of Washington, 1862-65. Plans of redoubts 2 and 3 and of the barracks, officers' quarters, and guardhouses located in these redoubts at Point Lookout, 1865. Copies of Coast Survey charts of the Potomac River near White House Point, Va., Lower Cedar Point, Md., Mathias Point, Va., and Rosier's Bluff, Md.; and detailed drawings of plans for obstructing the channel of the river near Fort Foote showing the kinds and placement of the obstructions, with a handwritten description on the proposed method for obstructing the channel, 1861-64. Plans of Fort Meigs and Battery Jameson located in Prince Georges County and forming a part of the temporary defenses of Washington, 1862-65. A plan of the defenses of Conowingo Bridge, Susquehanna River, 1864 (see entry 2.106).

Plans of the permanent Forts Carroll and McHenry dated before the war. Plans of additional buildings, barracks, and magazines at each fort dated 1861-65; and an armament sheet for each fort dated 1864. Plans of Fort Foote and its Facilities dated 1864. This fort was constructed in 1863 and became one of the permanently fortified sites following the war.

Other maps covering parts of Montgomery and Prince Georges Counties are described under the defenses of Washington, D.C.

WAR DEPARTMENT MAP COLLECTION

1.76. Antietam. 3 items.

Manuscript base maps of the Antietam battlefield: two prepared by the Antietam Battlefield Board in 1894 and 1897, and one without indication of origin.

MASSACHUSETTS

FORTIFICATIONS MAP FILE

1.77. Massachusetts Fortifications. 103 items.

A sketch of Boston Harbor showing the action of the eighteen 15-inch guns to be placed in the defending forts for the command of the channel into the harbor, 1862. Maps of Gloucester Harbor and vicinity showing fortified sites and sites for proposed fortifications, a map showing the ranges of the guns defending the harbor, plans of proposed batteries, plans for the alterations of old Fort Conant at Stage Head, and an armament sheet for the fort dated 1865, 1863-65. Plans and armament sheets for the year 1865 for Forts Phoenix and Rodman erected during the war for the defense of New Bedford Harbor, 1861-65. Maps of Newburyport and vicinity showing the range of guns and sites selected for quarters at Salisbury Point, a plan of the proposed works for the point, and an armament sheet for 1865 for these works, 1863-65. A map of Plymouth Harbor showing the ranges of the defending guns, plans of suggested works at Gurnet Point (Fort Andrew) and at Saquish Head (Fort Standish), and armament sheets for both these forts for the year 1865, 1863-65. Maps of Provincetown and vicinity including topographic maps, maps showing the ranges of guns defending the harbor, and a map showing boundaries of U.S. lands at Long Point; plans of temporary batteries; and an armament sheet for these batteries for the year 1865, 1862-65. A map of Salem Harbor showing ranges of defending guns, plans of Forts Glover and Miller, and armament sheets for these forts dated 1865, 1863-65. Plans of Fort Lee located at Salem Neck, one showing alterations to accompany heavy guns; and an armament sheet for the fort for 1865, 1863-65.

Plans of the permanent fortifications Independence, Pickering, Warren, and Winthrop dating before the war. Plans of alterations or additions to the forts dated 1861-65 include plans of batteries and a plan showing gun positions at Fort Independence. Plans of alterations to Fort Pickering. Plans of batteries and modifications of the defenses at Fort Warren. Plans of Fort Winthrop and its batteries including modifications or alterations. Armament sheets for each of these forts for the year 1865. See also entry 1.70.

MICHIGAN

FORTIFICATIONS MAP FILE

1.78. Michigan Fortifications. 23 items.
Plans of the facilities added to Fort Wayne, 1863-65.

MISSISSIPPI

CIVIL WORKS MAP FILE

1.79. General Information. 10 items.
The southern part of La Tourette's map of Mississippi with adjoining parts of Louisiana and Alabama, published in 1847 and annotated to show roads, new railroads, bridges, and additional places (S 28); a map of the Mississippi River from Rodney to Sargent's Bend prepared under the direction of Capt. P. C. Hains in October 1864 (M 119-1); a photoprocessed map of the northern part of the State compiled, surveyed, and drawn under the direction of Lt. J. H. Wilson, Chief Topographical Engineer, Department of the Tennessee (S 5); a large-scale unfinished manuscript map of northern Mississippi drawn by William Claypoole (Z 5); a manuscript map of townships 1 to 4 S., Rs. 6 to 11 E., Chickasaw Meridian (Z 30-3); a manuscript map of the area along the Mississippi River between Bolivar and Bunches Bend and extending eastward beyond the Yazoo River as far as Lexington and Carrolton (Z 30-1); a compiled manuscript map of Tishomingo County (Z 190) (see entry 2.124); a manuscript map of part of Mississippi and Louisiana showing the line of survey of the New Orleans, Jackson, and Great Southern Railway from Jackson to below the State boundary (Rds. 184); copies of Confederate maps of the Saltillo area (US 393-26; US 393-27); and a manuscript map of a survey of the road between Spring Hill, Salem, and Ripley (Z 26). For regional and other related maps, see also entries 1.29 and 1.62.

1.80. Township Plats. 142 items.
A group of manuscript plats of the public land surveys largely in the District west of the Pearl River, many of which were approved between 1846 and 1849 by the Surveyor General at Jackson (Z 29-1 through Z 29-46); a group of outline plats of townships in northern Mississippi, largely within the old Chickasaw cession, and a few of the areas across the Mississippi River in Arkansas, probably prepared to show rivers, streams, and swamp areas (Z 29-47 through Z 29-97 and unnumbered plats).

1.81. Corinth. 22 items.
A manuscript topographic sketch of Corinth and vicinity showing the Confederate entrenchments and the approach of the Union forces as surveyed from May 17 to June 6, 1862, by Capt. N. Michler and Maj. J. E. Weyss (S 13-1); a group of manuscript sketches showing roads leading out of Tennessee toward Corinth and Farmington and several sketches covering the Corinth and Farmington areas showing streams, fields, houses, roads, railroads, a few troop positions, encampments, and entrenchments (S 13-3 through S 13-18); a large-scale manuscript map of Corinth showing Union and Confederate lines (S 63-3); a photoprocessed map of the country around Corinth (S 63-2); a map of the battlefield of Corinth, October 4, 1862, received from Capt. Frederick E. Prime in August 1871 (S 63-1); and a photoprocessed map of the battlefield showing the street plan of Corinth, batteries, lines of works, roads, and railroads (Pub. 1862, No. 1).

1.82. Iuka. 11 items.
A topographic sketch of Iuka showing the site of the battle of September 19, 1862 (S 14-12) (see entry 2.122); a copy of the battlefield map accompanying General Rosecrans' report (S 14-1); a manuscript map of the battle showing troop positions, prepared for publication by the Office of the Chief of Engineers in 1876 (S 14-3); lithographed copies (S 14-4; S 14-5); a copy showing troop positions and annotated with contours transcribed from the Geological Survey Iuka quadrangle (S 14-6); and several other sketches of Iuka and vicinity, including one by Lt. Frederick Schraag (S 14-7 through S 14-11).

1.83. Operations in November and December, 1862. 5 items.
A manuscript map of the route taken by Col. T. L. Dickey's raid on the Mobile and Ohio Railroad (S 8) (see entry 2.123); a manuscript map of the country between Lamar and Lumpkins Mill made from surveys under the direction of 1st Lt. J. H. Wilson in November and December 1862 (S 9-2); a similar map of the country between Lumpkins Mill and Oxford, showing the headquarters of Maj. Gen. J. B. McPherson on December 25 and including an inset of a section of the Confederate works on the Tallahatchie River destroyed by Union forces on December 26 (S 9-1); a manuscript map showing camps of the right wing of the 13th Army Corps on the Yocona River (S 4-2) (see entry 2.131); and an annotated, colored, photoprocessed map on a smaller scale similar to the latter map (S 4-1).

1.84. The Vicksburg Campaign. 31 items.

A "bird's-eye view" of Vicksburg and vicinity on July 15 and 16, 1862, drawn by L. A. Wrotnowski, Civil Engineer, and showing the positions of Confederate defenses, gun boats, and rams in the Yazoo River, the position of Farragut's fleet in the Mississippi River, and the passage of the Confederate ram *Arkansas* through part of the fleet on July 15 (S 27); maps received with a letter of April 9, 1863, from Lt. J. H. Wilson, including a manuscript map of Yazoo Pass (S 11) and a manuscript map of Greenwood and vicinity showing Confederate batteries, camps, and other details, with an armament list of Fort Greenwood (Pemberton) and of the Union attacking forces (S 12); manuscript drawings of Confederate fortifications at Grand Gulf surveyed in May and drawn in October 1863 by H. A. Ulffers, Assistant Engineer (S 23-1 through S 23-3); manuscript maps of the country between Millikens Bend and Jackson showing the routes taken by the Army of the Tennessee and the sites of the battles in 1863 at Port Gibson, May 1, Raymond, May 12, Jackson, May 14, Champion Hill, May 16, and Black River Bridge, May 17 (S 19-1; S 19-13) (see entry 2.125); two annotated lithographed maps with the same title, and a copy of the edition published in 1876 (S 19-2; S 19-3); manuscript maps of the individual battlefields, except Raymond (S 19-10; S 19-11; S 15-2; S 15-4; S 29; S 62-2); a published map of the battlefield of Big Black River Bridge (S 15-1), and a manuscript map showing entrenchments in the vicinity (S 15-5) (see entry 2.119); manuscript maps showing roads and camps near Vicksburg, signal and observation stations, and the positions of batteries (S 19-6; S 19-7; S 19-9; S 19-12); a manuscript map by F. Tunica of parts of Madison and Tenasas Parishes, La., showing the route taken by a detachment of the 9th Division from Perkins' Plantation around Lake St. Joseph to Hard Times (S 19-8); and manuscript sketches

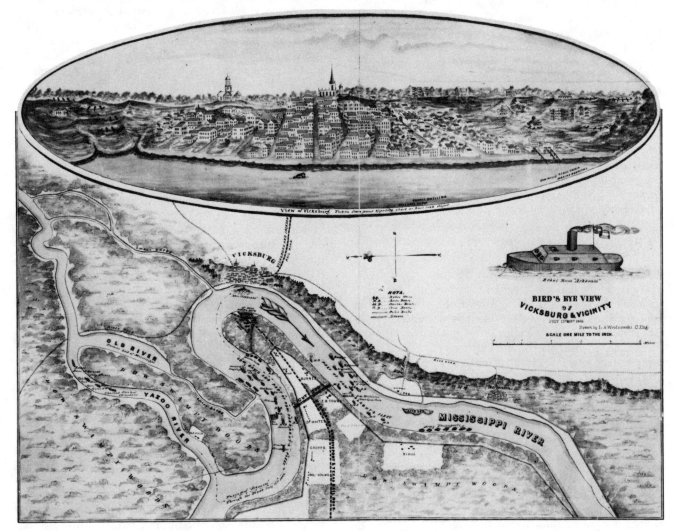

"Bird's-eye view" of Vicksburg and vicinity on July 15 1862. RG 77: S 27. See entry 1.84.

showing operations near Vicksburg, including one showing the center position of the 17th Corps, the Confederate line of defense, and the spot where the interview between Generals Grant and Pemberton took place on July 3, 1863 (S 35; S 37; S 38).

1.85. Operations After the Fall of Vicksburg. 15 items.

A manuscript map of Jackson and vicinity showing the Confederate and Union lines, dated Headquarters, Maj. Gen. W. T. Sherman near Jackson, July 1863 (S 63-3); a manuscript map of the siege of Jackson as surveyed by Lt. P. C. Hains and others and drawn by H. A. Ulffers in September 1863 (S 62-1); a large-scale topographic map of the new line of works at Vicksburg surveyed and drawn in November 1863 under the direction of Capt. C. B. Comstock and Capt. John M. Wilson by Lt. J. G. Patton and J. Fiedler (Z 328); manuscript maps of Yazoo City and vicinity showing Confederate batteries and fortifications and the route of advance of Major General Herron's Division in July 1863 as surveyd by Capt. A. Hoeppner and drawn by H. A. Ulffers in September 1863 (S 26-1 through S 26-4); maps of the country between Vicksburg, Yazoo River, and Haynes Bluff showing Union and Confederate defenses as surveyed under the direction of Capt. J. H. Wilson in 1864 by Lt. H. M. Bush and Charles Spangenberg (S 20); a manuscript map of the defenses of Natchez and vicinity surveyed and prepared under the direction of Capt. P. C. Hains in 1864 by Spangenberg and J. Fiedler (Z 271); and manuscript maps of Pascagoula and vicinity and nearby defenses prepared by order of Maj. Gen. Gordon Granger from surveys made by Capt. H. L. Wheeler and Lt. S. E. McGregory in January 1865 (S 25-a through S 25-d).

FORTIFICATION MAP FILE

1.86. Mississippi Fortifications. 56 items.

A map of the country between Vicksburg and Meridian showing the route of the 17th Army Corps, Union Army, under Major General McPherson, 1864 (see entry 2.130). Maps of Corinth and vicinity showing Confederate and Union entrenchments and the locations of batteries near Corinth (see entry 2.121), and panels of plans of Batteries Lothrup, Madison, Phillips, Powell, Robinett, Tannrath, and Williams, 1862-63. A map of Jackson and vicinity (Dr. 138-47) showing positions of Union and Confederate forces and the defenses of each, 1864. Maps of Natchez and vicinity showing defenses; plans of Fort McPherson, one of which is an inset on one of the vicinity maps of Natchez; and plans of the individual redoubts composing the fort, 1863-64. Maps of Vicksburg and vicinity showing Union and Confederate defenses during and after the siege (see entries 2.127 through 2.129), including a military map compiled and published by order of Gen. W. T. Sherman with annotations showing additional detail and the location of Sherman's headquarters, a map showing new or projected lines of work with a report on the land

defenses of Vicksburg by Lt. Peter C. Hains, a map of the peninsula opposite the city showing the canal and railroad line and eddies in the Mississippi River, plans of the traverse circle for heavy guns and of the platform for front pintle guns at Fort Grant, and plans of the battery opposite Vicksburg, 1863-65.

Plans of the permanent Fort Adams and of the permanent fort on Ship Island dating before the war. Items relating to the fort on Ship Island, 1861-65, including plans and alterations (some showing gun positions) and an armament sheet for 1865.

MISSOURI

CIVIL WORKS MAP FILE

1.87. General Information. 2 items.

A large-scale, unfinished manuscript map covering several counties in central and western Missouri and showing the drainage pattern, roads, railroads, and towns (Z 204); and a large-scale manuscript map of counties south of St. Louis to the Arkansas line showing proposed routes for the extension of the St. Louis and Iron Mountain railroad (Z 179). For regional maps, see also entry 1.30.

1.88. Battlefields. 8 items.

Maps of the Battlefield near Belmont, November 7, 1861, consisting of a manuscript map prepared for publication and copies of the edition published in 1876 (Q 286); a manuscript map of the battlefield of Wilson's Creek (Q 462) (see entry 2.141); a manuscript sketch of the ground near New Madrid showing the lines of fortifications and the location of gun boats (Q 86-4); and maps by Capt. Wm. Hoelcke showing the system of Confederate fortifications at Island No. 10 and New Madrid and the operations of the Union forces under Gen. John Pope (Q 86-1 through Q 86-3).

1.89. Local Defenses. 17 items.

A military map of the Cape Girardeau area accompanied by ground plans of four forts (Z 285); maps of Jefferson City and vicinity showing the line of defenses (Z 304); a map of New Madrid and vicinity showing Fort Thompson and other fortifications (Z 331); a contour map of Pilot Knob and vicinity showing abandoned Fort Curtis and spot elevations around Fort Davidson (Z 344); a military map of Rolla showing the location of Fort Wyman, government buildings, the post hospital, and post headquarters (Z 332), and a topographic manuscript map of the area (Z 187) (see entry 2.138); a large-scale draft and a finished manuscript military map of St. Louis and vicinity prepared in 1862 (Q 93) (see entry 2.139), and a map of the city and vicinity, published in 1864, annotated to show Camp Jackson, Benton Barracks, the Cavalry Depot and Corral, the Arsenal, the Marine Hospital tract, roads, and fortifications (Z 282); and a map of Springfield showing the forts around the city (Z 303), a manuscript

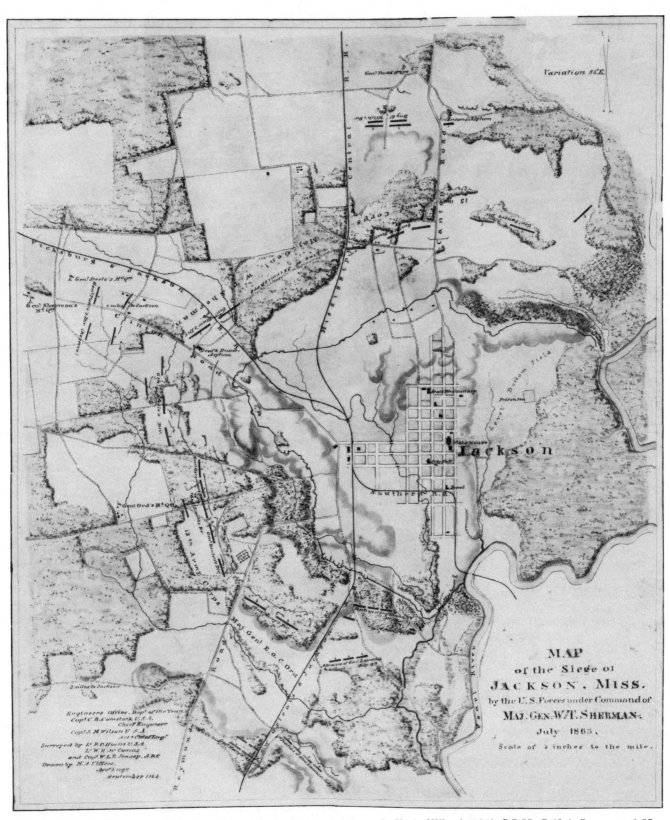

Siege of Jackson, Miss., as surveyed by Lt. P. C. Hains and others and drawn by H. A. Ulffers in 1863. RG 77: S 62-1. See entry 1.85.

map of picket roads and forts (Q 90) (see entry 2.140), and two sheets of plans of the forts dated November and December 1862, one of which includes profiles of gun platforms and entrenchments (Q 90-1; Q 90-2).

1.90. Reconnaissance Sketches. 17 items.

A set of penciled sketches, "Kern's reconnaissance notes from Rolla, Mo., westward to the Gasconade R., 1861," with a few remarks on the character of the country traversed (Z 223); manuscript, topographic sketches showing the routes from Little Piney Ford to Rolla (Q 88-1; Q 88-2) (see entry 2.137); and a plan for a railroad bridge across the Big River (Q 88-3).

FORTIFICATIONS MAP FILE

1.91. Missouri Fortifications. 28 items.

A map of Bloomfield and vicinity (Dr. 139-25) showing lines of defenses, and a plan and a profile of the fort located at the city, 1865. A map of Cape Girardeau showing defense lines, 1865 (see entry 2.132). A map of Jefferson City showing defense lines, 1865 (see entry 2.133). Maps of New Madrid showing Union and Confederate troop positions and defense lines in 1862 (see entry 2.134), defense lines in 1865 (see entry 2.135), and the character of the land; and an outline sketch and plans of Fort Thompson. A map of Pilot Knob showing defenses (see entry 2.136); and plans of Fort Davidson, one showing modifications to the fort, 1865. A map of Rolla and vicinity showing defenses; plans of Fort Wyman and of the powder magazine at the fort; and a plan of a blockhouse on the defense line, 1865. A topographic military map of St. Louis and vicinity, 1862 (Dr. 139-9). Two copies of a map showing defenses of Springfield (Dr. 139-74-2; Dr. 139-74-3), and copies of a plan of Fort No. 1, 1862.

WAR DEPARTMENT MAP COLLECTION

1.92. Battlefield of Wilson's Creek. 1 item.

A tracing of a map of Wilson's Creek battlefield showing troop positions, with a small inset map showing Sigel's and Lyon's routes, surveyed by Lt. N. Boardman and traced in the Office of the Chief Engineer, Military Division of the Missouri, 1865 (WDMC 21-Missouri).

NEW MEXICO TERRITORY

CIVIL WORKS MAP FILE

1.93. General Information and Operations near Fort Craig. 2 items.

Manuscript map reduced from a map furnished by General Getty, Commanding the District of New Mexico, showing the operations near Fort Craig in February 1862, the positions of Union lines, and Confederate camps, lines of battle, and route of march (W 109); and a pho-

toprocessed copy of the eastern part of a map of the Military Department of New Mexico annotated to show military posts (W 83-2). For regional maps, see also entry 1.30.

NEW YORK

FORTIFICATIONS MAP FILE

1.94. New York Fortifications. 178 items.

Maps of Sodus Bay and vicinity, Black River and Sacket's Harbor and vicinity, and the Genesee River and vicinity showing existing and proposed defenses, 1862. Maps and plans relating to defenses of New York Bay and Harbor, 1861-64, including plans for modifying existing batteries and for constructing additional batteries to defend the harbor, some showing the number of guns at each battery; a copy of a Coast Survey chart of The Narrows between Forts Richmond and Hamilton showing bottom contours; and plans for obstructing the channel.

Plans of the permanent Forts Gibson, Hamilton, Lafayette, Montgomery, Niagara, Ontario, Porter, Schuyler, Tompkins, Totten, Wadsworth, and Wood and Castle Williams dated before the war. Maps and plans, dated 1862-65, of each fort showing changes or modifications in batteries, the arrangement of guns, and additional buildings; and armament sheets for each fort, except Totten, for the year 1865.

NORTH CAROLINA

CIVIL WORKS MAP FILE

1.95. General Information. 6 items.

Manuscript maps of the western part of the State (H 79); a manuscript map of Beaufort Harbor, Core Sound, and Ocracoke Inlet compiled in the Bureau of Topographical Engineers in 1861 from surveys by Col. James Kearney and Capt. Hartman Bache and from Coast Survey maps (H 80); manuscript (H 85-1) (see entry 2.142) and published photoprocessed (Pub. 1862, No. 3) maps of the eastern part of the Military Department of North Carolina compiled in May 1862; and a published map with the same date and title having an inset map of the entrances to Cape Fear River and a panoramic view of the Confederate defense works (Pub. 1862, No. 2). For regional maps, see also entries 1.29 and 1.30.

1.96. Battlefields and Routes of March. 23 items.

A manuscript map of the Battle of Averysboro fought March 16, 1865, compiled under the direction of Bvt. Col. O. M. Poe by Maj. E. F. Hoffmann, showing Union and Confederate works, Confederate positions, and the positions of both forces on the night of March 16 (H 89); a manuscript map of the Battle of Bentonsville fought March 19, 1865, and of the operations of March 20 and 21 (H 90) (see entry 2.145), a map showing the position of the Army of the Tennessee on March 20 and 21 (H 90½); a manuscript map showing batteries and vessels at the attack on Fort Fisher, January 15, 1865 (G 443, vol. 8, p. 13); a published sketch of Fort Fisher and vicinity dated February 9, 1865, showing also a plan of the armament of Fort Buchanan, and a plan and sections of Fort Fisher taken by the Union forces under the command of Maj. Gen. A. H. Terry on January 15, 1865 (insets for map of the Military Department of the South, entry 1.30) (Pub. 1865, No. 7; Pub. 1865, No. 8); manuscript maps of Roanoke Island, one of which shows the action of February 8, 1862 (H 81-2) (see entry 2.154), and two with additional information about the engagement (H 81-3; G 443, vol. 9, p. 3½); a manuscript map of the battlefield of Roanoke Island, February 8, 1862, by Lieutenant Andrews, 9th N.Y. Regiment, copied from tracings in the Adjutant General Office (H 81-1), and a copy of the published edition (US 491-33); and manuscript campaign maps in book form showing the line of march of the 20th Corps from Savannah, Ga., to Goldsboro, N.C., January 17 to March 24, 1865 (US 280) (see entry 2.143), and the line of march of the 14th and 20th Corps from Goldsboro to Avens Bridge, April 10 to 15, 1865 (H 96) (see entry 2.144). See also entry 1.32.

1.97. Local Defenses. 10 items.

A manuscript plan showing fortifications and encampments around Wilmington and obstructions in the Cape Fear River (Z 94) (see entry 2.155); a manuscript chart showing soundings in the entrances to Cape Fear River and the location of Fort Caswell on Oak Island (H 85-5); a published copy of the preliminary chart of Frying Pan Shoals and entrances to Cape Fear River, annotated to show fortifications, batteries, shipwrecks along the coast above New Inlet, and other information received at the Coast Survey Office in December 1864 (H 86-2); a manuscript chart of the Cape Fear River to Wilmington drawn in 1864 by Brig. Gen. Charles K. Graham from Coast Survey charts, showing soundings and the position of forts and obstructions from observations and reports of pilots and deserters, and a copy showing fortifications in color (H 88); a sketch of the defenses of New Bern (H 82-1) (see entry 2.150), a manuscript map of the city (H 82-2), and a map of the area to the south and east made in 1864 (G 443, vol. 2, p. 11); and a manuscript map, dated October 26, 1863, of a survey of the approaches to Raleigh made by order of Governor Z. B. Vance (H 95) (see entry 2.152).

FORTIFICATIONS MAP FILE

1.98. North Carolina Fortifications. 39 items.

A view of the rebel defenses of Cape Fear River and a plan of Fort Anderson as captured by Union forces, 1865. Maps of Federal Point showing lines of defenses, ranges of defending guns, positions of blockading ships, and the position of the powder ship used to destroy Fort

Fisher (see entry 2.146); a report on the destruction of the fort; a plan of the powder ship; and plans of Battery Buchanan and Fort Fisher (see entry 2.147) as carried by assault of Union forces, 1864-65. A map of Hatteras Island showing defenses (see entry 2.149), and plans of Forts Clark and Hatteras, 1861-64. A plan of the fort at Morehead City, 1863. Photocopies of maps of New Bern (Dr. 143-24; Dr. 143-25) showing defenses and annotated with General Weitzel's approval; and plans of Forts Amory, Anderson (see entry 2.148), Chase, Gaston, Rowan, Spinola, Stevenson, and Totten, 1863-64. A map of Plymouth and vicinity showing lines of defenses (see entry 2.151); and a panel of plans of Forts Grey, Wessels, and Williams and Redoubt Compher, 1863. A map of Raleigh showing Confederate defenses, 1865 (see entry 2.153). Plans of the defenses of Washington, N.C., including Marine Battery and Forts Jack, McChesney, McKibbon, and Richter Jones, and the fort on Castle Island, 1863. A map of Wilmington and vicinity (Dr. 143-34) showing the inner and outer defenses as captured by Union forces in February 1865, and a plan of Fort Campbell, 1866.

Plans of the permanent Forts Caswell, Macon, and Johnston dated before the war. Two plans of Fort Caswell, one dated 1862 and the other dated 1866, showing the condition of the fort. A plan of Fort Johnston as it was when taken possession by the North Atlantic Squadron commanded by Admiral Porter, 1865, and a plan of the Confederate battery at the fort, 1866.

OHIO

FORTIFICATIONS MAP FILE

1.99. Ohio Fortifications. 7 items.

Part of a map of Lake Erie showing Sandusky Harbor, and plans of proposed defensive installations on Johnson's Island and Cedar Point, 1864-65. See also entries 1.60 and 1.61 for maps showing the defenses of Cincinnati.

OKLAHOMA (INDIAN TERRITORY)

FORTIFICATIONS MAP FILE

1.100. Oklahoma Fortifications. 2 items.

Two copies of a plan of Fort Gibson, also known in 1863 as Fort Blunt, formerly abandoned and reoccupied in 1863 for centralization and supply purposes.

PENNSYLVANIA

CIVIL WORKS MAP FILE

1.101. General Information. 7 items.

A manuscript map of the southern part of Franklin and Adams Counties, 1862 (E 66) (see entry 2.158); manuscript Confederate maps including a map of Franklin County (US 253-12) (see entry 2.157), a sketch map of York County (US 253-26), and a map of part of southern Pennsylvania (principally west of the Susquehanna River) and adjacent parts of Maryland showing roads and railroads (US 253-22); a manuscript map of Adams and Franklin Counties, Frederick and Washington Counties, Md., and Berkeley County, W. Va., captured from the Confederates (Z 265) (see entry 2.156); a rough plat of the turnpike between the Brandywine and Delaware Rivers with penciled notations of bearings and distances received from the Engineer Bureau in 1863 (E 75); and a manuscript map of the Susquehanna River from the confluence of the Juniata River to Havre de Grace received September 3, 1864, with Capt. C. N. Turnbull's report (US 245). For regional maps, see also entry 1.30.

1.102. Gettysburg. 39 items.

Maps of the battlefield of Gettysburg including an annotated published copy of Elliott's map, a manuscript sheet and profiles of routes or roads on the field, and a letter received October 22, 1866, with remarks by Bvt. Maj. A. H. Burnham on the plotting of certain lines and parts of the routes (E 73-1 through E 73-9); a manuscript map of the battlefield (E 72-1) and several annotated photoprocessed copies (E 72-3; E 105A-1) (see entry 2.159); a detailed, large-scale manuscript map of the battlefield surveyed and drawn under the direction of Bvt. Maj. Gen. G. K. Warren by 1st Lt. W. H. Chase and others in 1868-69 and revised and corrected in 1873 by P. M. Blake, Civil Engineer (E 81) (see entry 2.160), and a manuscript reduction of the map (E 105); a panoramic view of the battlefield and several shaded relief and contour proof sheets for a base map annotated by Warren, including final copies lithographed in January 1874 (E 105A-2 through E 105A-8; E 115-13 through E 115-15); a set of maps for July 1, 2, and 3, 1863, with troop positions by John B. Bachelder, printed in 1876 and approved in 1877 by the Secretary of War (E 119-1 through E 119-3) (see entry 2.161); a map of the third day's battle and an overlay sheet dated 1878 covering a part of the map, both with corrections and comments (E 120-1; E 120-2); a printed map of the second day's battle prepared by Capt. William H. Willcox (G 443, vol. 11, p. 1); a worksheet of the Gettysburg Extension Survey showing stations of 1880 and 1881, and an 1883 contour sheet of the same area by Frank O. Maxson (E 171-2; E 171-3); and three sets of published maps (the editions of 1876, 1883, and 1912) for the 3 days' battle (Pub. 1876; Pub. 1883; Pub. 1912).

1.103. Depots. 2 items.

A manuscript map of the eastern entrance of Erie Bay made from a survey in 1844, with a notation by Lt. Col. T. J. Cram in October 1864 that Erie would be an excellent site for a naval depot (E 140-1); and a manuscript plan for a "Rendezvous for Drafted Men" in Philadelphia (Z 432) (see entry 2.165).

FORTIFICATIONS MAP FILE

1.104. Pennsylvania Fortifications. 11 items.

Maps of the vicinity of Harrisburg showing defenses of and approaches to the city (L 162; L 163), and a plan of batteries located at these defenses, 1863-64 (see entry 2.164). A map of Pittsburgh and vicinity showing defenses, 1863 (see entry 2.166).

Plans of Fort Mifflin, a permanent fortification dating from before the war, including plans of the new magazine, sketches showing gun positions, and an armament sheet, 1863-65.

RHODE ISLAND

FORTIFICATIONS MAP FILE

1.105. Rhode Island Fortifications. 3 items.

A topographic map of Dutch Island, and a plan and an 1865 armament sheet of the battery (later known as Fort Greble) located on the island, 1863-65.

SOUTH CAROLINA

CIVIL WORKS MAP FILE

1.106. General Information. 1 item.

A manuscript map showing lines for railroads between Columbia and Spartanburg, Greenville, and Anderson, received from Capt. O. M. Poe. For regional maps, see also entries 1.29 and 1.30.

1.107. Charleston and Vicinity. 24 items.

A Coast Survey, annotated map of parts of the coast from Charleston to Savannah, and an accompanying sketch showing batteries near Charleston Harbor (US 208); a map of Charleston Harbor and the adjacent area surveyed from 1823 to 1825 by Capt. Hartman Bache and others, annotated to show Confederate works and siege operations from surveys made in April 1865 by Maj. John E. Weyss (I 34), and other manuscript maps and sketches (I 35; I 36); a Coast Survey chart of Charleston Harbor and its approaches published in 1858 and annotated to show underwater contours in the channels and the locations of Batteries Beauregard and Gregg and Fort Wagner (I 28-4); an annotated printed map relating to operations south of Charleston in June 1862 (G 443, vol. 7, p. 11); two manuscript maps of the defenses of Charleston City and Harbor, showing also the works erected by Union forces in 1863 and 1864: one of which accompanied the report of Maj. Gen. Q. A. Gillmore (I 58-1) (see entry 2.172) and the other of which is a finished map prepared for publication with a view of North Channel, February 18, 1865, and a note identifying the forts and batteries constructed by the Confederate forces and those by Union forces (I 58-10); an annotated printed map showing Union and Confederate batteries on July 11, 1863 (G 443, vol. 9,

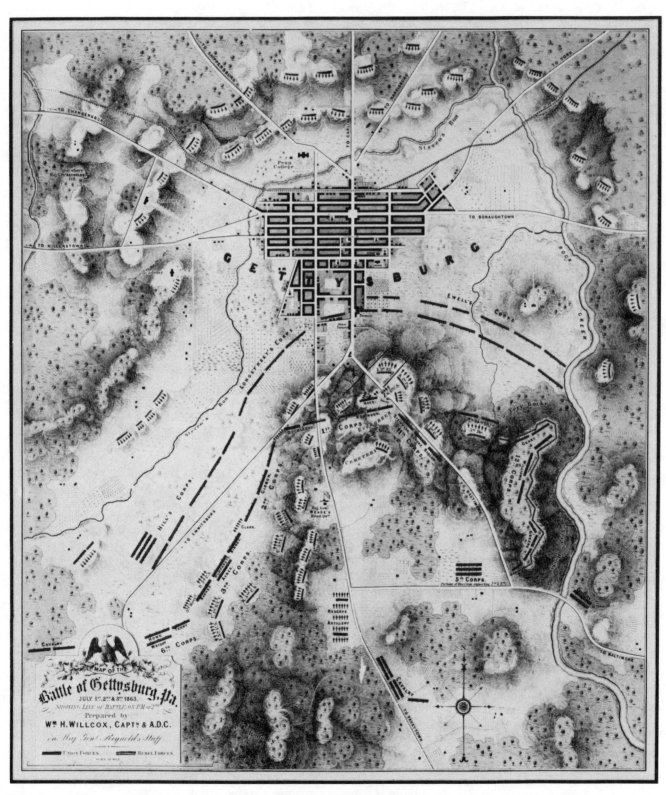

Printed map of the second day's battle at Gettysburg prepared by Capt. William H. Willcox. G 443, vol. 11, p. 1. See entry 1.102.

p. 17); annotated copies of the 1864 Coast Survey Chart of Charleston Harbor and its approaches received with Captain Suter's report of April 3, 1866, accompanied by a small sketch showing wrecks in the main channel near Forts Sumter and Moultrie (I 60-1; I 60-2) and a manuscript map of the shore line at the western extremity of Sullivan's Island (I 60-3); large-scale manuscript plans, elevations, and sections of Fort Sumter approved by Bvt. Maj. Charles R. Suter, with one noted as accompanying the report of Maj. Gen. Q. A. Gillmore, Commanding Department of South Carolina, Hilton Head, November 1, 1865 (see entry 2.173), and sections of forts and batteries on James and Sullivan's Islands (I 58-2 through I 58-6; I 58-8; I 58-9); a map of the middle part of Folly Island dated August 5, 1863, showing positions of Union troops and fortications and distances to Confederate fortifications on James Island as surveyed by order of Gen. J. Vodges (I 46-1), and a manuscript map of Long or Little Folly Island surveyed under the direction of Lt. Col. A. Wettstein and showing distances to batteries on James Island (I 46-2), both maps approved by Capt. Charles R. Suter; a sketch of Grimball's Plantation dated June 14, 1862, showing headquarters, a signal station, and volunteer engineers camp and fortifications (I 42); and a large manuscript map of the vicinity of Smith's Plantation, including Grimball's east of the Stone River and showing fields, marshes, pontoon bridge, and batteries farther inland (I 38).

1.108. The Port Royal and Beaufort Area. 17 items.

A Coast Survey chart of a reconnaissance of the Port Royal entrance and Beaufort Harbor published in 1855 and annotated to show underwater contours and names of islands (I 26); a manuscript map of the country around Port Royal showing fortifications at the entrance to Port Royal Sound as compiled for Brig. Gen. Thomas W. Sherman by 1st Lt. J. H. Wilson in November 1861 (I 28); manuscript copies of the 1862 Coast Survey charts of surveys for the naval coal depot at Bay Point and of the Peninsula of Lands End, St. Helena Island, both with annotated underwater contours (I 54; I 48); manuscript map of part of the Beaufort and Colleton Districts between the Broad and South Edisto Rivers (I 47) (see entry 2.169); a map of part of a tract of land known as Bowler's Island between the Ashepoo and Chehaw Rivers, copied in January 1862 from an 1834 survey (I 39); a manuscript map of Smith's Plantation on the Beaufort River showing acres reserved for the United States and the location of Spanish Fort, approved by Maj. James W. Abert on May 26, 1864 (I 33-3); plans of the city of Beaufort dated 1863 (I 41) (see entry 2.167); a manuscript map of Beaufort and its defenses, approved by Charles R. Suter (I 55); a manuscript plan of Beaufort entrenchments (I 44) (see entry 2.168); a large-scale map of Hilton Head Island showing the plan of the Union military installations and the village of Mitchelville (I 52) (see entry 2.174); another manuscript plan of a part of the island

(I 28-2); a map of Hilton Head, approved by James W. Abert, April 1864 (I 33-1); and a plan of the New York Volunteer Engineer camp and depot at Hilton Head (I 33-2).

1.109. Operations and Defenses Inland from Port Royal and Beaufort. 4 items.

A manuscript map showing the route of the expedition of October 22, 1862, with the battlegrounds of Pocotaligo and Coosawhatchie (I 40) (see entry 2.175); a copy of a map of a reconnaissance of the upper part of Broad River and its tributaries made in December 1864 and January 1865 under the direction of C. O. Boutelle of the Coast Survey (I 50); and manuscript maps of the Confederate lines in 1865 on the Pocotaligo, Combahee, and Ashepoo Rivers (I 53-1; I 53-2) (see entry 2.176). See also entry 1.32.

FORTIFICATIONS MAP FILE

1.110. South Carolina Fortifications. 245 items.

Charleston Harbor and vicinity: maps of Charleston Harbor showing Confederate and Union defenses and positions during the siege, positions of blockading vessels, and the range of fire of guns (see entries 2.170 and 2.171); plans of temporary forts and batteries including Forts Green, Putnam, Shaw, Strong, and Wagner, Batteries Barton, Chatfield, Dahlgren, Gregg, Holbrook, and Seymour, and the marsh battery; a unit of 43 loose sheets filed and identified as an atlas, containing drawings of the outer defense lines, rifle pits, defenses within the city of Charleston (particularly in the wharf area), plans of forts and batteries composing the defenses (among these Forts Ripley and Sumter and Castle Pinckney), and plans of torpedoes, torpedo boats, and the Blakely gun used in the siege, 1863-66. A plan of Castle Pinckney dated 1865 showing changes made by the Confederates, and two plans of Fort Sumter showing arrangements made to resist attack, 1861. A map of part of James Island as occupied by Union forces and showing defenses built in June 1862; and 93 sheets filed and identified as an atlas, including plans of Forts Johnson, Pemberton, and Pringle and of numerous batteries, rifle pits, and siege and defense lines, 1862-65. A collection of maps and plans relating to the defenses on Sullivan's Island filed and identified as an atlas, consisting of maps showing defense lines and rifle pits and plans of the forts and batteries composing these lines, among these Forts Moultrie and Beauregard, 1865.

Plans of the permanent fortifications of Forts Johnson, Moultrie, and Sumter and Castle Pinckney, some dated before the war.

The Georgetown area: a copy of a Coast Survey chart of a reconnaissance of the Bottle Channel entrance to Georgetown Harbor, 1862.

The Port Royal and Beaufort area: a map of the Port Royal entrance to Beaufort Harbor (Dr. 146-23) showing the fort at Bay Point, Fort Welles on Hilton Head Island, and the areas reserved for proposed military reservations, 1866. Map of Beaufort and vicinity (Dr. 146-20) showing defenses, and plans of Fort Stevens, 1866. Maps of Hilton Head showing entrenchments, and plans of Forts Howell and Welles (Dr. 146-14; Dr. 146-16 through Dr. 146-18). A map of Pocotaligo and vicinity (Dr. 146-19) showing defense lines, 1866. A map of Port Royal and vicinity showing lands reserved for military purposes and plantations (Dr. 166-22) (see entry 2.177), apparently related to other maps of Port Royal made or used during the Reconstruction period that are among the records of the Collector of Internal Revenue for South Carolina. See also entry 1.7.

TENNESSEE

CIVIL WORKS MAP FILE

1.111. General Information. 12 items.

A manuscript military map of Kentucky and Tennessee begun under the authority of Maj. Gen. Don Carlos Buell, Department of the Ohio, by Capt. N. Michler and completed under the authority of Maj. Gen. Ambrose E. Burnside by Lt. Col. J. H. Simpson in July 1863 (T 68) (see entry 2.11); a manuscript map of part of the Department of the Cumberland revised and corrected to emphasize railroads and noted as official by Capt. O. M. Poe on June 17, 1863 (T 116-19); an unfinished manuscript map of middle and western Tennessee received from Poe (T 103); an unfinished manuscript map of middle and western Tennessee made under the authority of Gen. J. H. Wilson (Z 4); a manuscript map of part of east Tennessee compiled under the direction of Lt. Col. N. Bowen (Z 234) (see entry 2.179); a manuscript map of east Tennessee prepared under the direction of Poe in 1864 (T 87-1) (see entry 2.178) and an annotated photoprocessed copy (T 87-2); an incomplete manuscript map of middle Tennessee compiled under the direction of Col. W. E. Merrill by Edward Ruger in 1865 with additional manuscript pieces (T 84½); and a manuscript map of middle Tennessee and parts of east Tennessee made under the direction of Merrill in 1865 (T 84-2) (see entry 2.180). For more local maps of surveys and reconnaissances, on which many of the above maps are based, see entries 1.113 and 1.114. For regional maps, see also entries 1.29 and 1.30.

1.112. Railroads in Tennessee and Adjoining States. 63 items.

Maps showing routes, maps of surveyed lines, or profiles (most of which were received from Capt. O. M. Poe) for the following railroads: Central Southern (Rds. 185); Covington and Lexington (Z 261); East Tennessee and Virginia (Rds. 183; Rds. 187; Z 85); Edge-field and Kentucky (Rds. 182); Hiwassee (Rds. 173); Knoxville and Charleston (Rds. 189); Knoxville and Kentucky (Rds. 178; T 116-7; Z 86; Z 87-1 through Z 87-13); Louisville and Nashville (Z 263); Mobile and Ohio (Z 100); Nashville and Decatur (Rds. 191); Sewanee Mining Company (Z 235); and Tennessee and Alabama (Rds. 179; Z 99; Z 257; Rds. 180; Rds. 181; Rds. 192; Z 93; G 443, vol. 7, p. 4).

1.113. Reconnaissances and Surveys in Western Tennessee. 16 items.

A manuscript map of Memphis and vicinity surveyed and drawn by Lieutenants Pitzman and Frick by order of Maj. Gen. W. T. Sherman showing features of the terrain, railroads, and roads (T 125-1), and a similar photoprocessed map annotated to show bridges (T 125-4); a topographic map of Bolivar and vicinity annotated to show roads, bridges, and ferries (T 24); a manuscript map of the country between Memphis and Bolivar showing roads and railroads, partly copied from a captured Confederate map and compiled from reconnaissances made under the direction of Lt. J. H. Wilson, Chief Topographical Engineer, Department of the Tennessee (T 43); a manuscript sketch map of western Tennessee showing roads and railroads (T 106-2); other manuscript maps of surveys made under the direction of Wilson by H. A. Ulffers for La Grange and vicinity, by Chas. Spangenberg for the country north of Grand Junction, and by J. Fiedler and Otto H. Matz for the country west of La Grange and the country between La Fayette and Collierville (T 35-1; T 44; T 45; T 46); a topographic map of La Grange, Grand Junction, and vicinity made by Chas. Spangenberg in April 1863 under the direction of Wilson (T 35-3); a photoprocessed map of La Grange and vicinity annotated to show the location of a fort and with a note stating that the erection of field works was begun in February 1863 (T 35-2); a manuscript map of the vicinities of Moscow, La Grange, and Grand Junction showing roads, the route of the Memphis and Charleston Railroad, and its junction with the Tennessee and Ohio Railroad (Rds. 199-1), and a manuscript map of the road from Moscow to Memphis showing parts of the Memphis and Charleston Railroad surveyed and drawn by order of Sherman by Pitzman and Frick (Rds. 199-2); and a manuscript map of the road from La Grange to Chewalla compiled and drawn by Pitzman from information gathered by Lt. I. G. Kappner (Z 30-2).

1.114. Reconnaissances and Surveys in Middle and Eastern Tennessee. 70 items.

Maps made under the direction of Capt. N. Michler including a topographic sketch of the vicinity of Nashville surveyed in March 1862 and September and December 1863 for use by the Armies of the Ohio and the Cumberland, annotated to show railroads, turnpikes, and roads leading out of Nashville, particularly to the south (Z 62-2); a photoprocessed map of the country along the Gallatin-Hartsville turnpike compiled from original recon- naissances and emphasizing roads (Z 64-2); photopro- cessed copies of topographic sketches of Nashville and Murfreesboro surveyed in 1862 and annotated to show roads and railroads (T 34; T 29-1); manuscript topo- graphic sketches of Murfreesboro and vicinity surveyed in 1863, showing railroads, roads, and turnpikes (T 29- 3; T 29-5); a topographic sketch of the country adjacent to the Nolensville-Chapel Hill turnpike compiled from original reconnaissances (T 36) (see entry 2.198); and a topographic sketch of Sparta and vicinity made from in- formation received from W. Bosson, Esq. (T 52-2).

A group of topographic maps, some of which show fortifications, prepared under the direction of Col. Wil- liam E. Merrill, Chief Engineer of the Department of the Cumberland, by Maj. James R. Willett, Chief In- spector of Railroad Defenses, and drawn from surveys made in October and December 1864 and January through April 1865, showing the vicinities of Clarksville (T 79; Z 74), Cleveland (Z 75), Columbia (Z 75; T 101), De- cherd (Z 68), Duck River Bridge (T 115), Fort Donelson (T 78; Z 69) (see entry 2.190), Gallatin (Z 46-11), Lou- don (Z 79), Nashville (Z 62-1), Pulaski (Z 78), Straw- berry Plains (Z 80-2), and Tullahoma (Z 67); and an un- dated topographic map of Franklin and vicinity (N 218).

Maps received from Capt. O. M. Poe including man- uscript maps of parts of counties in the northern part of the State east of the Tennessee River and west of La- fayette (T 98-1 through T 98-5), of Carthage and vicinity (T 111), of the coal and iron region in Campbell County (T 95), of the Cumberland Gap region (T 116-4; T 116- 5), of the Hiwassee and Ocoee Districts north and south of the Hiwassee River and east of the Tennessee River (T 109; T 112), of roads from Georgetown by way of Decatur, Morganton, and Maryville to Knoxville (T 110- 1 through T 110-8), of Knox County and its boundaries (T 108-1 through T 108-3), of Knoxville and vicinity (T 90; T 93; T 99; Z 104), of part of Cocke County (T 96), and of Bridgeport, Ala., and its defenses (T 114); sketches of the valleys of the Holston and French Broad Rivers (T 116-6; T 116-8; T 116-9; T 116-12) and of the routes from Knoxville to the South Fork of the Cumberland River in Kentucky (T 116-11); and a topographic report from the Headquarters of the 2d Brigade, November 13, 1863, on new roads traveled by the brigade (T 116-14) and a draft of the roads and picket posts surrounding Russellville and Cheek's Cross Roads (T 116-13).

An unfinished manuscript map of a topographic survey near Kingston made by engineers of the 9th Corps under the direction of Lt. Col. N. Bowen in November 1863, progress on which was interrupted by the advance of a Confederate force under General Longstreet (T 54); a manuscript plat of the lands of the University of the South on the Sewanee Plateau in Franklin County, showing roads and railroads surveyed and drawn in 1858 and later copied by A. McCafferty (Z 237-2); a manuscript map of the Ocoee District made August 18 and 19, 1863, by

McCafferty (Z 426-1), and a duplicate tracing (Z 426-2); a manuscript Confederate map of mountain passes prac- ticable for wagon roads from Cumberland Gap to Winters' Gap (N 219-1) (see entry 2.188); and manuscript copies of Confederate maps, one showing the gaps in the moun- tains from Winters' Gap to Louisa (Levisa) Fork, Va. (US 393-17), one of the country between Kingston and Knoxville (US 393-18), and one showing bridle paths and roads in the valleys of the Clinch and Powell Rivers between Kingston, Tazwell, Jacksboro, and Cumberland Gap (US 393-14).

1.115. River Surveys. 21 items.

Manuscript tracings of a survey of the Tennessee River drawn by Lt. S. P. Heintzelman and copied by C. Ham- berg (Z 425); a sketch map of the Watauga River (Z 95); a compiled map of a reconnaissance of the Tennessee, Holston, and French Broad Rivers by Poe (Z 101); and manuscript maps received from Poe of the Tennessee, Little Tennessee (in North Carolina and Tennessee), French Broad, Holston, and Nolichucky Rivers (T 91; T 94; T 97; T 98-6; T 100; T 113).

1.116. Construction Plans. 8 items.

A manuscript plan of the railroad junction and depots at Knoxville and a large-scale plan showing positions of freight houses, engine house, proposed Union passenger station, car works, and the Knoxville Iron Company (Cons. 115-1; Cons. 115-2); ground plans and elevations of the depot at Jonesboro and an unidentified plan for a turntable (Cons. 115-3 through Cons. 115-5); a plan and section of the pontoon bridge used for crossing the Little Tennessee River at Loudon (Z 266); a plan of the U.S. Military Bridge at Chattanooga surveyed and drawn under the direction of Lt. Col. P. V. Fox (Z 81); and a general plan with sections of Magazine Granger at Nashville, prepared under the direction of Col. William E. Merrill by Maj. James R. Willett in November 1864 (Z 76-1).

1.117. Forts Henry and Donelson. 4 items.

A sketch of Fort Donelson (T 88-5) (see entry 2.189); a published sketch showing the relative positions of Forts Henry and Donelson and the road connecting them (T 88- 4); and plans of the two forts drawn under the direction of Lt. Col. J. B. McPherson and published by authority of the Secretary of War in the Office of the Chief of Engineers, 1875 (T 88-1; T 88-2).

1.118. Shiloh. 4 items.

A manuscript sketch of the battlefield (T 31-3) (see entry 2.199); a photoprocessed map showing the position of the Confederate troops and roads in the vicinity (T 31- 2); a manuscript map showing the positions of Union forces under Grant and Buell on the mornings and eve- nings of April 6 and 7, 1862, surveyed under the direction of Col. George Thom, Chief of Topographical Engineers, and drawn by Otto H. Matz, Assistant Topographical

Engineer (T 20); and a copy of a Confederate map of the battle area (US 393-16).

1.119. Cumberland Gap and Vicinity. 6 items.

A manuscript contour map, with sketches in the margins, of Cumberland Gap and vicinity from surveys made by Capt. Sidney S. Lyon under the orders of Gen. G. W. Morgan, showing the locations of works constructed by Confederate and Union forces (T 63-1) (see entry 2.186); a manuscript map of the vicinity by Lyon showing the fortified area on a larger scale (T 63-2); and a manuscript map, with an overlay sheet, compiled for publication by Edward Ruger to illustrate the operations of the Seventh Division under Morgan's command during a part of 1862, and a copy of the edition published in 1877 (T 141-1; T 141-2; Pub. 1877, No. 3).

1.120. Stones River. 16 items.

Manuscript topographic sketches (sheets 1 and 2) of the battlefield of Stones River near Murfreesboro showing positions of Union troops on December 31, 1862, surveyed under the direction of Capt. N. Michler (T 28-1; T 28-3; T 28-4) (see entry 2.200); annotated photoprocessed copies of sheet 1 and of a similar map showing troop positions on December 31, 1862, and January 2, 1863 (T 28-2; T 28-6; T 28-7); a manuscript sketch showing Bragg's troops on December 31 compiled from various newspaper accounts and official Confederate reports (T 28-10); manuscript sketches showing Union troop positions on January 1 and 2 (T 33); a colored, reduced, photoprocessed copy of a map of the battlefield showing both Union and Confederate positions (T 28-9); a manuscript map of the battlefield as surveyed under the direction of Michler made in the Office of the Chief of Engineers and bearing Engineer Department stamps of 1879 and 1880 (T 28-11), and several photoprocessed copies with troop positions added in color and with corrections and notations by officers (T 28-12 through T 28-19); a manuscript topographic sketch of the battlefield by Capt. Francis Mohrhardt, Topographical Engineer of Sheridan's division (Z 338-1) (see entry 2.201); a manuscript map drawn by Helmuth Holtz in September 1865 under the direction of Bvt. Maj. G. L. Gillespie, Chief Engineer of the Military Division of the Gulf, showing the positions and movements of Sheridan's troops (Z 338-2); and a manuscript map of the Battle of Murfreesboro, December 30, 1862, to January 3, 1863, copied in the Engineer Department in 1865 from the original received from Colonel Comstock (T 28-30).

1.121. Blue Spring. 2 items.

A manuscript sketch drawn by Poe showing troop positions in the affair at Blue Spring, near Bulls Gap, between that part of the Army of the Ohio under the com-

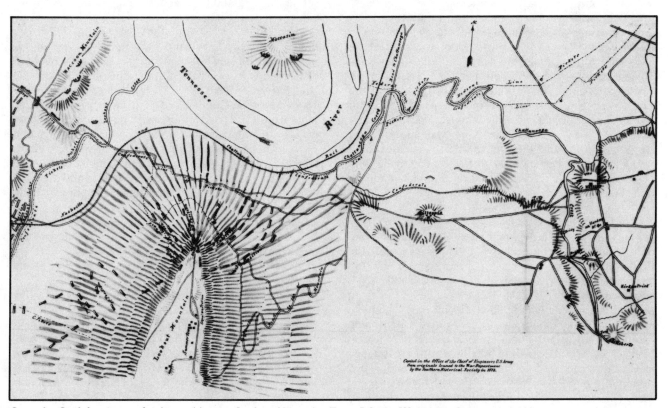

Copy of a Confederate map showing positions on Lookout Mountain, Tenn. RG 77: US 393-23. See entry 1.122.

mand of Maj. Gen. A. E. Burnside and the Confederate forces in October 1863 (T 120-1); and a copy made in the Engineer Bureau (T 120-2).

1.122. Chattanooga. 8 items.

A copy of a map of the country near Brown's Ferry made November 5, 1863, to accompany the report of Brig. Gen. Wm. F. Smith, showing the positions of troops, bridge equipage, and batteries (T 67) (see entry 2.181); a manuscript map of the area around Chattanooga dated January 4, 1864, made by direction of Smith to accompany Grant's report (T 73-1) (see entry 2.183); a manuscript map of the battlefield dated January 23, 1864, made to accompany Grant's report (T 73-2) (see entry 2.184); a photoprocessed map of the battlefield sent to the Engineer Department by Smith (T 73-7), a manuscript map of the battlefield redrawn from the original for publication (T 73-3), and a published edition of 1875 (Pub. 1875, No. 3); a manuscript map of the summit of Lookout Mountain as surveyed in April and May 1865 under the direction of Col. W. E. Merrill, showing works and fortifications, General King's Headquarters, the Topographical Engineer Office, the hospital, and army camps near Summertown (US 261); and a copy of a Confederate map showing positions on Lookout Mountain (US 393-23).

1.123. Knoxville. 6 items.

A manuscript map of the approaches and defenses of Knoxville showing troop positions during the siege (T 71-1) (see entry 2.192), a photoprocessed copy with notations added in 1868 and in 1874 regarding errors (T 71-2), an undated manuscript map prepared for publication (T 71-3), and a copy of the published map (Pub. 1864, No. 1); a copy of a Confederate sketch map of the area of the advance on Knoxville in November 1863 (US 393-20); and a manuscript map from the Topographical Engineer Office, 11th Corps, accompanying Maj. Gen. O. O. Howard's report and showing the route of march from near Cleveland, Tenn., to the vicinity of Knoxville from November 29 to December 5 and return to Chattanooga from December 6 to 17, 1863 (T 122).

1.124. Franklin. 6 items.

Maps of the battlefield of Franklin including a manuscript sketch map drawn by H. S. Hebard showing the field works and positions of troops of the 4th and 23d Corps during the engagement of November 30, 1864, approved by Capt. William J. Twining (T 80); a manuscript topographic map (Z 77) (see entry 2.191) and an annotated lithographed map (T 89-1) of the battlefield compiled by Edward Ruger under the direction of Col. William E. Merrill, a manuscript map with an attached revised title prepared for publication (T 89), and a copy of the edition published in 1874 (Pub. 1874, No. 9); and a copy of a Confederate map showing the positions of Stewart's Corps (US 393-15).

1.125. Nashville. 6 items.

Maps of the battlefield of Nashville including an annotated photoprocessed map signed by Brig. Gen. Z. B. Tower, showing the positions of the Union and Confederate forces during the battles of December 15 and 16, 1864 (T 86-8); annotated photoprocessed maps of the battlefield surveyed and drawn under the direction of Tower with legends describing the actions of December 15 and 16, one of which has information added October 22, 1865, from a map in the Adjutant General's Office (T 86-1; T 86-2); a manuscript reduction prepared in the Engineer Bureau (T 86-5); a copy of a Confederate map showing the positions of Stewart's Corps on December 15 and 16 (US 393-19); and a topographic map of the battlefield (Z 76½) (see entry 2.198).

FORTIFICATIONS MAP FILE

1.126. Tennessee Fortifications. 71 items.

A published map of middle and eastern Tennessee and adjacent parts of Alabama and Georgia (Dr. 147-18) annotated to show additional information about roads, 1863. A map of Chattanooga and vicinity (Dr. 147-41) showing defenses proposed by Capt. W. E. Merrill; a topographic map showing the line of defenses as established; a location map, ground plan, and drawings of the waterworks constructed at Chattanooga by the Department of the Cumberland; and plans of Forts Creighton, Jones, and Phelps, Batteries Erwin and Taft, Redoubt Putnam, Lunette O'Meara, and the swing ferry in use, 1864-65. Maps showing the defenses of Columbia and of the Duck River Bridge (Dr. 147-26; Dr. 147-27) located at Columbia, 1865. Maps of Cumberland Gap and vicinity showing Union and Confederate defenses and campsites (see entry 2.187), and a plan of Fort Farragut (formerly Churchwell) forming a part of the defenses. (For defenses of Cumberland Gap in Kentucky and Virginia, see entries 1.61 and 1.151.) Maps of Franklin and vicinity (Dr. 147-48) showing roads and defenses, and a plan of Fort Granger. Maps of Gallatin and vicinity (Dr. 147-47) and Johnsonville and vicinity (Dr. 147-49) showing defenses, 1864. Maps of Knoxville and vicinity showing defenses and positions during the siege of 1864 (see entry 2.193), and plans of Forts Byington, Dickerson, Fearns, Lee, Sanders, Smith, and Wiltsie, 1864-65.

A panel of plans of the six redoubts at McMinnville, 1865. A map of Memphis showing the status of defensive works with recommendations for additional work (Dr. 147-16), a sketch of the fortifications at Memphis (see entry 2.196), a topographic map of Fort Pickering, and plans of the fort, 1863-64. Maps of Fortress Rosecrans located at Murfreesboro showing details of the fortress and the range of fire of the guns, 1863-65. Maps of Nashville and vicinity (Dr. 147-37; Dr. 147-38; Dr. 147-46) showing defenses; plans of Forts Dan McCook, Garesche, Harker, Houston, Morton, Negley, and Sill; plans of several batteries including Battery W. L. Whipple; plans of several redoubts including the Hyde Ferry Redoubt, the redoubt designed for Hill 210, and the redoubt on the north side of the Cumberland River; plans of blockhouses on the lines of defense; a plan of Magazine Granger; a plan of a flanking redan for ditches of redoubts; a plan for a bastionet designed for flanking unswept faces of Forts Houston and Morton; and plans of pontoon bridges across the Cumberland River, 1864-65.

WAR DEPARTMENT MAP COLLECTION

1.127. Battlefield of Shiloh. 1 item.

A large-scale tracing of the Shiloh battlefield showing the boundary of the military park without date or indication of origin (WDMC 15-Tenn).

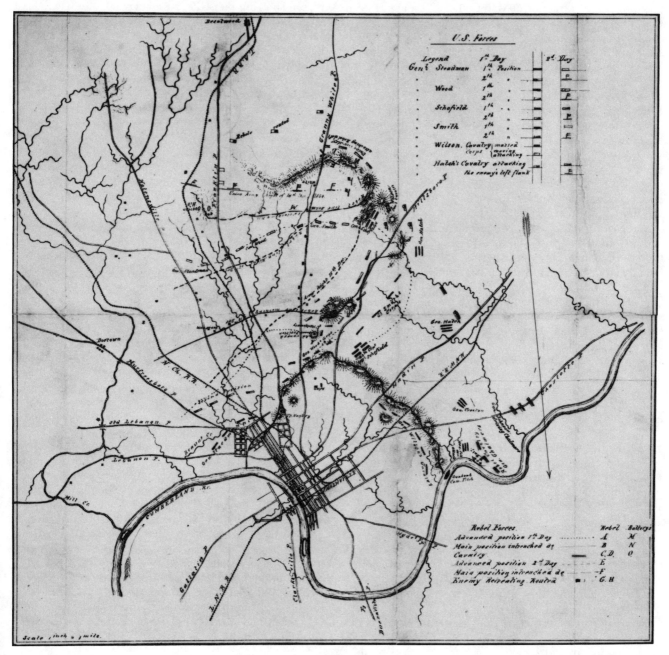

Annotated photoprocessed map of the battlefield of Nashville, 1864, signed by Brig. Gen. Z. B. Tower. RG 77: T 86-8. See entry 1.125.

TEXAS

CIVIL WORKS MAP FILE

1.128. General Information. 23 items.

A detailed manuscript map of Texas and adjoining States and territories showing hydrography, early routes of explorations, roads, forts, post offices, place names, and information about the character of the country, prepared under the direction of Maj. G. L. Gillespie in 1865 from Pressler's map of Texas, from Confederate surveys, and from a military map of Texas and New Mexico (Q 122); a manuscript map of the principal part of the Eastern Military Subdistrict of Texas (Z 49); manuscript maps of the country between the Sabine and Neches Rivers north of the Texas and New Orleans Railroad to Tyler and Starrville in Smith County and the adjoining part of Louisiana, prepared by Capt. W. Von Rosenberg from surveys made in 1863 and 1864 in connection with a reconnaissance of the Sabine (Z 50-1 through Z 50-10); manuscript maps of the country between the San Antonio and Colorado Rivers (Z 49-1 through Z 49-3) (see entry 2.203); and a manuscript Confederate map of Burr's Ferry and vicinity (Z 54-5) (see entry 2.207).

Manuscript maps of the coastal region showing bays, harbors, and islands (Z 39); of the area along the coast from the Colorado River to Galveston Bay and extending inland to Richmond, Houston, and Liberty showing roads and information about the country and supplies available (Z 347); of the area along the coast between the Brazos and Colorado Rivers with particular emphasis on roads leading inland from Sargent, Quintana, and the mouth of the San Bernard River (Z 51-8); of the town of Liberty showing the Texas and New Orleans Railroad across the Trinity River and the swamp to the south (Z 42); of Chambers County (Z 51-10) (see entry 2.208); and of Brazoria County (Z 55-2). For regional maps, see also entry 1.29.

1.129. Battle at Mouth of Sabine River. 1 item.

A manuscript map showing the positions of gunboats and transports at the mouth of the Sabine River at the beginning and close of the engagement on September 8, 1863 (Q 105) (see entry 2.213).

1.130. Local Coastal Defenses. 44 items.

A manuscript map of the gulf coast of Texas (Z 298) (see entry 2.204) and a large-scale map of the coast from Matagorda Bay to Galveston Island showing the locations of signal stations and forts, signed by Capt. Tipton Walker (Z 343).

For that part of the coast from the Sabine River to Galveston: a map of the area (Z 54-2); a map showing obstructions in Sabine Pass, a fort, and railroads (Z 51-2); a plan of Fort Sabine (Z 54-7); maps and sketches showing the defenses of Sabine Pass, Sabine City, and the lower Sabine River as far inland as Orange (Z 54-4; Z 54-6; Z 54-8; Z 54-9; Z 54-11); a map of the lower part of the Sabine River copied from a map in the Texas General Land Office (Z 54-13); manuscript maps of the eastern part of Galveston Island showing its defenses (Z 53-9); a coast and land sketch of the west side of Galveston Bay dated September 2, 1863, showing forts on Virginia Point (Z 53-10); a map of western Galveston Bay and the entrance to the bay showing soundings (Z 53-1); a sketch of the entrance to Galveston Harbor showing a proposed fort on Pelican Spit (Z 53-11); a map of Galveston showing piers (Z 53-2); several scale drawings of obstructions in the main channel and plans of Forts Point, Magruder, Bankhead, the fort on Pelican Spit, and South Battery (Z 53-3 through Z 53-8); and a manuscript map of Galveston and vicinity (Q 102) (see entry 2.209), and detailed plans of the city (see entry 2.210) and the line of works around the city (see entry 2.211).

For that part of the coast from the Brazos River to Brownsville: a manuscript map showing Forts Quintana and Velasco at the mouth of the Brazos, the piling across the mouth of the river, and the ferry and inland fortifications at Quintana (Z 51-9); a sketch of Matagorda and Lavaca Bays (Z 51-1) and sketches of Pass Cavallo showing fortifications and old field works along the channel as surveyed in 1863 by Felix A. Bluecher, Major of Artillery and Assistant Engineer, C.S.A. (Z 51-3 through Z 51-5); a map showing fortifications near the mouth of Caney (Cany) Creek (Z 51-6); two Confederate manuscript maps dated July 1, 1862, one of Pass Cavallo and Matagorda Island showing lighthouses, channel depths, and forts (Z 43), and the other of the entrance to Aransas Bay showing channel depths, a lighthouse on Harbor Island, wharves on St. Joseph's Island, and a fort on Shell Bank Island (Z 44); maps showing the vicinity of Brazos Island (one dated February 1864) including a ground plan of the fort (Z 357; Z 284-3), and maps of the north end of the island showing plans of works (one with an armament list and signed by Capt. P. C. Hains) (Z 248-1; Z 248-2); a map of Brownsville and vicinity including a plan of the fortifications along the Rio Grande copied by order of Maj. Gen. F. J. Herron from a map drawn in May and June 1864 (Z 356); and a Spanish map of Matamoros copied in 1864 showing the fortifications on the opposite side of the Rio Grande (Z 60).

1.131. Local Inland Defenses and Surveys. 18 items.

Manuscript maps, many of which are unfinished, of the vicinities of Marshall, Carthage, Austin, and San Antonio (Z 38-1 through Z 38-6; Z 52-1 through Z 52-5; Z 55-3 through Z 55-6), including a plan of San Antonio showing the interior and exterior lines of entrenchments, locations of magazines near the main square, and forts (Z 55-29); and a map of the San Antonio River valley region (Z 299).

1.132. Military Routes. 11 items.

A printed map of the eastern half of Texas prepared by order of Maj. Gen. N. P. Banks under the direction of Maj. P. C. Hains in April 1865, annotated to show distances and military routes between major towns (Q 110); and a set of manuscript maps with descriptions of the best routes for military movements between these towns (Q 107-1 through Q 107-4; Q 107-6 through Q 107-10).

FORTIFICATIONS MAP FILE

1.133. Texas Fortifications. 32 items.

A copy of a Coast Survey chart of Aransas Pass showing locations of Confederate batteries captured by Union forces, November 17, 1863 (see entry 2.206). A map of the north end of Brazos Island showing defenses, with enlarged plans of the defenses; and a map showing proposed work at the fort located on the island, with an inset giving details of the fort. A map showing Confederate defenses near Galveston; plans of Forts Bankhead, Eagle Grove, Green, Hebert, Jackson, Magruder, Moore, Nelson, Point, Scurry, and Sidney Sherman or South Fort; plans of batteries including Battery Cook, the battery on Pelican Spit, Batteries No. 1 and No. 2, and the unfinished sand battery at the east end of obstructions in the channel; plans of Redoubt No. 2 and an unidentified redoubt; and plans of Bastions 1 through 9 in the main line of works. A copy of a Coast Survey chart of Pass Cavallo showing the positions of Confederate defenses in December 1863 (see entry 2.212).

VIRGINIA

CIVIL WORKS MAP FILE

1.134. General Information. 41 items.

Maps of the State: a copy of Herman Boye's map of Virginia corrected by Buckholtz in 1859 (G 61); annotated, reduced photoprocessed copies of Boye's map, one annotated to show coalfields and the relations of geological formations and roads by Thomas S. Ridgeway, formerly of the Geological Survey of Virginia, for Maj. A. A. Humphreys (G 74), and the other annotated to show map coverage for Virginia and West Virginia (G 66-2); an annotated copy of C. Crozet's 1855 map of the internal improvements of Virginia (Z 110); a map of the State showing the distribution of the slave population by county and other population information from the 1860 census (G 103); and a photoprocessed map of the State compiled by the Coast Survey and annotated to emphasize roads and railroads (G 463-3).

Maps of counties: a copy of John Wood's 1821 map of Culpeper County with roads shown in color and with annotations in pencil (Z 416); a published map (G 82-1) and annotated photoprocessed maps (G 82-2; G 87; G 455) of Henrico County; an 1862 copy of Yardley Taylor's 1853 map of Loudoun County (G 98), and an 1861 map of the county (G 64); a photoprocessed map of Rockbridge County compiled under the direction of Lt. J. N. MaComb in 1862, with roads added in color (G 75-2); a Confederate manuscript map of Rappahannock, Madison, Culpeper, and Orange Counties (G 296); an anno-

tated Confederate map, dated April 1864, covering the same counties and adjoining counties to the south (Z 404); a manuscript map of part of Spotsylvania and adjoining counties compiled by Capt. W. H. Paine in 1863 (G 138); a group of manuscript Confederate maps of Albemarle (US 253-20), Caroline (US 253-25), Culpeper and Madison (US 253-17; US 253-21) (see entry 2.238), King William (US 253-23; US 253-24), Loudoun (US 253-29), Orange (US 253-18), and Page, Warren, and Shenandoah (US 253-30) Counties, and the town of Orange (US 253-8) (see entry 2.244); a group of manuscript maps made by Jed. Hotchkiss, 1865-66, under the direction of Maj. P. S. Michie for the War Department, for Augusta (G 180), Greene (G 189), Madison (G 191), Rappahannock (G 190), Rockingham (G 187), and Shenandoah, Page, and part of Warren Counties (G 188); and photoprocessed copies of Hotchkiss maps of parts of James City, York, Warwick, and Elizabeth City Counties (Pub. 1867, No. 21), parts of Rappahannock, Madison, Greene, and Nelson Counties (Pub. 1867, No. 22).

1.135. Roads and Railroads. 5 items.

A manuscript map of the turnpike from Alexandria to Difficult Run (Z 371); manuscript profiles for the following railroads in Virginia: Norfolk and Petersburg, Petersburg and Lynchburg, Richmond and Danville, Richmond and Fredericksburg, Richmond and York River, and Seaboard and Roanoke (G 88-1 through G 88-4); and two maps of the Virginia and Tennessee Railroad (Z 418; Rds. 193).

1.136. Engineer Compilations and Surveys. 52 items.

Lithographed, photoprocessed, annotated, and manuscript versions of part of the map of the Military Department of S.E. Virginia and Fort Monroe, compiled in August 1861 and in 1862 after the Peninsula Campaign and in 1864 at the beginning of the campaign against Richmond and Petersburg (G 112-1; G 112-2; G 112-a; G 112-b; G 115; Pub. 1862, No. 4); manuscript (G 211 Portfolio) (see entry 2.215) and a few lithographed (G 285; G 443, vol. 3, pp. 13 through 15) maps with corrections on a scale of 1 inch to 1 mile made by the Engineer Department, Army of the Potomac, covering a large part of Virginia and often referred to as "campaign maps," including an 1862 revised copy of Lloyd's map of Virginia annotated to show the coverage of the separate maps; field sketches and annotated printed maps principally for the area north of the Rapidan River, probably used in the compilation of the 1-inch-to-1-mile maps (G 463); and a detailed manuscript military map copied from a Coast Survey tracing of Suffolk and vicinity for Maj. Gen. J. J. Peck by Lt. Oscar Soederquist of the 99th N.Y. Volunteers (G 321).

1.137. Battlefields and Campaign Areas. 146 items and 2 atlases.

The following sets of related manuscript maps show rivers and streams, roads, railroads, towns, churches, houses, names of residents, relief, vegetation, land use, earthworks, and fortifications.

Manuscript survey and preliminary compilation sheets for the Richmond-City Point-Petersburg area west to Appomattox Court House on a scale of 2 inches to 1 mile (Z 390, 15 sheets), for some of the major battlefields on a scale of 4 inches to 1 mile (Z 412-a through Z 412-i), for areas around Richmond on a scale of 8 inches to 1 mile (Z 395-index and sheets 1 through 19), and Fredericksburg, Chancellorsville, the Wilderness, and Mine Run (Z 402-1 through Z 402-6; Z 404½).

Manuscript maps compiled under the direction of Bvt. Brig. Gen. N. Michler and Bvt. Lt. Col. P. S. Michie including sheets on a scale of 2 inches to 1 mile for Amelia Court House (G 204-7), Appomattox Court House (G 204-3), Burkesville (Junction) (G 204-6), City Point (G 204-14), Clover Hill (G 204-11), Dinwiddie Court House (G 204-12), Farmville (G 204-5), Goodes Bridge (G 204-9), Nottoway Court House (G 204-8), Petersburg (G 204-13), Prospect Station (G 204-4), Richmond (G 204-15), and Wilson's Station (G 204-10); maps of battlefields and campaign areas on a scale of 4 inches to 1 mile for Antietam (G 204-31), Chancellorsville (G 204-28), Cold Harbor (G 204-21), Five Forks (G 204-22), Fredericksburg (G 204-27), Harpers Ferry (G 204-30), High Bridge and Farmville (G 204-24), Jetersville and Sailors Creek (G 204-23), Mine Run (G 204-29), North Anna (G 204-26), Spotsylvania Court House (G 204-19), Totopotomoy (G 204-20), and the Wilderness (G 204-17) (see entry 2.254); and maps of the Richmond-Petersburg area on a scale of 8 inches to 1 mile (G 204-33 through G 204-60) (see entry 2.246). There are index maps for each of the three sets.

Maps published in 1867 by order of Bvt. Maj. Gen. A. A. Humphreys, Chief of Engineers, on a scale of 3 or 4 inches to 1 mile for Antietam, Appomattox Court House, Bermuda Hundred, Chancellorsville, Cold Harbor, Fredericksburg, Harpers Ferry, High Bridge and Farmville, Jetersville and Sailors Creek, Mine Run, North Anna, Petersburg and Five Forks, Richmond, Spotsylvania Court House, Totopotomoy, and the Wilderness (Pub. 1867); and a map of the region between Gettysburg and Appomattox Court House showing the relation between the battlefield and the campaign maps, published in 1869 by the Office of Chief of Engineers (Pub. 1869).

Two editions of an atlas entitled *Military Maps illustrating the Operations of the Armies of the Potomac & James May 4th 1864 to April 9th 1865 including Battlefields,* published by the Office of the Chief of Engineers, War Department, 1869, containing most of the maps mentioned above (Pub. 1869—2 atlases).

1.138. Campaign Routes, 1864-65. 9 items.

Four versions of a map of central Virginia, three showing by color and symbols Grant's campaign and the marches of the armies under his command in 1864-65, the first a copy of the published edition (Pub. 1865, No. 1), the second an annotated map showing the route of the 19th Corps as delineated by General Emory (G 165-4) (see entry 2.216), the third a printed proofsheet with changes (G 165-2), and the fourth a photoprocessed copy of a revised copy of a map accompanying the November 30, 1865, report of the Chief of Engineers (WDMC, 161-Virginia); maps of central Virginia annotated to show the routes of Sheridan's raids in May and June 1864 and in February 1865 (G 128-1; G 163), and a published map of central Virginia showing his campaigns and the marches of the cavalry under his command in 1864-65, with additional routes added in manuscript and an attached printed list describing the routes of the seven raids (G 195-1) (see entry 2.217); and maps of central Virginia annotated to show the route of the 6th Corps in 1864 as delineated General Wright, July 19, 1865 (G 195-5; G 195-6).

1.139. Northern Virginia. 16 items.

A published map of northeastern Virginia and the vicinity of Washington compiled from surveys for military defenses in the Topographical Engineer Office at the division headquarters of Gen. Irvin McDowell in January 1862 and corrected in August from surveys and reconnaissances under the direction of the Bureau of Topographical Engineers (Pub. 1862, No. 7) (see entry 2.218); photoprocessed copies of a map of a military reconnaissance of Virginia made by Capt. A. W. Whipple and Lt. H. S. Putnam, annotated to show roads and railroads in the area between Alexandria, Leesburg, Haymarket, and Dumfries (G 485; similar versions filed as G 443, vol. 4, pp. 6 and 14); a photoprocessed sketch of the seat of war in Alexandria and Fairfax Counties made by V. P. Corbett on May 31, 1861, and showing camps, entrenchments, roads, railroads, and houses in the vicinity of Alexandria and Washington (G 483); a manuscript map of the 12th Regiment Camp between Alexandria and Arlington Heights (G 443, vol. 3, p. 13); an annotated photoprocessed copy of a Coast Survey map of the ground of occupation of the army under the command of McDowell showing roads, camps, and fortifications in the vicinities of Alexandria and Arlington as surveyed in June and July 1861 (F 100-3); a manuscript sketch map of the area south and west of Alexandria showing division roads and camps near Brentsville (G 443, vol. 4, p. 1); a copy of a map of reconnaissance, October 20, 1861, by Maj. W. R. Palmer between Lewinsville, Vienna, and Flint Hill (G 62); a manuscript map of the action at Drainsville, December 20, 1861, drawn by H. H. Strickler, Company A, 9th Pa. Reserve, prepared for publication (G 72), and a copy of the map published in 1875 (G 72 Duplicate); a manuscript map and profile of the Washington and Alexandria Railroad and its connections (Rds. 195) (see entry 2.225), and a manuscript map of the military railroad station in Alexandria (Rds. 194) (see entry 2.224), both drawn in 1865 in the Alexandria Office of the Chief Engineer and General Superintendent of Military Railroads in Virginia; a manuscript map by Maj. Gen. G. K. Warren showing the extent of published information about the country between Cedar Run and Broad Run in the vicinity of

Bristoe Station, Brentsville, and Warrenton in October 1863 (G 283), and a detailed map showing more information in the same area and to the north along the Manassas Gap Railroad, prepared by the Office of Surveys and Maps for the Army of the Potomac in November 1863 (G 284); a map of a reconnaissance on June 6, 1861, of White House Point by Capt. W. R. Palmer, copied from the Archives of the Coast Survey and sent to Gen. Joseph G. Totten on June 17, 1861 (F 52); and an annotated map of Jones Point surveyed for the Engineer Department by the Coast Survey in April 1863 (G 443, vol. 4, p. 5).

1.140. General Information, the Shenandoah Valley and the Upper Potomac Region. 26 items.

A manuscript map of the Shenandoah and Upper Potomac including parts of Virginia, West Virginia, and Maryland compiled in 1864 from surveys made under the direction of Lt. J. R. Meigs and other sources (G 150-3); a manuscript map accompanying the report of Brig. Gen. Lander in February 1862 showing turnpikes and country roads between Harpers Ferry, Winchester, Martinsburg, and points to the west (G 71); a photoprocessed map of Loudoun and Frederick Counties, Va., and Jefferson and Berkeley Counties, W. Va., with roads emphasized in color, received from Lt. Nicolas Bowen in November 1862 (G 96); an annotated published map of Frederick, Berkeley, and Jefferson Counties (G 121-3), and a similar manuscript copy showing roads in color west of Harpers Ferry and southward to Strasburg (G 121-2); unfinished manuscript maps showing roads in the Harpers Ferry area and along the Upper Potomac, one including Berkeley County, W. Va., and a large part of Washington County, Md. (G 61); a manuscript map of the Shenandoah Valley captured from the Confederates (G 154) (see entry 2.249), an Engineer Bureau manuscript copy (G 155-1), and a photoprocessed copy annotated to show the routes of the 1864 expeditions in the valley (G 155-2) (see entry 2.250); a manuscript sketch map of the Massanutten Mountain area entitled "Sketch of Powells Big Fort" drawn by Thomas S. Ridgeway, formerly of the Geological Survey of Virginia (G 79); a manuscript map of the Shenandoah River from Harpers Ferry to Port Republic (Z 116); and a manuscript Confederate map of the "Valley of Virginia" showing the area south of the Potomac River between Harpers Ferry and Cumberland, west of the Shenandoah River and as far south as Luray (Z 403½).

A manuscript map of the Upper Potomac from McCoy's Ferry to Conrad's Ferry and adjacent parts of Maryland, Virginia, and West Virginia, compiled in the Engineer Department in 1863 (US 224-1); a published copy with an inset of the area from Strasburg to Manassas Gap (US 224-2); and detailed manuscript maps of the Potomac River from Harpers Ferry to Great Falls showing topography along the north bank in 1865 and from Bolivar Heights to Shepardstown showing topography along both

banks in 1864-65 (F 90-1 through F 90-4; F 93-1 through F 93-3; F 94).

1.141. Battlefields in the Shenandoah Valley. 7 items.

A manuscript Confederate map of the Battle of Winchester, June 13-15, 1863 (US 253-5) (see entry 2.256); a map of the Waynesboro battlefield published in 1873 showing troop positions and other details prepared by Bvt. Lt. Col. G. L. Gillespie from surveys made under his direction by order of Lt. Gen. P. H. Sheridan, March 2, 1865 (Pub. 1873, No. 1); an annotated copy of the Winchester map (G 265) and a manuscript version of the Waynesboro map (G 196); a manuscript copy of a sketch map of the approach to Fisher's Hill showing the relative positions of works of the 19th Corps and of Confederate works and rifle pits on September 24, 1864, as surveyed by J. G. Oltmanns of the Coast Survey (G 152-2); an annotated map of the battlefield of Cedar Creek showing also the October 9 cavalry fight at Tomsbrook (G 266); and a manuscript copy of a map of the battleground of Cedar Creek and vicinity showing the positions of the 19th Corps on October 19, 1864, as surveyed by Oltmanns (G 152-1).

1.142. Operations and Defenses in the Shenandoah Valley and the Upper Potomac Region. 5 items.

A manuscript map of Winchester by Capt. J. W. Abert in 1861 (G 463-9); a manuscript map of defense reconnaissances in the vicinity of Strasburg by Abert in 1862 (G 94), and a map of the Strasburg-Middletown area showing lines of works near Cedar Creek, Fisher's Hill, and Strasburg, inscribed on the reverse "belonging to Genl. Sheridan" (G 166-1); a manuscript plan for the defense of Lexington (Z 126) (see entry 2.242); and a map of the Upper Potomac from McCoy's Ferry to Conrad's Ferry showing the operations of the Army of the Shenandoah commanded by Sheridan, drawn and lithographed under the direction of Bvt. Maj. G. L. Gillespie in 1865 and hand-colored to show routes along the Upper Potomac, routes from Halltown into the Shenandoah Valley, and points of encounter with the Confederate forces in August 1864 (G 193-1). See also entry 1.155.

1.143. First Bull Run. 12 items.

Two manuscript copies of a picturesque map of the battles on Bull Run near Manassas on July 21, 1861, made from observations by Solomon Bamberger and published by West and Johnson, Richmond (G 57-1; G 57-2); a manuscript copy of a Confederate survey of the battlefields of Manassas (G 136) (see entry 2.230); a map of the vicinity of Bull Run Bridge (G 205½); photoprocessed sketch map of a reconnaissance of the battlefield with annotations regarding positions of troops (G 443, vol. 2, p. 15); a manuscript map of the battlefield of Young's Branch, or Manassas Plains, showing the positions of troops (Z 396) (see entry 2.229); a detailed terrain map of the battlefield of Bull Run compiled from a map accompanying the report of Brig. Gen. Irvin McDowell

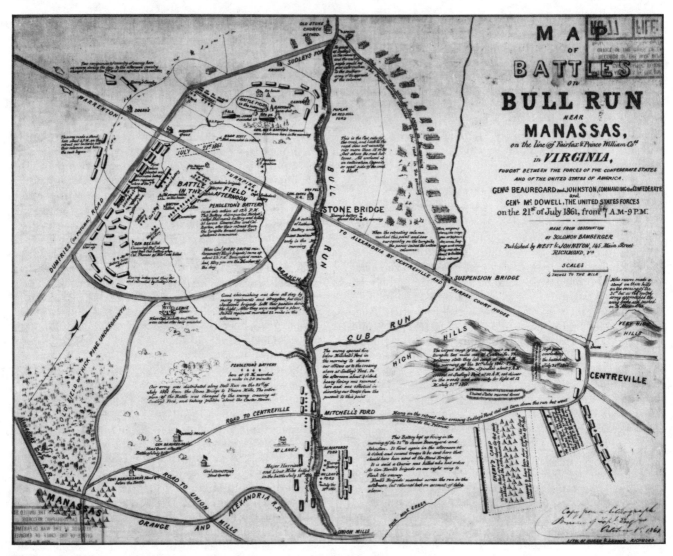

Battle on Bull Run near Manassas, Va., July 21, 1861. RG 77: G 57. See entry 1.143.

and from a map made under the direction of General Beauregard prepared for publication in 1877 (G 276-1), with an overlay showing the positions of the forces in colors (G 276-2), and a copy of the published edition (G 276-3); a manuscript outline map of the battlefield area (G 463-26); a manuscript map (G 73-2) (see entry 2.228) and a photoprocessed copy, annotated to show troop movements, of the reconnaissance of the battlefield at Bull Run made by Lt. Henry Abbot on March 14, 1862 (G 73-1); a manuscript map showing the Confederate position and works at Centreville from a reconnaissance of March 14, 1862, by Lt. M. D. McAlester (G 443, vol. 4, p. 20); and a photoprocessed copy of a map of Manassas Junction and vicinity as surveyed by a Coast Survey party under the orders of Lt. Col. J. N. Macomb with field work under the direction of H. L. Whiting in April 1862, annotated to show Confederate

regimental camp in the winter of 1861-62 and other information added by Maj. Gen. G. K. Warren in 1878 (G 122).

1.144. Cedar Mountain and Second Bull Run. 32 items.

A set of four manuscript maps showing the operations of the Army of Virginia under Maj. Gen. John Pope, copied in November 1868 from the originals on file in the Adjutant General's Office, consisting of the battlefield of Cedar Mountain on August 9, the positions of the troops on the night of August 27 in the area around Warrenton, the positions of troops at sunset on August 28 in the vicinity of Centreville, Groveton, and Haymarket, and the battlefield of Manassas at the close of action on August 29 (G 205-1 through G 205-4); related manuscript copies (G 205-6 through G 205-8); a copy of the published edition having the four maps on one sheet (G 205-5); a copy of a map by Maj. Franz Kappner showing the route taken by Major General Sigel's Corps from Middletown on July 7 to the Battle of Bull Run and to Fort deKalb near Washington on September 10 (G 206); a manuscript map of the battlefield of Bull Run, August 29 and 30, as surveyed by order of Sigel under the direction of Kappner in November 1862 (G 122½) (see entry 2.231); maps and related records received from Gen. Fitz John Porter in 1871 and 1879 regarding the strength and movements of his corps on August 29 and 30, 1862, some of which are copies of those used by him in the investigation of his case before the Army Board of West Point in 1878 (G 222-1 through G 222-4; G 290-1 through G 290-6); records received from Maj. Gen. G. K. Warren in 1879 including maps with numerous annotations, profiles, and maps of resurveys of the battlefield by Warren in 1878-79 (G 281-2 through G 281-10); and a published map of the 1878 survey of the battlegrounds of August 28-30, 1862, in the vicinity of Groveton (Pub. 1878, No. 1).

1.145. The Peninsular Campaign. 71 items.

Preliminary maps include a manuscript copy of a sketch map of Hampton Roads and vicinity received in the Engineer Bureau in 1861 (G 443, vol. 12, p. 6); a manuscript military reconnaissance map of the peninsula and adjacent areas prepared by Col. T. J. Cram (G 443, vol. 12, p. 10); two photoprocessed copies of an extract from a map of the Fort Monroe, Norfolk, Suffolk, and Yorktown area compiled under the direction of Cram in February 1862, annotated in color to show Confederate defenses on the peninsula and dated Bureau of Topographical Engineers, March 22 (G 77-1) and March 27 (G 77-2), respectively, the latter including information added on April 2; a composite map consisting of parts of printed Coast Survey maps of the York River with manuscript additions (G 78-2), a related manuscript map of the country between the York and James Rivers compiled in the Bureau of Topographical Engineers in April 1862, and a photoprocessed copy (G 178; Pub. 1862, No. 4); and a manuscript map and an annotated copy showing the approaches to Richmond and Petersburg also compiled in the Bureau in April 1862, the manuscript having additions from Edwin Sheppard's published map of the battlegrounds of the Chickahominy.

The Yorktown and Williamsburg areas: a photoprocessed map of the country between the York and James Rivers with annotated corrections (G 113-4); a manuscript map of part of the peninsula (G 113-6); a manuscript Coast Survey map of part of the York River (G 113-5); a manuscript map of a reconnaissance of the Warwick River made by Lieutenants Merrill and Bowen in April (G 443, vol. 12, p. 11); annotated photoprocessed sketch maps made from reconnaissances between April 5 and 18 by command of Maj. Gen. George B. McClellan (G 80; G 443, vol. 2, p. 17), and a manuscript map dated April

21, 1862, of the position of Yorktown and its approaches (G 113-11); a manuscript copy of the official plan of the siege of Yorktown, April 5-May 3, prepared under the direction of Brig. Gen. J. G. Barnard by Lt. Henry L. Abbot (G 106-1); manuscript sketches showing the armament designed for the defenses at Yorktown and Gloucester Point (G 443, vol. 12, pp. 4 and 5); manuscript maps dated May 4, 1862, of reconnaissances of Confederate works at Yorktown (G 443, vol. 12, pp. 2 and 12); a manuscript map showing the position of Williamsburg (G 447) (see entry 2.255); manuscript field sketches of the vicinity of Williamsburg (G 113-14; G 113-15); and a manuscript map of the battlefield in front of Williamsburg, May 5 (G 207-1), and an 1876 published copy (Pub. 1876, No. 1).

The Richmond area: photoprocessed maps of Henrico County (G 443, vol. 13, p. 12; G 443, vol. 2, p. 5) or parts of the county (G 443, vol. 2, p. 4), some with manuscript additions and corrections, one prepared under the direction of Lt. Col. J. N. Macomb; photoprocessed maps, most of which have manuscript additions, prepared from reconnaissances and surveys made by order of McClellan between May 18 and June 21, 1862 (G 82; G 87; G 443, vol. 2, pp. 4 and 5; G 443, vol. 13, p. 12), including sketches showing the approaches to Richmond between the Pamankey and Chickahominy Rivers (G 83; G 443, vol. 13, p. 11), maps of the Chickahominy from Mechanicsville to Bottom's Bridge (G 85; G 95-2; G 113-13; G 443, vol. 13, pp. 2, 3, 8, and 19), a map of the position of Richmond (G 84), and a sketch of the approaches to Richmond from the Pamunkey River (G 443, vol. 13, p. 5); manuscript maps of surveys around Richmond (G 113-1 through G 113-10), including a map of the White Oak Swamp area (G 113-12) (see entry 2.253); manuscript and photoprocessed maps of field works around Seven Pines and Fair Oaks Station (G 443, vol. 12, p. 1) and Fair Oaks and Chickahominy (G 443, vol. 13, p. 1); copies of Confederate maps of the Richmond area and its defenses (US 393-2; US 393-4; US 393-18); a manuscript copy of a Confederate map of the battle at Mechanicsville and Cold Harbor (US 393-8); and a copy of Edwin Sheppard's map of the battlegrounds of the Chickahominy River with an annotation concerning its origin (G 95½).

The Malvern Hill and Harrison's Landing area: a manuscript copy of a Confederate map of the battle at Frazier's Farm showing the Union positions at Malvern Hill (US 393-7); manuscript (G 90) and annotated photoprocessed (G 443, vol. 13, p. 13) maps of the country between Haxall's Landing and Charles City Court House and extending northward around Malvern Hill; a manuscript map of the position of the Army of the Potomac at Harrison's Landing as surveyed on July 30 by order of Brig. Gen. D. P. Woodbury (G 443, vol. 2, p. 12); and manuscript maps of reconnaissance surveys in the area on August 12 (G 113-7; G 113-8; G 443, vol. 12, p. 9).

A detailed manuscript map of the Norfolk and Portsmouth vicinities (Z 208); a photoprocessed map of the navy yard at Gosport showing the condition of buildings after the evacuation of Confederate forces from Norfolk and vicinity as surveyed in June 1862 (G 443, vol. 10, p. 10); and an annotated photoprocessed map of parts of Chesterfield and Charles City Counties showing the position of Richmond and Petersburg, dated Headquarters Army of the Potomac, Camp at Harrisons Point, August 11, 1862 (G 443, vol. 13, p. 16).

Three manuscript maps summarizing the Peninsular Campaign prepared for publication by order of Maj. Gen. George B. McClellan and compiled under the direction of Brig. Gen. A. A. Humphreys by Capt. H. L. Abbot for the phases of the campaign from Yorktown to Williamsburg (G 97-1), from Williamsburg to White House (G 97-5), and from White House to Harrison's Landing (G 97-10; enlarged version filed as G 97-14 through G 97-22); an annotated photoprocessed copy of the latter (G 443, vol. 1, p. 23); and a manuscript (G 115) and a published (Pub. 1862, No. 4) copy of part of the map of the Military Department of Southeast Virginia and Fort Monroe showing the approaches to Richmond and Petersburg, with additions and corrections in 1862 showing fortifications and lines of works of the Peninsular Campaign.

1.146. Fredericksburg and Vicinity. 22 items.

A manuscript map of part of the north bank of the Rappahannock River showing the approaches to Fredericksburg prepared under the direction of Capt. R. S. Williamson and Lt. Nicolas Bowen in December 1862 for the use of the Army of the Potomac (G 114-1), a photoprocessed copy with manuscript additions (G 118-2), and a map of the river in the vicinity of Fredericksburg copied from a Coast Survey map for Lt. Col. J. N. Macomb in April 1862 (G 114-2); a manuscript map showing roads between Fredericksburg, Gordonsville, and Culpeper Court House, including a statement that it was copied in the Bureau of Topographical Engineers on December 1, 1862, from a map in the possession of Lt. Hains that was found among the papers of Gen. J. E. Stuart (G 101-1); a similar map with a notation stating that it was copied from a map captured from Stuart in August 1862 (G 101-2); a manuscript map showing the railroad and roads between Fredericksburg and Aquia Station as modified by Capt. W. H. Paine (G 81); two lithographed maps of part of the Rappahannock River above Fredericksburg and the Rapidan River and adjacent country compiled under the direction of Macomb by Paine in December 1862 and issued by the Office of Surveys and Maps for additions and corrections (G 102-1), and a small section of the area above Fredericksburg dated April 8, 1863, with additions and corrections (G 102-2); a manuscript map of the Battle of Fredericksburg, December 10-16, 1862 (G 117) (see entry 2.239); manuscript copies of Confederate sketches of the battle on December 13 (G 131; G 443, vol. 9, p. 3) (see entry 2.240); a manuscript map showing the positions of the divisions of Humphreys, Whipple, Griffin, and Sykes on December 13, with two annotated blueprints (G 119-1 through G 119-3); a manuscript map showing the positions of Humphrey's division, December 13-16 (G 130-1) (see entry 2.241), a similar map on a smaller scale drawn by J. J. Young (G 130-2), a version prepared for publication in 1876 (G 130-3), and two published copies (one with corrections) (G 130-4; G 130-5). See also entry 1.137.

1.147. Chancellorsville. 12 items.

A manuscript map of the Rappahannock River from Fredericksburg to Port Royal copied in February 1863 from surveys by the Coast Survey for Capt. C. B. Comstock, Chief Engineer of the Army of the Potomac (Z 423); a manuscript map of the field of occupation of the Army of the Potomac in the vicinities of Fredericksburg, Port Royal, Aquia Creek, and Chancellorsville (Z 399) (see entry 2.221); a manuscript map showing the positions of the 5th and part of the 3d Corps of the Army of the Potomac, received on April 30, 1863 (G 120); manuscript maps of the field of operations of the Army of the Potomac under Maj. Gen. Joseph Hooker in the battles with the army of General Lee near Chancellorsville and Fredericksburg between April 27 and May 7, 1863, prepared from surveys and reconnaissance made in the field by Brig. Gen. G. K. Warren and others (G 125-1 through G 125-3); manuscript sketches showing the positions of the Army of the Potomac from May 1 to 5 and the positions of the units of the 11th Corps on May 2 and 5 by Lt. E. F. Hoffmann of Maj. Gen. O. O. Howard's staff (G 209-1; G 209-2); and a manuscript map of the battlefield received from Major King, August 22, 1865 (US 532-7). See also entry 1.137.

1.148. Operations in the Fall of 1863. 3 items.

Manuscript copies of Confederate maps including: a map of a reconnaissance in Fauquier and Prince William Counties, October 16-18, 1863 (US 393-1); a sketch of the area east of Culpeper Court House showing the position of the Army of Northern Virginia on November 8 (US 393-10); and a map of Orange County and adjoining areas showing the plan of operations of the Confederate and Union forces at Mine Run and the Rapidan River (US 393-28).

1.149. The Wilderness Campaigns in 1864: to Richmond and Petersburg. 135 items.

Joined photoprocessed maps issued by the Engineer Department, Army of the Potomac, annotated to show the routes of the 2d, 5th, 6th, 9th, and 18th Corps and of the cavalry in the march toward Richmond, with a table of distances between the successive camps of the commanding general from May 4 to July 12 (G 159-1 through G 159-5; G 454-1 through G 454-3); a group of detailed photoprocessed maps of the area from the Rapidan to Petersburg issued by the Engineer Department,

Army of the Potomac, in May and June, with an index map and a few manuscript copies of road reconnaissances; similar photoprocessed maps annotated to show lines of operations and odometer readings (G 160-1 through G 160-58); and other related items (G 132; G 133-1; G 133-2; G 284).

Manuscript maps of battlefields surveyed under Col. J. C. Duane, Chief Engineer, Army of the Potomac, including the Wilderness from May 5 to 7 (G 184-1), Spotsylvania Court House from May 8 to 21 (G 181-1), North Anna from May 23 to 27 (G 181), and Totopotomoy and Bethesda Church from May 28 to June 2 (G 182) (see entry 2.252); annotated photoprocessed maps of the last two battles (G 182-3; G 181-2); a manuscript map of

the country in the vicinity of Todd's Tavern showing the position of the 2d Corps on May 8, surveyed under Duane (G 185); a manuscript sketch showing lines near new Cold Harbor (G 134) (see entry 2.235); a manuscript map of the Cold Harbor and Gaines' Mill area prepared by direction of Maj. Gen. J. G. Barnard and showing General Burnside's headquarters in June, lines of works and fortifications, and other details (Z 395-19); an annotated photoprocessed map of the Cold Harbor area showing Union and Confederate lines (G 443, vol. 1, pp. 13 and 21); and a map of the battlefield of Cold Harbor (Z 412-C) (see entry 2.236).

Maps of Henrico County showing the defensive lines and works around Richmond in 1864 (G 443, vol. 2, pp. 4

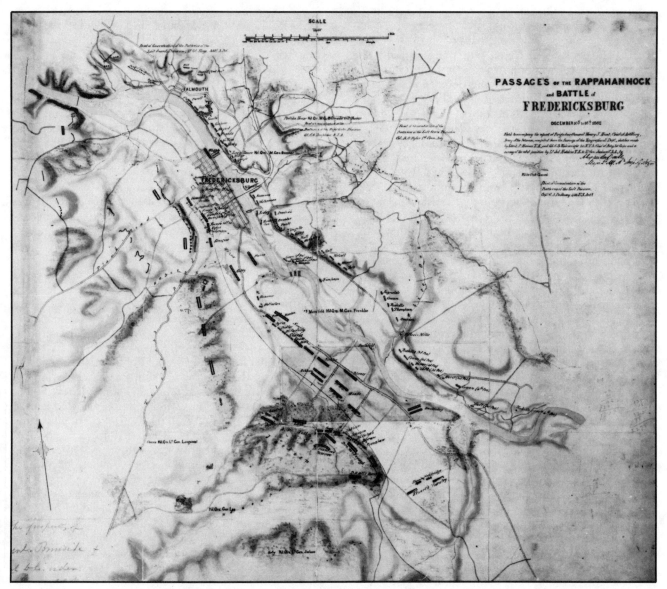

Manuscript map of the Battle of Fredericksburg, Va., Dec. 10-16, 1862. RG 77: G 117. See entry 1.146.

and 5); a two-part published map of part of the Military Department of Southeast Virginia and Fort Monroe showing the approaches to Richmond and Petersburg, with additions and corrections to May 1864 showing batteries north of Petersburg and other information from Brig. Gen. G. Weitzel's sketch of operations against Fort Darling (Dr. 150-13; Dr. 150-14); a manuscript copy of a Confederate map of the area east of Swift Run between Richmond and Petersburg showing lines of works in the vicinity of Drury's Bluff and Fort Darling (US 393-9); manuscript maps from Brig. Gen. G. Weitzel and Maj. Peter S. Michie, Army of the James, dated May, June, and August, 1864, showing roads, railroads, and field works in the James and Appomattox River areas north and east of Petersburg, west of Bermuda Hundred, and in the vicinity of Drury's Bluff (G 129; G 157; G 443, vol. 6, p. 29; G 443, vol. 1, pp. 6 and 8), including a map of the Union line of works and the left of the Confederate line between the two rivers (G 158) and a plan showing the position of Union forces on the north side of the James River (G 156); two similar manuscript maps of lines of entrenchments for the defense of camps at City Point (Z 407) (see entry 2.234); a copy of a captured Confederate photoprocessed map showing the country adjacent to Richmond and defenses around the city (G 151-1) (see entry 2.248), and two similar photoprocessed copies dated October 15 and 31, 1864, and annotated to show lines and fortifications north of the James River in the vicinity of Dutch Gap and Deep Bottom (G 151-3 and G 151-3 copy); an annotated photoprocessed Coast Survey map of the James River (G 443, vol. 1, p. 15); and an annotated printed map of Richmond and the James River taken by a paroled prisoner (G 156-2).

A manuscript and a photoprocessed copy of the 1854 James Keily map of Petersburg (G 164); a Confederate sketch map of the vicinity of Petersburg and City Point showing roads and railroads (G 140); a photoprocessed copy of a Confederate map of the Petersburg area compiled in 1864 under the direction of Capt. A. H. Campbell, C.S.A. (Z 404-2); a manuscript map showing the area of General Kautz's attack on Petersburg (G 160-42); a copy of a Confederate map showing the defense lines around Petersburg, the position of the Union forces on June 15, and the line captured on June 16 (US 393-11); a manuscript map showing the Confederate lines south of the Appomattox River and east of Petersburg in the possession of the Army of the Potomac on June 18 (G 443, vol. 1, p. 12); a photoprocessed copy of a Coast Survey map of the Appomattox River from City Point to Petersburg annotated to show bars and fortifications (G 443, vol. 1, p. 4; G 443, vol. 12, pp. 7 and 8); various annotated photoprocessed sheets of the area in the vicinity of Petersburg on scales of 8 inches, 2 inches, and 1 inch to 1 mile issued by the Engineer Department, Army of the Potomac, and annotated to show lines (G 142; G 153-2; G 160-26; G 160-35; G 148-1; G 149; G 443, vol. 1, pp. 2, 3, 7, 9 through 11, and 19; G 443, vol. 2, pp. 1

and 2; G 443, vol. 13, pp. 20 through 22); a detailed manuscript map of the vicinity of Petersburg from the Appomattox River to the Weldon Railroad, surveyed under the direction of Maj. N. Michler between July 9 and September 25 and showing Confederate defense lines and positions of the Union forces besieging the city (G 186-1), and photoprocessed copies relating to the survey (G 186-3; G 169); a manuscript map (G 458) and a photoprocessed copy (G 443, vol. 2, p. 16) showing the position of Union forces around Petersburg on September 21; and manuscript maps and sketches in the Richmond and Petersburg areas by Capt. E. B. Cope and others (US 532-1 through US 532-6), including one by Gen. G. K. Warren showing the Confederate line west of Globe Tavern on the morning of September 30 (US 532-2).

1.150. Richmond, Petersburg, and Appomattox, 1865. 39 items.

A map published by the Engineer Bureau in 1865 showing the area of operations against Richmond and Petersburg (Pub. 1865, No. 1); a photoprocessed map dated January 18 showing the forts west of the Weldon and Petersburg Railroad (G 462); a manuscript map showing the position of the Confederate units between Richmond and Petersburg on January 26 (G 179); a manuscript and a photoprocessed map showing the relative positions of the Union and Confederate lines around Petersburg in February (G 459); a manuscript copy dated March 1 of a campaign map of the Army of the James for the use of the Army of the Potomac, showing entrenched lines and fortifications west of Bermuda Hundred, north of the James River, and in the vicinity of Drury's Bluff (G 160-49); a manuscript map of the area between Richmond and Petersburg dated March 24 (G 171) (see entry 2.247); two manuscript maps of the defenses of Chaffin's Bluff made by direction of Maj. Gen. J. G. Barnard in June and July showing batteries constructed in 1862-63 and 1864-65 (Z 391); an annotated photoprocessed copy (G 186-2) and a manuscript copy (G 186-4) of part of the map of the vicinity of Petersburg from the Appomattox River to the Weldon Railroad showing the positions of regiments and brigades immediately before the capture of Petersburg; and a photoprocessed map of the siege of Petersburg, 1864-65, surveyed under the direction of Brig. Gen. N. Michler (Pub. 1865, No. 9). There are also manuscript items from the Office of the Chief Engineer and General Superintendent of Military Railroads of Virginia consisting of a map and profile of the City Point and Army Line and its branches and connections around Petersburg (Rds. 196) (see entry 2.232) and a military railroad map of City Point (Rds. 197) (see entry 2.233); a manuscript plan, section, and elevation of a pile bridge across the James River at Varina dated January 1865 (G 443, vol. 2, p. 10); and a manuscript plan of a signal tower constructed near Peebles' House about four miles south of Petersburg (Cons. 113).

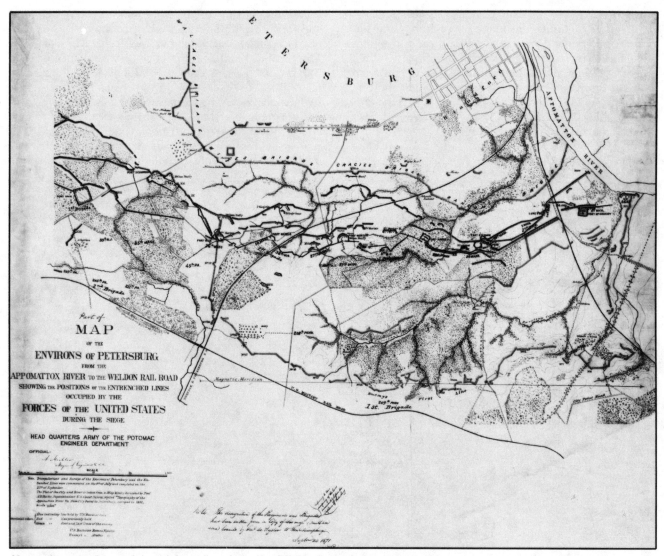

Manuscript copy of map of the vicinity of Petersburg, Va. RG 77: G 186-4. See entry 1.150.

Items for the operations after the fall of Richmond and Petersburg include a large-scale manuscript map showing the area of the operations of the Army of the Potomac between March 29 and April 9 (G 170-1), and a reduced photoprocessed copy annotated in color to show headquarters and routes of march of the 2d, 5th, 6th, and 9th Corps in pursuit of the Confederate Army (G 170-2); manuscript sketch maps showing roads in the area east of Appomattox Court House (G 170-5; G 170-6); a composite map on which the lines of march of the corps were annotated in 1871 (G 170-4); a manuscript map of the battlefield of Dinwiddie Court House, March 31 (G 173), and a manuscript map of the battlefield of Five Forks, April 1 (G 172), both surveyed and drawn under the direction of Maj. G. L. Gillespie by Henry C. Koch; and a group of manuscript and annotated maps, some of which were received in 1881 from Gen. G. K. Warren, relating to the investigation of the Battle of Five Forks and consisting of maps of surveys made in December and January, 1879-80, by J. P. Cotton (G 304-1 through G 304-3), annotated lithographed and partial tracings of the Michler surveys (G 304-4 through G 304-7), and maps of a part of the battlefield plotted by Frank O. Maxson from surveys and notes made in March and April, 1880, for the Chief of Engineers (G 304-11; G 304-12). See also entry 1.137.

FORTIFICATIONS MAP FILE

1.151. Virginia Fortifications. 340 items.

The Fredericksburg and Rappahannock River area: a map showing pontoon bridges and positions of covering guns at Fredericksburg, 1862 (Dr. 150-29). Maps showing defenses of Aquia Creek, Brook's Station, and Potomac Run Bridge. A map of the area north of the Rappahannock River showing the ground occupied by the Army of the Potomac in January 1863 (Dr. 150-38); and a map of the Rappahannock River and vicinity showing bridges from Port Royal to Richard's Ferry, Hooker's lines for May 1-3, and the site of the battle at Salem Church, May 3, 1863 (Dr. 150-42).

The Hampton Roads, Norfolk, and Yorktown area: sketches of Hampton Roads and vicinity, one showing soundings, and a plan of Camp Butler showing defenses and facilities, 1861-62. A copy of a Coast Survey chart of Craney Island showing defenses, 1862. Maps of Forts Monroe and Wool dated before the war. A map of Fort Monroe and vicinity showing positions occupied in front of the fort, 1861 (Dr. 158-153½); plans of the fort and its facilities including plans showing gun positions; and an armament sheet for 1865, 1861-65. Plans of Fort Wool and its facilities, 1862, and an armament sheet for 1865. A map of Norfolk and vicinity showing a plan for the defense of the city, old "rebel" lines, and rifle pits, n.d.

Published map of Richmond, Va., and surrounding country showing rebel fortifications, 1864. Dr. 150-44. See entry 1.151.

(Dr. 150-86). Maps of Yorktown and vicinity showing roads and defenses during the siege in 1862, and plans of Confederate and Union defenses constructed after the occupation, 1862.

The Richmond, City Point, and Petersburg area: maps of the Richmond area (Dr. 150-44) and the area between the Appomattox and James Rivers showing defenses. A photocopy of a map showing fortifications at Bermuda Hundred (Dr. 150-50) annotated with General Weitzel's approval, and a plan of a lookout and signal tower at Crow's Nest near Bermuda Hundred, 1864 (Dr. 150-62). A map of the Chickahominey River from Mechanicsville to Bottoms Bridge showing adjacent roads and place names (Dr. 150-18), and a plan of a permanent bridge built over the river by an Engineer brigade, 1862. Maps of City Point and vicinity showing defensive works and plans of Forts Abbott, Craig, Gould, Graves, Lewis O'Morris, MacKeen, Merriam, and Porter, 1864. A photocopy of a map showing defensive works at Deep Bottom, annotated with General Weitzel's approval, 1864. Maps showing the site of the Dutch Gap Canal and the status of work on the canal and its defenses, and a plan showing the cross sections of the canal, 1864. Maps of the area along the James River showing defensive positions, the position of a pontoon bridge erected and used by the Army of the Potomac, and defensive works at Harrison's Landing and Wilson's Wharf; and plans of Fort Powhatan, a battery near Fort Brady, log casemates at Fort Burnham, King's Bridge at Richmond, and a pile bridge near Varina, 1862-64. Maps of Petersburg and vicinity showing troop positions and defenses; plans of the mine constructed in front of the 2d Division's lines to destroy the Confederate defenses at that point (see entry 2.245); and plans of the forts defending the city as follows: Alex. Hayes, Blaisdell, Bross, Clark, Cummings, Davison, Emory, Fisher, Gregg, Haskell, Howard, Keene, McGilvery, Meikle, Patrick Kelly, Morton, McMahon, Prescott, Rice, Sampson, Sedgwick, Seibert, Urmston, Wadsworth, Welch, and Wheaton, 1862-64. A photoprocessed copy of a map of the defenses of Richmond and vicinity noted that it accompanied General Barnard's report on the defenses of Washington, 1862.

Southwestern Virginia: plans of forts located in Virginia and defending Cumberland Gap including Forts Edgar (formerly Green), Halleck, and Nat. Lyon (formerly Pitt); and plans of Batteries 3, 4, 5, and 6. For defenses of Cumberland Gap located in Kentucky and Tennessee, see entries 1.61 and 1.126.

The vicinity of Washington, D.C.: maps of the area from Alexandria to Leesburg showing roads, fortifications, and campsites particularly in the vicinity of Washington. Maps of Alexandria and vicinity showing defense lines (see entry 2.223); plans of Forts Blenker, Ellsworth, Ward, Williams, and Worth forming part of the defenses of Washington; a plan for a projected fort, probably Williams; plans for defenses of Traitor's Hill; a plan of the sunken battery on a point below Alexandria; several plans of Battery Rodgers and of guns mounted in the battery;

plans showing the results of test firings conducted at Battery Rodgers; and plans of the defenses of Hunting Creek, 1861-65. Plans of forts and batteries located within the boundaries of the present day Arlington County and composing part of the defenses of Washington, including Forts Albany, Barnard, Bennett, Berry, Cass, C. F. Smith, Corcoran, Craig, Ethan Allen, Haggerty, Jackson, McPherson, Morton, Richardson, Runyon, Scott, Strong or DeKalb, Tillinghast, Whipple (later Fort Myer), and Woodbury and Battery Garesche, 1861-65. Maps and plans relating to defenses in Fairfax County including maps showing the positions of blockhouses at Fairfax Court House and at Vienna and defenses at Prospect Hill; and plans of Forts Farnsworth, Lyon, Marcy, O'Rourke, Ramsay, Weed, and Willard, 1861-65. See also entries 1.44 and 1.45.

WAR DEPARTMENT MAP COLLECTION

1.152. General Information and Battlefields. 10 items.

An annotated published map of northern Virginia identified as Department of Northeastern Virginia Map 1 accompanying an 1861 letter of General Meigs, a manuscript sketch of the vicinity of Hatcher's Run and a general map of Bermuda Hundred and vicinity given by Mrs. Peter S. Michie to the General Staff, Second Section, in 1909, a manuscript map without authority or date showing Gen. Fitzhugh Lee's route to Richmond, and a manuscript sketch of Kelly's Ford dated March 17, 1863; undated manuscript maps of the battlefield of Second Bull Run showing troop positions and a manuscript copy of the 1878 survey of the vicinity of Groveton used in the rehearing of General Porter's case; a published map of the battlefield of Cold Harbor with annotations, probably by Maj. L. M. Koehler (Cav.), showing additional troop positions for June 3-6, 1861; and a manuscript map showing the routes taken in the march to North Anna, May 20-22, 1864, compiled in the Army War College in 1913.

WEST VIRGINIA

CIVIL WORKS MAP FILE

1.153. General Information. 41 items.

A manuscript shaded relief map of part of West Virginia and adjoining parts of Virginia compiled under the direction of Lt. John R. Meigs of the Department of West Virginia in 1864 (G 203-1), and an undated map of the Panhandle of West Virginia and several other items related to the Meigs map described above (G 203-2 through G 203-10); an unfinished large-scale manuscript map of part of West Virginia showing roads between the principal towns (G 155-2); two similar undated manuscript maps turned in by Lt. Meigs of the area between Oakland, W. Va., and Hancock, Md., showing names of rural residents and a comparison of roads drawn from the "Nine

Sheet Map" and from more recent surveys (Z 119; Z 143-2); a manuscript copy of John P. Kearfott's map of Berkeley County (G 59-2), and manuscript and annotated photoprocessed versions of a map of Berkeley County compiled under the direction of Lt. Col. J. N. Macomb (G 59-3; G 59-4); copies of maps of Harrison County by John Wood in 1821 with roads shown in color (Z 145; Z 138); a manuscript map of Jefferson County (G 139); a manuscript map of a large part of Kanawha County drawn in 1865 by Henry Topping, Assistant Engineer, Department of West Virginia (Z 167); a manuscript map of parts of Pleasants and Wood Counties showing the vicinity of Parkersburg and islands in the Ohio River (Z 124) (see entry 2.267); map of Pocahontas County by H. Boye in 1825 (Z 139); manuscript maps of surveys along the routes between Fairmont, Grafton, Clarksburg, Weston, Glenville, Buchannon, Beverly, and Philippi (Z 113-1 through Z 113-4) and of a railroad from Parkersburg to Grafton (Z 121); manuscript maps of the Ohio River from Wheeling to below the mouth of the Great Kanawha River (Z 159-1 through Z 159-3); manuscript maps of Charleston and vicinity with a description of the country (G 202-1; G 202-2; G 168); manuscript maps of the vicinity of Clarksburg (Z 161; Z 113-5) and a published map (WDMC 4-W. Va.) (see entry 2.261) of the vicinity surveyed and drawn under the direction of Lt. J. R. Meigs by Henry Topping in September 1863; a manuscript map of the vicinity of Berkeley Springs (G 463-16) (see entry 2.260); and a map of Martinsburg made by Capt. J. W. Abert in 1861 (G 463-11) (see entry 2.264). For regional and other related maps, see also entries 1.71, 1.134, and 1.140.

1.154. Battlefields and Expeditions. 11 items.

A manuscript sketch map of operations on July 10-12, 1861, at Rich Mountain near Beverly (G 63) (see entry 2.266), and a copy of a Confederate map showing Camp Garnett and Rich Mountain (US 393-3); a manuscript map of the battlefield of Carnifex Ferry on the Gauley River showing camps and troop positions, September 10, 1861 (copied from a map accompanying the report of

General Rosecrans and prepared for publication in 1876) (G 274-2), and a copy of the published edition (G 274-3); a manuscript map of Brig. Gen. W. S. Rosecrans' reconnaissance in the vicinity of Gauley Bridge from September 11 to November 15, 1861, and the 1879 published edition (G 292; Pub. 1879, No. 1); a manuscript map of the battlefield of New Creek, August 4, 1864 (Z 125½) (see entry 2.265); a manuscript map of parts of Virginia and West Virginia showing the routes of Gen. W. W. Averell on his expeditions in August, November, and December 1863, drawn under the direction of Lt. J. R. Meigs (G 123-2) (see entry 2.259); a manuscript map showing only the November route as surveyed by Henry Topping (G 123-1); and an unfinished map of the routes, apparently a compilation sheet by Meigs (Z 113-1).

1.155. Harpers Ferry and Defenses. 5 items.

A sketch of the vicinity of Harpers Ferry (F 78) (see entry 2.262); a manuscript map of the country adjacent to Harpers Ferry including Maryland, Loudoun, and Bolivar Heights and parts of South and Short Mountains, showing the positions of the defensive works as surveyed between August 3 and September 30, 1863, by Maj. John E. Weyss under the direction of Capt. N. Michler (G 135-1), and a photoprocessed copy with an attached manuscript sheet showing the positions of Sheridan's lines at Hall town (G 135-2); a large-scale preliminary map of the defenses on Maryland Heights and adjacent country surveyed by Weyss and drawn by Theodore von Kamecke (F 106) (see entry 2.263); and a manuscript map of Harpers Ferry and vicinity drawn under the direction of Meigs in 1864 from the Michler survey (Z 125). See also entries 1.137 and 1.140.

FORTIFICATIONS MAP FILE

1.156. West Virginia Fortifications. 1 item.

A map of Harpers Ferry and vicinity (Dr. 150-32) covering parts of Virginia and Maryland and showing defenses and a ford across the Potomac River, 1863.

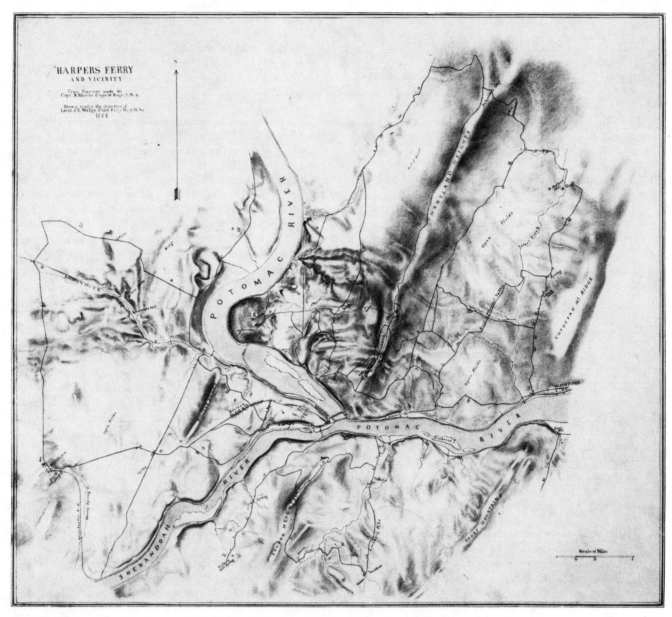

Manuscript map of Harpers Ferry, 1864. RG 77: Z 125. See entry 1.155.

Records of the Office of the Judge Advocate General (Army). RG 153

The following cartographic records of the Office of the Judge Advocate General were produced for the Gouveneur K. Warren Court of Inquiry.

1.157. Battlefield of Five Forks, Virginia. 1879-80. 5 items.

Maps appearing in part 3 of the published report on the Gouveneur K. Warren Court of Inquiry relate to the Battle of Five Forks, Va., April 1, 1865, and include: a map of Five Forks and vicinity compiled by order of the Court of Inquiry from official maps by Maj. N. Michler and Frank O. Maxson and maps prepared by J. P. Cotton, Civil Engineer; copies of Cotton's maps of the battlefield and of the White Oak Road area that the corps commanded by General Warren was supposed to secure during the battle; a map showing the formation of the 5th Army Corps south of Gravelly Run Church on the afternoon of April 1, 1865; and a published copy of the photographic map exhibited in the court and referred to by General Warren in his testimony.

Records of the Office of the Quartermaster General. RG 92

The Post and Reservation Map File of the Quartermaster General's Office consists of maps and plans relating to Quartermaster installations, plans of equipment used by the Quartermaster Corps, and a few miscellaneous maps. There are 1,235 items in this file that relate to the Civil War. They are described in the following three series: maps and plans of Quartermaster installations; other maps pertaining to the Civil War; and general building and equipment plans.

1.158. Quartermaster Installations. 1861-66. 1,165 items.

City maps and maps of parts of cities showing locations of Quartermaster installations including hospitals; stables and corrals; offices; barracks; camps; warehouses and other storage facilities; repair and maintenance shops; magazines; quarters for military personnel, laborers, and refugees; prisons; recruiting depots; supply depots; and related facilities. Ground plans of hospitals and depots show the locations of the different buildings. Some of the city maps and hospital and depot ground plans include floor and vertical plans of the buildings; other floor and vertical plans are separate items. Many of the plans include notes on the location of the facilities, dates of construction, construction materials and costs, rental costs if the buildings were not owned by the Government, condition of the structures, and sometimes the name of the troops occupying a building. Most of these facilities were located in the Northern and Border States; a few were established in the occupied areas of the Confederacy.

These records, which are mostly manuscript, are described below in greater detail by State.

1.158-a. Alabama. 2 items. A sketch map showing the railroad and steamboat terminals and Confederate defenses of Bridgeport, 1863, and an 1852 published map of Montgomery annotated to show rail facilities, the soldiers cemetery, and a U.S. Army camp.

1.158-b. Connecticut. 3 items. A map of part of New Haven showing the buildings occupied by the State hospital, names of adjacent streets, and other buildings; a vertical plan of a guardhouse; and a floor plan of a post hospital, 1862.

1.158-c-1. District of Columbia. 183 items. Plats of part of Washington and Georgetown showing locations of Quartermaster installations including offices, hospitals, barracks, camps, prisons, corrals, stables, warehouses, shops, and wharf facilities. These location plats usually show names of streets and ground plans of the installations, some include vertical drawings. Building measurements, costs of construction, and estimates for changes or modifications are often given. In addition to the city plats there are ground plans of Quartermaster installations located at the temporary forts erected for the defenses of the city. Most of these items are in watercolors, 1865-66 (see entries 2.42 through 2.45).

1.158-c-2. Georgia. 1 item. A sketch of Andersonville and vicinity showing fort, prison pen, sheds, Confederate hospital, and Negro cabins, 1868.

1.158-d. Indiana. 18 items. Floor and vertical plans of stables, ordnance and clothing storerooms, barracks, and a U.S. hospital; and ground plans of Camps Carrington,

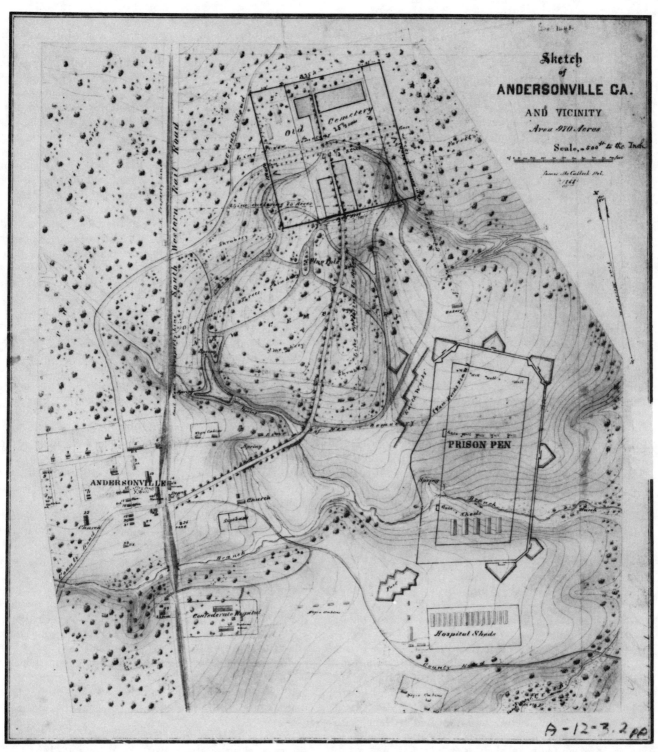

Sketch of Andersonville, Ga., and vicinity showing fort, prison pen, sheds, Confederate hospital, and Negro cabins, 1868. RG 92: Map 265. See entry 1.158-c-2.

Morton, Noble, and Shanks located in Indianapolis, 1861-62 (14 items). Floor and vertical plans of stables and hospital facilities located in New Albany, 1864 (4 items).

1.158-e. Iowa. 19 items. Location plans of Camps Kearney and McClellan at Davenport showing barracks, prisons, hospitals, and other Quartermaster installations; floor and vertical plans of these facilities; and pencil-sketched views of Camp McClellan and of the individual buildings at both camps, 1861-65.

1.158-f. Kentucky. 111 items. A view and floor plans of a hospital located at Ashland, n.d. (5 items). Ground, floor, and vertical plans of facilities located at Bowling Green including the barracks at Camp Baker and other barracks, officers' quarters, hospitals, commissary warehouses, stables, and corrals, 1862-64 (5 items). A location plan of Camp Nelson showing homes for refugees, hospitals, warehouses, and other Quartermaster installations, received in 1866. Views and floor plans of barracks, stables, and a warehouse located at Catlettsburg and vicinity, 1863-64 (10 items). A map of Columbus showing locations of Government buildings and Fort Halleck; and vertical and floor plans of barracks, railroad station facilities, and other Government buildings, 1865 (5 items). Views and floor and vertical plans of barracks, hospitals, shops, stables, warehouses, and a prison in and around Covington; and views of Forts Burbank, Kyle, McLean, Mitchell, Shaler, and Whittelsey, Battery Coombs, and the Tunnel Battery forming the defenses of Covington and Newport, Ky., and Cincinnati, Ohio, 1863-65 (60 items). Floor and vertical plans of the prison, commissary warehouse, the post Quartermaster's office, workshops, and the barracks at Fort Clay; and a view of the barracks and fortifications at Fort Clay near Lexington, n.d. (6 items). Floor and vertical plans of barracks, the buildings at Taylor Barracks, a warehouse, and a hospital at Louisville; and a ground plan of Taylor Barracks, 1864-65 (8 items). Floor and vertical plans of offices, shops, a forage house, barracks, and stables located in Munfordville, 1864 (4 items).

1.158-g. Louisiana. 33 items. Floor and vertical plans and view of warehouses, shops, and the railroad depot at Brashear City, 1864-65 (4 items). Views and floor plans of headquarters, Adjutant's quarters, officers' quarters, barracks, warehouses, and a hospital at Port Barrow in the vicinity of Donaldsonville; a house at Fort Butler; and a markethouse at Donaldsonville, 1864-65 (10 items). A view of the barracks and stables located at Napoleonville, 1864. Floor plans and views of barracks, stables, warehouses, and hospitals located at New Orleans, some of which are dated 1863 (15 items). Floor plans and views of the guardhouse, the Quartermaster Office, and the headquarters of the commanding general of the Union forces located at Shreveport; and a plat of part of the city showing the ownership of lands occupied by the Union forces, 1865 (3 items).

1.158-h. Maine. 12 items. Floor and vertical plans of the wards and messroom of the hospital located in Augusta; a ground plan of Camp Coburn near Augusta, with an inset photograph of the camp, and floor plans of barracks and stables composing the camp; and a ground plan of Camp Keys, also near Augusta, and floor plans of the barracks at the camp, 1864-65 (8 items). A ground plan of Camp Berry near Cape Elizabeth, and floor plans of the buildings composing the camp, n.d. (4 items).

1.158-i. Maryland. 65 items. Floor and vertical plans of barracks, hospitals, and stables located in the City of Baltimore; ground plans of Camps Bradford, Cheeseborough, Donaldson, Meade, Newport, and Rank and of Belger, Birney, and Lafayette Barracks, also located in Baltimore; floor and vertical plans of the buildings located in these camps and barracks; a ground plan, floor and vertical plans, and views of Relay House Barracks located south of Baltimore City; and a ground plan, floor and vertical plans, and views of the U.S. smallpox hospital located south of Baltimore in Anne Arundel County, 1861-64 (51 items). A ground plan of the hospital and floor and vertical plans of the barracks located at Clarysville, 1862-64 (5 items). A ground plan of the barracks at Cumberland, 1864. Ground plans, some with vertical drawing of buildings, of the hospital, wharf, shops, warehouses, prison, barracks, and livestock yards at Point Lookout, 1865 (8 items) (see entry 2.112).

1.158-j. Massachusetts. 22 items. Location plan of the buildings composing the draft rendezvous at Gallups Island, Boston Harbor, and floor and vertical plans of the buildings composing the camp, 1864 (3 items). A ground plan of the buildings at Eastern Point, Gloucester Harbor, 1863. A ground plan and vertical plans of the barracks located at Groton Junction, 1862 (2 items). Floor and vertical plans of the hospitals, barracks, and other buildings of the fort at Clark's Point and Fort Phoenix, New Bedford Harbor, 1863-71 (5 items). Floor and vertical plans of the barracks at Long Point Batteries, Provincetown, 1864 (3 items). A location plan and floor plans of the buildings at Camp Meigs, Readville, 1863 (2 items). A location plan of the barracks at Fort Pickering on Winter Island near the entrance to Salem Harbor, 1863. Floor and vertical plans of the barracks at Wenham, 1863 (1 item). A location plan of the barracks at Worcester, 1863, and plans for converting the Eclectic College into a general hospital, n.d. (4 items).

1.158-k. Michigan. 10 items. Floor and vertical plans of the general hospital and barracks at Detroit, 1864.

1.158-l. Minnesota. 33 items. Ground plans and views of the following: Garden City barracks and stables located at Mankato, Blue Earth County; the camp at Lake Hanskah and Camps Cottonwood and Cox, Brown County; Fort Pomme de Terre, Andy Johnson (Douglas) County;

the buildings at Winnebago Agency and the camp at Winnebago City, Faribault County; the granary and storehouse at Glencoe, McLeod County; the barracks at Camp Chanyuska, Martin County; Fort Ridgely and the stable at St. Peter, Nicollet County; Fort Goodhue, Sibley County; barracks at Richmond, stables at St. Cloud, and the post at Sauk Centre, Stearns County; and Camp Wilkin on the Watonwan River, 1862-64.

1.158-m. Missouri. 23 items. A location map showing shops and storage buildings in Jefferson City with views of the buildings, n.d. Ground and vertical plans of the warehouse and carpenter shop located in Kansas City, 1864 (2 items). Ground and vertical plans of facilities located at Rolla including a hospital, veterinary hospital, barracks, messhouses, corral, and miscellaneous shops, 1863-65 (8 items). A textual description of the hospital at Benton Barracks, St. Louis; ground plans of Quartermaster and Commissary Department facilities located at Benton Barracks; a ground plan with views of the officers' quarters at the Camp of Instruction, St. Louis; and ground and vertical plans of other barracks located in the city, 1864 (6 items). A ground plan of the corral at Springfield showing adjoining buildings, n.d. A ground plan and a view of Camp Grover located at Warrensburg, and floor and vertical plans of the buildings in the camp, 1864 (5 items).

1.158-n. New Hampshire. 2 items. A ground plan of the barracks at Concord, 1862, and a ground plan of the hospital at Manchester with vertical views of the buildings, n.d.

1.158-o. New Jersey. 9 items. A ground plan of the hospital at Newark and floor plans with views of the different parts of the hospital, 1863 (8 items). A ground plan of Camp Perrinne located at Trenton with photographs and views of the buildings inserted, 1863.

1.158-p. New York. 42 items. Ground and vertical plans of the barracks and hospital located in Albany and vicinity, 1861-64 (7 items). Ground, vertical, and floor plans of the Soldier's Rest located at Buffalo, n.d. (2 items). Ground, vertical, and floor plans of the hospital, prison, and barracks located at Elmira, n.d. (9 items). Ground and floor plans and vertical views in watercolors of storehouses, barracks, hospitals, and offices (including the Headquarters Office for U.S. troops, the Medical Director's Office, the Paymaster's Office, and the Quartermaster's Office) located in New York City, 1863 (23 items). A ground plan with vertical building plans of the hospital located two miles north of Troy, 1864.

1.158-q. North Carolina. 3 items. A view and a ground plan of Camp Russell Barracks at Raleigh, formerly the Confederate Hospital Pettigrew, and floor and vertical plans of the buildings, 1865.

1.158-r. Ohio. 121 items. A map of the lands appropriated for Camp Dennison showing the owners of the lands, houses, and fields (often giving the crops raised); and a ground plan of the buildings at the camp, 1861 (2 items). A map of Cincinnati annotated to show the locations of Quartermaster properties, and floor and vertical plans and photographs of the individual properties including hospitals, barracks, warehouses, and stables, 1864 (39 items). A location map showing the hospital and Quartermaster buildings in part of Cleveland, and views and floor plans of the hospital, 1862 (3 items). Ground plans with vertical views of Camp Chase, Tod Barracks, and Tripler Hospital, all located in Columbus, 1863-65 (3 items). Ground plans and vertical views of facilities in Gallipolis including a hospital, barracks, storehouses, stables, forage sheds, and miscellaneous shops, 1862 (50 items). Ground and floor plans of barracks, shops, warehouses, officers' quarters, and other facilities located on Johnson's Island, 1863-65 (24 items).

1.158-s. Pennsylvania. 57 items. Ground plan with views of Camp Copeland, 10 miles east of Pittsburgh, Alleghany County, 1864. A ground plan of U.S. properties located at Pittsburgh, and views of the buildings, n.d. (2 items). Floor plans of numerous hospitals located in and near Philadelphia and of other Quartermaster installations including barracks, storehouses, a laboratory, and offices; a ground plan and views of Camp William Penn and floor plans of the barracks at the camp; and a ground plan and views of Camp Cadwalader, 1863-64 (47 items). A watercolor view of Pottsville Barracks, and ground, vertical, and floor plans of the barracks, 1863 (5 items). A ground plan of the hospital near Reading, n.d. A ground plan with photographic views of the hospital near York, 1865.

1.158-t. Rhode Island. 2 items. Ground and floor plans of the hospital located at Portsmouth Grove, 1863.

1.158-u. South Carolina. 4 items. Two maps of Hilton Head, each showing the locations of army buildings near the city including Quartermaster properties, the Engineer depot and quarters, Commissary Department buildings, the hospital, the post office, the Provost Guard's buildings, and the Fort Welles Reservation, 1864. Ground, floor, and vertical plans of the machine and marine works located on St. Helena Island, 1865 (2 items).

1.158-v. Tennessee. 260 items. A ground plan of the facilities at Chattanooga built by the Construction Corps of the U.S. Military Railroad during Sherman's campaign, 1864-65; ground, floor, and vertical plans of hospitals, barracks, shops, and warehouses located at Chattanooga; and a cross section of a military bridge also at Chattanooga, 1863-65 (89 items). Floor and vertical plans of a hospital and officers' mess located at Decherd, 1865 (3 items). Vertical plans of a sawmill, bridge, corral, and other buildings located at Knoxville, 1865 (22 items). A map of Lookout Mountain showing roads and railroads approaching the mountain and positions of army buildings (see entry 2.194), and ground and floor plans and vertical views in watercolors of the hospital and buildings serving the hospital, 1864-65 (16 items). A map of Memphis annotated to show the general area in the navy yard that was occupied by the Quartermaster Department; a plan of part of the navy yard showing buildings used by the Quartermaster; ground and vertical plans of many of these buildings; and ground and floor plans of Quartermaster buildings at Fort Pickering, 1863 (8 items). Ground, floor, and vertical plans of numerous hospitals located at Nashville; and ground plans of barracks, storehouses, corrals, and other Quartermaster buildings in the city, 1864 (122 items).

1.158-w. Vermont. 16 items. Ground plans and vertical views of the hospitals and barracks at Brattleboro (7 items) and Burlington (5 items), the hospital at Montpelier (3 items), and the barracks at Saint Albans (1 item), 1862-65.

1.158-x. Virginia. 90 items. Watercolor plats of parts of the City of Alexandria showing ground locations of and sometimes vertical plans of buildings used by the Quar-

termaster Departments, including a bakery, prisons, hospitals, offices, and shops; ground plans of Quartermaster facilities around the different forts composing the defenses of Washington located south of the Potomac; plans of the buildings at Soldiers Rest (see entry 2.226); and floor and vertical plans of several of the hospitals, 1865-66 (40 items). Ground plans in watercolors, some with vertical building plans, of Quartermaster installations located in Arlington; ground plans of several Government farms; ground plans with vertical building plans of the buildings at the entrance to the Government cemetery and of the headquarters office buildings at Freedman's Village (see entry 2.227); and ground plans of Quartermaster facilities located at the different forts composing the defenses of Washington and located in Arlington, 1865 (44 items). A map of City Point showing the location of wharves, the railroad, warehouses, and other Government properties, 1865. Ground plans in watercolors, with vertical building plans of the hospitals and the rendezvous of distribution located at Fairfax Court House, and a map of the railroad station located there, 1863 (5 items).

1.158-y. West Virginia. 25 items. Floor and vertical plans of the hospital, warehouses, and stables located at Grafton, 1863-64 (10 items). A map of New Creek Station

Watercolor view of Pottsville, Pa., Barracks, 1863. RG 92: Map 60-A. See entry 1.158-s.

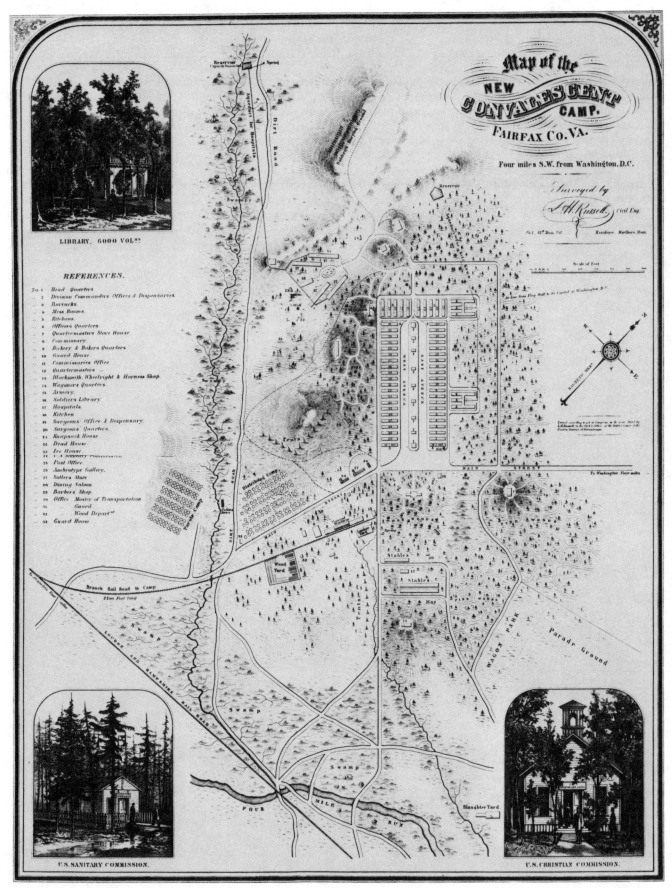

Published map of convalescent camp, Fairfax, Va. RG 92: Map 112-5. See entry 1.158-x.

showing the location of Government and private buildings, and a plan of a building to be erected, 1864 (2 items). Views with ground plans of the hospital, quarters, and stables at Parkersburg, 1865 (4 items). Floor and vertical plans of shops, warehouses, and quarters at Webster, 1861 (9 items).

1.159. Other Maps Pertaining to the Civil War. 1862-65. 4 items.

A railroad map of the Southern States annotated to show the different railroad gauges, 1862 (see entry 2.5).

A map of the defenses and approaches to Moorhead City and Beaufort Harbor, N.C., and a map of Moorhead City and vicinity also showing defenses, 1865. A map of the coast of Texas showing the points of occupation of the Union forces under Gen. N. P. Banks in 1863 (see entry 2.205).

1.160. General Building and Equipment Plans. 1861-65. 66 items.

Floor and vertical drawings of barracks, chapels, and hospitals and plans of wagons and ambulances.

DEPARTMENT OF THE NAVY

Records of the Hydrographic Office. RG 37

During the Civil War the Hydrographic Office functioned principally as a distributor of Coast Survey and foreign nautical charts to naval operating squadrons. The Civil War map described herein is among a large number of manuscript and annotated maps later collected by the Archives Section of the Office.

1.161. Mobile Bay, Alabama. N.d. 1 item.
A manuscript chart of the entrance to Mobile Bay showing soundings, bottom conditions, aids to navigation, and defenses. This chart was compiled in the Bureau of Ordnance and Hydrography of the Confederate Navy and bears the approval of John M. Brooks, Commander in the Confederate Navy.

DEPARTMENT OF THE INTERIOR

Records of the Geological Survey. RG 57

The Geological Survey has issued a special series of maps of national parks, monuments, military sites, and battlefields. Described below are maps pertaining to Civil War sites that were surveyed and mapped under the direction of the Topographic Division of the Survey and maps that were collected by the Survey Library.

TOPOGRAPHIC DIVISION

1.162. Battlefields, National Military Parks, and National Military Monuments. 1913-35. 8 items.

Topographic maps of the Chickamauga and Chattanooga, Shiloh, and Vicksburg National Military Parks showing positions of monuments and markers by numbers keyed to lists of the markers and monuments; topographic maps of the battlefields of Gettysburg, Chancellorsville, Salem Church, and Fredericksburg (the latter also showing locations of defenses and Lee's headquarters); and a topographic map of the Fredericksburg-Spotsylvania Battlefield National Monument area showing locations of monuments.

GEOLOGICAL SURVEY LIBRARY

1.163. Census Maps of Arkansas, Louisiana, Mississippi, and Missouri. Ca. 1861-65. 2 items.

A published post route map of Arkansas, Louisiana, and Mississippi annotated to show, by county or parish, population by race (free colored and slaves are distinguished), agricultural production, and kinds and numbers of livestock. A published post route map of Illinois and Missouri annotated to show population by race in the counties of Missouri; again, free colored and slaves are distinguished. These maps are believed to have been compiled by the Census Office for the use of the Army during the Civil War. Similar maps are in the Civil Works Map File of the Office of the Chief of Engineers, Record Group 77.

Records of the National Park Service. RG 79

In 1933 the National Park Service was given jurisdiction over military and battlefield parks and monuments that were formerly the responsibility of the War Department. The records described below were created by various commissions before jurisdiction was transferred to the Park Service.

1.164. Campaigns and Battlefields. 1874-1921. 9 items.

A published military map of the theater of operations of the Chickamauga, Chattanooga, and Tullahoma campaigns compiled by the Chickamauga and Chattanooga National Park Commission, 1896-1901, from surveys and maps prepared by the Corps of Engineers, U.S. Army; maps published by the Gettysburg National Park Commission consisting of maps of the battlefield from original surveys by engineers of the Commission, a perspective view of the Gettysburg National Military Park, a topographic map of the battlefield in 26 sheets copied by the Commission from an original map by G. K. Warren of the Corps of Engineers, and two maps of the area between Fredericksburg, Va., and Harrisburg, Pa.—one showing the itinerary of the Army of Northern Virginia (Confederate) and the other of the Army of the Potomac (Union) in the Gettysburg campaign; and a map of the battlefield of Shiloh, Tenn., showing troop positions on the second day of battle, April 7, 1862, compiled and published by the Shiloh National Military Park Commission.

DEPARTMENT OF COMMERCE

Records of the Coast and Geodetic Survey. RG 23

As a result of the Civil War, the normal field operations of the Coast Survey (renamed the Coast and Geodetic Survey in 1878) were partially suspended, and the work of the central office in Washington was substantially modified. In 1861 Army and Navy personnel could no longer be detailed to the Survey as they had been in peacetime. A number of the staff of civilian assistants were assigned to special duties in strategic areas, notably with Federal blockading squadrons off the southeastern and gulf coasts, with Federal forces conducting operations on the Mississippi, Ohio, and Tennessee Rivers, and with the troop and territorial commands, especially with the Army of the Potomac. The maps prepared by these assistants that have survived are for the most part included with the records of military agencies.

The published nautical charts of the Coast Survey, resulting from nearly three decades of survey work, were available for war purposes, and the Survey quickly increased the reproduction and distribution of these charts. The Survey also made available to the Armed Forces copies of manuscript material in its holdings not incorporated on published charts. The original manuscript hydrographic and topographic sheets remain in the custody of the National Ocean Survey (NOAA), but manuscript tracings copied during the war are in both the Civil Works and Fortifications Map Files of the Office of the Chief of Engineers, Record Group 77. The divisions of the Survey responsible for drawing, engraving, photography, electrotyping, and lithography also reproduced maps prepared under the direction of the military organizations; many of these maps are among Records of U.S. Army Continental Commands, 1821-1920, Record Group 393.

The Civil War maps of the Coast Survey herein described consist of two groups: published nautical charts and special Civil War maps.

PUBLISHED NAUTICAL CHARTS

Before and during the Civil War the Coast Survey prepared and published nautical charts of the coasts of the United States on several scales, the scales varying with the use of the charts. Sailing charts of the coast were published on a scale of 1:1,200,000; general charts of the coast for inshore navigation on a scale of 1:400,000; preliminary seacoast charts for inshore navigation on a scale of 1:200,000; coast charts and charts of navigable rivers on a scale of 1:80,000; and harbor charts on scales, varying from 1:10,000 to 1:80,000.

At the beginning of the war the Survey had surveyed and published sailing and general charts covering most of the Atlantic and gulf coasts and many harbor and river charts. During the war many of these were revised and republished. The 1864 annual report of the Survey contains a list of the published charts available at that date. The record set of published charts in the National Archives was compared with this list and is complete; however, many of the editions published during the war have been hand corrected to show later information.

The hydrographic information shown on these charts consists of soundings, aids and dangers to navigation, and occasional remarks about the composition of the bottom of the coastal waters. In addition, the charts show the outline of adjacent shore lines, roads, habitations, and sometimes topography. Many of the harbor and coastal charts include sketches of views of prominent coastal features.

Until about 1875 the Coast Survey did not assign consecutive numbers to the published charts as is the current practice. At that time the annual reports of the Superintendent of the Coast Survey included copies of most of the charts published during the year, and the records include a set of these charts arranged chronologically. The annual reports also included charts showing the progress of the systematic surveys by well-defined areas and charts prepared from special studies of coastal areas and tides and from related nautical information. Indexes to the charts appear in each report. The few charts not appearing in the annual reports are also arranged by year of publication. Many of the earlier charts were corrected by hand and became the basis for later numbered editions; the earlier editions were filed with the later ones.

The nautical charts published from 1861 through 1865 covering areas along the South Atlantic and gulf coasts of the United States that were incorporated with the regular charts of the Survey are described below by area.

1.165. Eastern and Gulf Coasts. 1861-64. 15 items.
Sailing charts of the coast from Nantucket, Mass., to Cape Hatteras, N.C., from Cape Hatteras to Mosquito Inlet, Fla., from Mosquito Inlet to Key West, Fla., and from Key West to the Rio Grande, Tex.; general charts of the coast from Cape May, N.J., to Cape Henry, Va., and from the entrance to the Chesapeake Bay to Ocracoke Inlet, N.C.; a preliminary seacoast chart from the Savannah River, Ga., to the St. Mary's River, Fla.; a chart

of the lower part of Delaware Bay; a six-sheet chart of the Chesapeake Bay; and a chart of the middle part of the Mississippi Sound.

1.166. Mobile Bay, Ala. 1864. 2 items.

A published chart and a copy of an 1851 edition of a published chart hand-corrected to 1864.

1.167. Florida. 1861-64. 11 items.

Coast charts of the Florida Reefs and harbor charts of Charlotte, Key West, and St. Augustine Harbors, the Cedar Keys, Indian River Inlet, and Escambia and Santa Maria de Galvaez Bays.

1.168. Georgia. 1860-62. 5 items.

Charts of Wassaw, Ossabaw, and Sapelo Sounds, St. Simon's Sound, Brunswick Harbor and Turtle River, and the Savannah River.

1.169. Southwest Pass of the Mississippi River, La. 1862. 1 item.

1.170. Potomac River, Md. 1861-62. 5 items.

A small-scale chart of the river from Point Lookout, Md., to Washington, D.C., and four charts covering the river from its mouth to Little Falls Bridge.

1.171. North Carolina. 1861-64. 7 items.

Coast charts of Core Sound and Straits, Cape Lookout Shoals, and Cape Fear River and approaches to Wilmington; and harbor charts of Beaufort Harbor, Oregon and Hatteras Inlets, and the mouth of the Roanoke River.

1.172. South Carolina. 1862-64. 8 items.

Charts of Charleston Harbor, Lighthouse and Stono Inlets, St. Helena Sound, the entrance to Port Royal, the mouth of Beaufort River, Calibogue Sound, and Skull Creek.

1.173. Virginia. 1861-62. 7 items.

A harbor chart of Metomkcon Inlet, and a series of six charts covering the Rappahannock River.

SPECIAL CIVIL WAR MAPS

During the Civil War the headquarters offices in Washington compiled special maps for the use of the Armed Forces, including maps of the States in insurrection, and other informational maps for general distribution. Other special maps were compiled by Coast Survey personnel assigned to the Armed Forces and were printed by the Coast Survey. Many maps compiled by Coast Survey personnel on assignment to the territorial and troop commands were printed under the direction of these commands, and copies of these maps are to be found among the records of the command authorizing the publication of the maps (Record Group 393) or among the engineer

records relating to those commands (Record Group 77).

Since the first edition of this guide in 1964, certain maps have been reassigned to Record Group 77. These reassignments are noted.

1.174. "Historical Sketches of the Rebellion." 1862-63. 3 items.

A map showing the limits of the loyal States in July 1861 and the limits occupied by Union forces in March, May, and July 1862; and a map showing the limits of the loyal States in July 1861 and the limits occupied by Union forces in July 1863, plus the extent of the blockade of the South Atlantic and gulf coasts (see entries 2.1 and 2.2).

1.175. Southeastern States. 1863-65. 20 items.

Maps of parts of or groups of States showing topography, roads, railroads, cities, and towns. Among these are maps of Virginia with parts of adjacent States (see entry 2.214) and maps of southeastern Virginia and part of North Carolina (see entry 2.219); maps of North Carolina; maps of South Carolina and parts of Georgia; maps of the mountain region of Tennessee and North Carolina (see entry 2.12); and maps of parts of Florida, Louisiana, Mississippi, and Alabama, (see entries 2.13, 2.46, and 2.86). Several of these maps appear in more than one edition.

1.176. Coastal Area of the Southeastern States. 1861-63 6 items.

Maps of the coastal areas of Virginia, North and South Carolina, and Georgia showing the shoreline and such features as roads, railroads, settlements, swamp areas, and defenses. See also under the various States in the following entries.

1.177. Tennessee River. 1864-65. 18 items.

A map of the Tennessee River in 16 sheets with an index sheet and a title page. Prepared under the direction of F. H. Gerdes of the Coast Survey for the use of the Mississippi Squadron (see entry 2.14).

1.178. Fort Hindman, Ark. 1863. 1 item.

A map showing approaches to the fort as captured by the Mississippi Squadron with an inset landscape view of the fort, surveyed by C. Fendall under orders of Admiral Porter of the Mississippi Squadron.

1.179. The Approaches to Washington, D.C. 1863. 1 item.

A road map.

1.180. Georgia. 1862-ca. 1865. 3 items.

Maps of Ossabaw and Wassaw Sounds and vicinity prepared by C. O. Boutelle of the Coast Survey under the direction of Adm. S. F. DuPont of the South Atlantic Blockading Squadron, consisting of a sketch showing

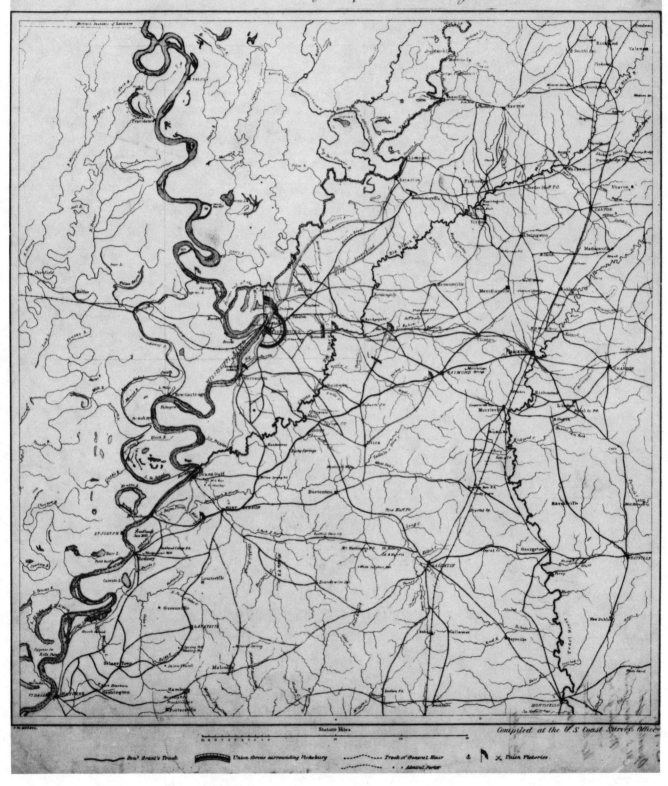

Operations of Union forces in the advance on Vicksburg, Miss., and sites of Union victories. RG 77: S 18. See entry 1.182.

depths and sailing lines on Wassaw Bar and a sketch of
the Wassaw and Ossabaw Sounds showing the relative
positions of the U.S. ironclad steamer *Montauk* and the
Confederate Fort McAllister during the bombardment of
the fort, February 1, 1863; and a map showing operations
of Sherman's forces in the Atlanta campaign, compiled
in the Coast Survey from information furnished by Capt.
O. M. Poe of Sherman's staff and from Sherman's published report (reassigned to RG 77: Z 166).

1.181. Louisiana. 1862-63. 3 items.

A map of part of southern Louisiana from New Orleans
west to Vermillion Bay and north to Port Hudson showing

roads; railroads, drainage features, and place names; a
sketch of the approaches to Fort Butte La Rose captured
by Union forces, showing positions of Union and Confederate ships and including an inset plan of the fort,
drawn by J. G. Oltmanns under orders of Maj. Gen.
N. P. Banks (reassigned to RG 77: G 443, vol. 11, p. 7);
and a map of a reconnaissance of the Mississippi River
below Forts Jackson and St. Philip, made by F. H. Gerdes
before the forts were reduced by the Union fleet under
Adm. D. G. Farragut, and showing the positions of the
mortar flotilla and gunboats (reassigned to RG 77: G 443,
vol. 11, p. 6).

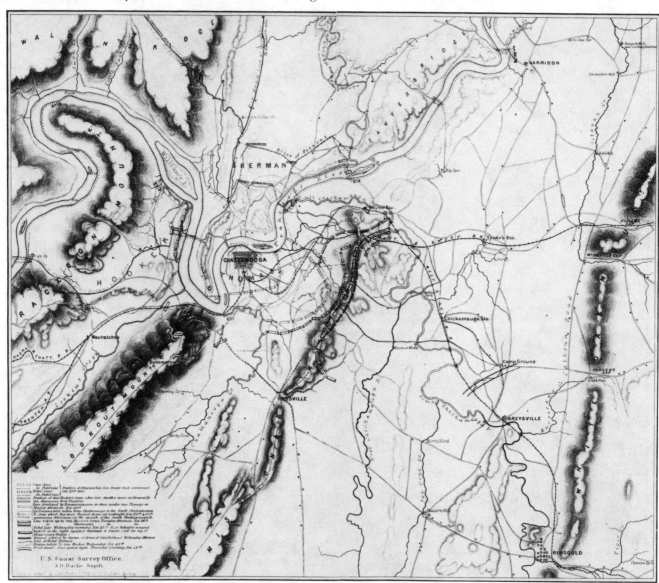

*Map of the battlefield at Chattanooga, Tenn., showing Union and Confederate troop positions and defense. RG 23: Special Civil War Maps:
Tennessee. See entry 1.184.*

1.182. Vicksburg and Vicinity, Miss. 1863. 6 items.

A map showing the operations of Union forces in the advance on Vicksburg and sites of Union victories (reassigned to RG 77: S 18); and maps drawn by C. Fendall and A. Strausz under the direction of Adm. D. D. Porter, commander of the Mississippi Squadron, showing the approaches to the city and Confederate defenses (reassigned to RG 77: G 443, vol. 11, p. 17; S 22), sketch maps showing defenses of the Yazoo River at Walnut Hills and positions of the attacking gunboats on April 30 and May 1 at Haines (Haynes) Bluff, a survey of a canal connecting Walnut Bayou with the Mississippi River (reassigned to RG 77: G 443, vol. 10, p. 3), and a map showing Admiral Porter's attempted route into the Yazoo River by way of Steels Bayou and Deer Creek (reassigned to RG 77: G 443, vol. 10, p. 5).

1.183. South Carolina. 1862-65. 14 items.

Maps of Charleston Harbor showing positions of Confederate defenses and of the blockading Union ships, 1863; a map showing siege operations against Forts Sumter and Wagner between July 13 and September 7, 1863 (reassigned to RG 77: I 31-2); and a sheet of plans and views of Confederate defenses along the coast consisting of forts or batteries located at Bay Point, Botany Bay Island, Fenwick Island, Otter Island Point, and Sam's Point. Although most of the forts are unnamed, Fort Beauregard is at Bay Point, and Fort Walker is at Hilton Head Island. A plan of the rebel battery at St. Helena also shows the locations of the *Pennsylvania* and the *Raritan*, which were burned by the Union Navy.

1.184. Chattanooga, Tenn. 1863. 1 item.

Map of the battlefield showing Union and Confederate troop positions and defenses (a different version of the map is filed as RG 77: T 75).

1.185. Virginia. 1861-65. 11 items.

A topographic map of the area in the vicinity of Arlington, Alexandria, and Falls Church showing defenses of Washington and camps of military units, 1861 (reassigned to RG 77: G 124); several editions of a map of the southeastern part of the State showing roads, railroads, place names, some topographic features, drainage features, and swamp area; plans of the Confederate forts located on Craney Island and on Sewall's Point; and a city plan of Richmond showing street names, the home of Jefferson Davis, city facilities, industrial areas and warehouses, and public buildings (reassigned to RG 77: G 142).

1.186. Cape Fear River Entrances and Frying Pan Shoals, N.C. 1864. 1 item.

A copy of a published chart annotated to show Confederate defenses and locations of wrecked ships (reassigned to RG 77: H 86-2). Unlike the maps described above, this chart bears the notation that it was received in the Coast Survey, December 6, 1864, from J. S. Bradford, Assistant in the Coast Survey and Aide-de-Camp to Admiral Porter.

OTHER

National Archives Gift Collection. RG 200

This record group consists of private papers given to the National Archives and accepted as "appropriate for preservation by the Government as evidence of its organization, functions, policies, decisions, procedures, and transactions." The cartographic records that pertain to the Civil War are those of William Henry Paine, a native of New Hampshire, who in 1862 was appointed an aide-de-camp with the rank of captain and continued in his duties as a topographical engineer under the Headquarters Department of the Rappahannock. From January 1863 to June 1865 he served as the assistant to the Chief of Topographical Engineers, Army of the Potomac. Of Paine's service, Maj. Gen. G. K. Warren wrote: "To his previous great knowledge of the country he added by constant laborious and oftentimes daring reconnaissances, and applied it in unfailing efforts to correct our imperfect maps and in guiding our columns on the marches

night and day along the secret paths he had discovered." Paine was breveted a Colonel of Volunteers after the war. He died in 1890. His papers were given by his daughter in 1932 to the American Geographical Society, which presented them to the National Archives in 1954.

1.187. Virginia. 1862-65. 85 items.

Three published maps of parts of Virginia showing roads, topography, wooded areas, and names of residents compiled by Captain Paine; manuscript and annotated terrain maps of parts of Virginia, particularly the central and northern parts; and manuscript and annotated maps showing routes and operations of the Army of the Potomac. These maps are arranged with a letter-number designation assigned before they were received in the National Archives and are accompanied by a typewritten, descriptive list.

War Department Collection of Confederate Records. RG 109

This record group consists of records of the Confederate States of America acquired by capture or surrender at the close of the Civil War or acquired later by donation or purchase. The cartographic records include maps and drawings of campaigns and fortifications in various States. Some of the maps are untitled. All are manuscript except when noted below as being published. The entries are arranged alphabetically by State; miscellaneous maps relating to more than one State appear at the end.

1.188. Alabama. 4 items.

Maps of Demopolis, n.d.; the country south and west of Mobile, n.d.; Blakely, n.d.; and Demopolis, 1863.

1.189. Arkansas. 6 items.

Maps of a reconnaissance between St. Francis and White Rivers, 1863; the Battle at Prairie Grove, n.d.; the approaches to Little Rock, 1863; the vicinity of Fayetteville and Fort Smith (2 sketch maps), n.d.; Helena and its approaches, 1863; and Little Rock and its approaches, 1863.

1.190. Georgia. 19 items.

Maps of Atlanta and vicinity (2 sections), ca. 1864; roads between Marietta and Dalton, 1864; the battlefield of Chickamauga (copied from the original loaned by the Southern Historical Society), 1863; roads between Chattanooga and Ringgold, ca. 1863; New Hope and vicinity, ca. 1863; the battlefield of Chickamauga, n.d.; the country from Augusta to Sister's Ferry, n.d.; the movement of B. R. Johnson's Division in the Chickamauga campaign, 1863; roads between the Chattahoochie River and Atlanta, ca. 1864; Atlanta and its environs, with the location of French's Division, ca. 1864; Marietta to Pace's Ferry, ca. 1864; Marietta to Pace's and Defoe's Ferries, ca. 1864; the country northwest and southwest of Atlanta (2 maps), 1864; the country between Marietta and Cartersville, ca. 1864; the country between Marietta, Atlanta, Newnan, and Van Wert (2 versions of the same map), ca. 1864; the vicinity of Atlanta and Newnan, ca. 1864; and the vicinity of Marietta and Dallas, 1864.

1.191. Kentucky. 2 items.

Maps of Perryville and the surrounding country (Louisville to Lexington), 1862, and the vicinity south and east of Shepherdsville, n.d.

1.192. Maryland. 1 item.

A map of the battlefields of Harpers Ferry and Sharpsburg, 1864.

1.193. Mississippi. 17 items.

Maps of the battlefield of Baker's Creek (near Jackson), 1863; fortifications at Columbus, ca. 1862; the vicinity of Corinth and the adjacent part of Tennessee, n.d.; the vicinity of Saltillo and Guntown, n.d.; the vicinity of Corinth, 1862; and fortifications near Vicksburg, 1861. A military map of Mississippi by Robertson, n.d. Maps of northeastern Mississippi, including Corinth and Iuka, 1863; the vicinity of Corinth and Rienzi, n.d.; the vicinity of Columbus, n.d.; the vicinity of Corinth, n.d.; the vicinity of Raymond and Clinton, n.d.; the vicinity of Grenada, n.d.; northeastern Mississippi and part of Ten-

nessee (2 items), n.d.; northeastern Mississippi, Corinth to Columbus (for General B. R. Johnson), n.d.; and the battlefield of Iuka, 1862.

1.194. Missouri. 6 items.

Maps of southeastern Missouri in the vicinity of St. Francis River, n.d.; the vicinity of Farmington, n.d.; the vicinity of Ironton, n.d.; fortifications near Belmont, n.d.; and the vicinity of Belmont, n.d. A "New Sectional Map of the State of Missouri," published by George F. Cram, Chicago, 1876.

1.195. Oklahoma. 1 item.

A map of the vicinity of Boggy Depot (near Red River), n.d.

1.196. South Carolina. 7 items.

Maps of Broad River mouth, with fortifications and fleets artistically drawn, n.d.; Fort Drayton on New River,

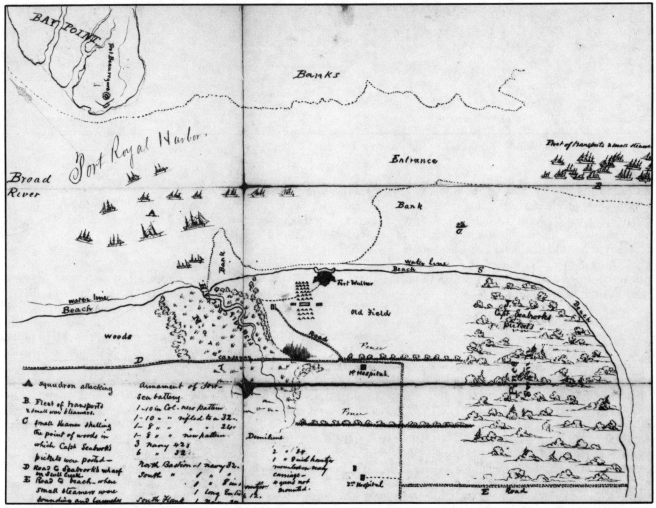

Drawing of the mouth of the Broad River and Port Royal Harbor showing fortifications. RG 109: South Carolina 1. See entry 1.196.

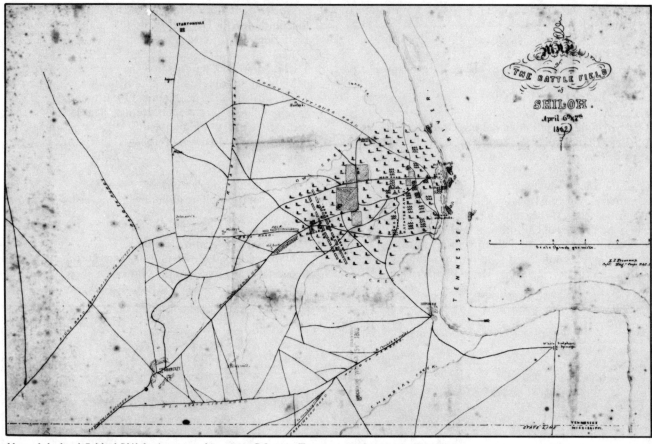

Map of the battlefield of Shiloh, Apr. 6 and 7, 1862. RG 109: Tennessee 11. See entry *1.197.*

n.d.; and the mouth of Broad River (plan of Fort Beauregard on reverse), n.d. A map from Barnwell's report on troops to protect the railroad in the area between Charleston and the Savannah River, n.d. Plans of fortifications at South Island and Cat Island Redoubts, n.d.; of Winyaw Bay and vicinity, 1861; of James Island fortifications near Charleston, 1862; and of Combahee Ferry works (north of Beaufort), n.d.

1.197. Tennessee. 17 items.

Maps of the lower Hiwassee River Valley, n.d.; Knoxville and the vicinity to its north, n.d.; the battlefield of Murfreesboro, 1862-63; and Cumberland, Franklin, and surrounding areas, n.d. A rough sketch and a printed map of the battlefield of Murfreesboro, 1863. Maps of the vicinity of Nashville and Murfreesboro, 1862; the vicinity of the Battle of Shiloh, n.d.; the area west and south of Knoxville, 1863; the area west of Nashville, n.d.; and the battlefield of Shiloh, 1862 (2 items). A sketch of the battlefield of Shiloh for General Beauregard, 1862. Maps of the western part of Tennessee, n.d.; the country between Kingston and Knoxville, n.d.; the vicinity of Wartrace, n.d.; and the vicinity of Nashville and Edgefield, n.d.

1.198. Texas. 2 items.

Plans of defense near Gonzales, with fortifications artistically drawn, n.d., and of Fort Waul near Gonzales, n.d.

1.199. Virginia. 22 items.

Maps of the vicinity of Quantico, n.d.; the Malvern Hill battlefield, n.d.; Coggins Point on the James River, 1862; and the Potomac River near Quantico Creek, n.d. Two versions of a sketch map of the route of General McLaw's Division in Orange County, 1863. Maps of the battlefield of Frazier's Farm and positions at Malvern Hill, 1862; battlegrounds in the vicinity of Groveton, 1862; the battlefield of Winchester, 1863; the route of the Army of the Valley from Pendleton County to the Battle of Winchester, 1863; the area north of Petersburg, n.d.; Slaughter's Mountain battlefield, 1862; Cross-Keys battlefield, n.d.; the area east of Petersburg, n.d.; the vicinity of Richmond showing fortifications, 1862; the city of Richmond and its defenses, 1862; the vicinity of Petersburg, 1864; the vicinity of Richmond and part of the peninsula, 1864; Petersburg with its defenses, ca. 1862 (1874 also appears); and Malvern ("Malvoin") Hill battlefield and vicinity, 1862. A "Map of the Seat of

War" (in Virginia), published by Hart and Mapother, Louisville, n.d.

1.200. Miscellaneous maps relating to more than one State. 11 items.

A chart of Sabine Pass (between Texas and Louisiana) also showing shore fortifications, 1861. A map showing gaps in the mountains from Winter's Gap to Louisa Fork in the vicinity of Cumberland Gap, n.d. A map of Tennessee, Mississippi, Alabama, and part of Georgia, 1862. A plan of the route from Columbus, Miss., to Decatur, Ala., n.d. A map of Kentucky and Tennessee published by O. Lederle, Memphis, 1862 (2 copies). A map of parts of Mississippi and Alabama (in the vicinity of Tuscaloosa) with a description of the route of General French, 1864. A small sketch map of western Kentucky and Tennessee, n.d. Another sketch map of parts of Kentucky and Tennessee from Frankfort to Knoxville, n.d. A map of the fall campaign of the Army of the Missouri under Maj. General Price in Missouri, Arkansas, Oklahoma, and Kansas, 1864. A rough sketch map of mountain gaps in the vicinity of Bristol, on the border of Virginia and Tennessee, n.d.

PART II

Part II consists of detailed descriptions of maps of exceptional interest that have been selected from the records described in part I. They were selected for several reasons: they represent the major geographical areas in the Civil War; they possess intrinsic historic value; they contain the highest concentration of information; they are easier to read than other maps covering the same area; and they are of artistic value.

Maps of the United States as a whole or of large areas, such as military departments, are listed under United States; maps of States or smaller areas are listed under individual States, which are arranged alphabetically.

The numbered entries include the map title; usually the name of the surveyor, compiler, draftsman, or producing agency; date; scale; dimensions to the nearest inch; a brief description of the map; the record group to which it belongs; and the file designation.

The information in the first paragraph of each entry, other than that enclosed in brackets, is quoted directly from the the map being described, although the information may not always be in the map's title block. Information enclosed in brackets has been supplied by the archivist. Spellings, abbreviations, and most capitalizations are given as they appear on the map, but punctuation has been inserted for greater ease in reading.

UNITED STATES

2.1. Historical Sketch of the Rebellion. Published at the Office of the U.S. Coast Survey, A. D. Bache, Supdt. [Edition of] July 1862.

1 inch to about 90 miles. 22 x 19. Published. A map of the United States east of about the 98th Meridian showing by blue lines the limits of loyal States as of July 1861. Purple, red, and yellow lines indicate limits of areas occupied by Union forces on March 1, 1862, May 15, 1862, and July 15, 1862, respectively. Reassigned to RG 77: Dr. 154-32.

2.2. [Same title as above. Edition of July 1863.]

Limits of loyal States as of July 1861 are shown by blue lines and limits of areas occupied by Union forces in July 1863 by red lines. The extent of the coastal blockade is indicated by blue ship symbols. Reassigned to RG 77: US 225.

2.3. Limit of Territory Controlled by U.S. Forces, Novr. 1864.

1 inch to 50 miles. 34 x 41. Annotated published. The loyal States and areas controlled by Union forces are shaded pink and areas remaining under control of the Confederacy are shaded blue. Other annotations read: "Prepared for the Military Committee of the Senate" and "Engineer Bureau, War Department, November 30th, 1864." The map is signed "Richd. Delafield, Genl. & Chief Engineer, U.S. Army." The area covered by this map is east of the 100th Meridian. An inset map, scale 1 inch to about 230 miles, covers the western portion of the country. G. Woolworth Colton's "New Guide Map of the United States," edition of 1864, was used as the base map. RG 46: 38th Congress. Military Committee Map 9.

2.4. Map of the United States Showing the Military Divisions and Military Departments of _____ [1865].

1 inch to 50 miles. 34 x 49. Annotated published. Boundaries and names of military departments are in red and those of military divisions in blue. Other annotations read: "For the Military Committee of the Senate" and "Engineer Bureau, War Department, December 13th, 1865." The area covered by the base map and inset map are the same as described under entry 2.3 above. G. Woolworth Colton's "New Guide Map of the United States," edition of 1865, was used as the base map. RG 46: 38th Congress. Military Committee Map 26.

2.5. Gauges of Southern Railroads. Compiled under the direction of Lieut. Col. J. N. Macomb, A.D.C., Chf. Top. Engr.

1 inch to 30 miles. 32 x 55. Annotated published. Varying gauges are distinguished by colors added to a published copy of a "Rail Road Map of the Southern States Shewing the Southern & Southwestern Railway Connections with Philadelphia 1862. Prepared by Thomas Kimber, Jr., Chairman of the Committee on Inland Transportation of the Board of Trade of Philadelphia." RG 92: Map 119.

2.6. Portions of the Military Departments of The Cumberland . . . of the South . . . and of The Gulf . . . Compiled in the Bureau of Topog'l. Eng's., War Department, January 1863, by Denis Callahan Delt.

1 inch to 5.524 miles. 67 x 51 (2 sections). Manuscript. Covers Alabama, western Georgia, and western Florida. Railroad lines are in red with symbols differentiating existing from contemplated routes. A blue line along the Chattahoochee and Oconee Rivers to Athens, Ga., indicates part of the route surveyed in 1828 by William Jerome for a line of communication by canals and railroad between the Tennessee and Altamaha Rivers. Mail stage routes are in brown. "Uncertain" roads are distinguished from other roads; and canals, swamp lands, prairie lands, post offices, county seats, mills, forts, and names of some residents are included. Sections reserved for the use of public schools in each township in Alabama are located by asterisks. Some relief is indicated by shading. RG 77: US 215.

2.7. Portions of the Military Departments of [the] Missouri and [the] Ohio compiled in the Bureau of Topographical Engineers, War Department, from the best and latest authorities, Feby. 1862.

1 inch to about 5½ miles. 59 x 51 (2 sections). Manuscript. Covers eastern Missouri, northeastern Arkansas, western Kentucky and Tennessee, the southern tip of Illinois, and a small part of northern Alabama and Mississippi. Railroads are in red. Mines, mills, forts, post offices, towns and villages, and roads are shown. RG 77: US 209.

2.8. Part of the Military Department of the South . . . compiled in the Engineer Bureau, War Department, September 1864. [Continuation sheet dated October 24, 1864.]

1 inch to 5.524 miles. Map: 59 x 52 (2 sections); continuation sheet: 25 x 25. Manuscript. Covers South Carolina, eastern Georgia, and southern North Carolina. Railroads are in red with symbols differentiating existing from contemplated routes. A blue line along the Oconee River to Milledgeville, Ga., shows part of the route surveyed by William Jerome in 1828 for a line of communication by canals and railroad between the Tennessee and Altamaha Rivers. Names of some residents, mills, post offices, towns and villages, railroad stations, churches, ferries, swamp areas, and forts are shown. RG 77: US 244.

2.9. Map of portions of the Military Departments of Washington, Pennsylvania, Annapolis, & North-Eastern Virginia. Compiled in the Bureau of Topogl. Engs., War Department, from the best and latest Authorities, July 1861.

1 inch to about 3⅕ miles. 58 x 51 (2 sections). Man-

uscript. Railroads are in red with symbols differentiating existing and contemplated lines. Turnpike roads are in brown; stage roads and common roads are shown by different kinds of line symbols. Drainage features are in blue and county boundaries in different colors. Names of towns, villages, churches, and mills are included. Some relief is indicated by shading. RG 77: US 203.

2.10. Map Prepared to exhibit the Campaigns in which the Army of the Cumberland took part during the war of the Rebellion by order of Major Genl. Geo. H. Thomas, U.S.A. Compiled under the direction of Brvt. Majr. Genl. Z. B. Tower, Chief Engr., Milty. Div. of the Tenn., by Ed. Ruger, Supt., Topl. Engr. Office at Nashville. Assistants: Capt. A. Kilp & Lieut. R. Flach, 3 U.S.C.A. (Heavy) & Assist. Topl. Engrs.

1 inch to 10 miles. 55 x 85 (4 sections). Manuscript. Covers area from southwestern Virginia to Savannah, Ga., and from north-central Kentucky to northern Alabama. Routes of the different campaigns and of Jefferson Davis' flight are shown in different colors and symbols. Sites of military engagements are shown in colors corresponding to those which distinguish the different campaign routes. Printed descriptions of the campaigns in Alabama, Georgia, Kentucky, Mississippi, the Carolinas, Tennessee, and the western part of Virginia are pasted on the margins of the map. RG 77: US 275-l.

2.11. Military Map of the States of Kentucky and Tennessee within eleven [m]iles of the 35th Parallel of Latitude or Southern Boundary of Tennessee . . . Commenced under the Authority of Major General Don Carlos Buell, Commanding the Department of the Ohio, by Capt. N. Michler, Corps Topogl. Engrs., U.S.A., continued under Major General H. G. Wright by Maj. L. Sitgreaves, Corps Topogl. Engrs., USA., and completed under Major General Ambrose E. Burnside, Commanding the Department, by Lieut. Col. J. H. Simpson, U.S.A., Chief of Engrs. in the Department, July 1863.

1 inch to 5.524 miles. 51 x 84 (3 sections). Manuscript. Railroads in red and drainage features in blue. The States of Kentucky and Tennessee and adjoining parts of other States are shaded in different colors. County seats, other towns and villages, ironworks, forges, saltworks, mills, post offices, improved roads, and common roads are shown. RG 77: T 68.

2.12. Mountain Region of North Carolina and Tennessee. Compiled by W. L. Nicholson & A. Lindenkohl, 1863, With corrections to May 1864. U.S. Coast Survey, . . . Drawn by A. Lindenkohl, H. Lindenkohl & Chas. G. Krebs, Lith.

1 inch to 10 miles. 25 x 42. Published. Also includes parts of Alabama, Georgia, Kentucky, South Carolina, and Virginia. State boundaries and railroad lines in red. Drainage features, roads, and place names are included. Relief is indicated by hachures. A list of authorities is

included. RG 23: Special Maps.

2.13. Southern Mississippi and Alabama Showing the Approaches to Mobile. U.S. Coast Survey Office . . . 1863. Edw. Molitor, Lith.

1 inch to about 11 miles. 25 x 28. Published. Covers area from Choctawhatchee Bay, Fla., to Lake Ponchartrain, La., and extends inland to about 33° N. Latitude. Railroads in red and drainage features in blue. Also shows roads and place names. Reassigned to RG 77: G 443, vol. 11, p. 8.

2.14. Map of the Tennessee River for the Use of the Mississippi Squadron under Command of Acting Rear Admiral S. P. Lee, U.S.N., From Reconnaissance by a party of the United States Coast Survey [under F. H. Gerdes] . . . 1864-65.

1 inch to about ⅔ mile. 18 sheets averaging 22 x 18. Includes a title sheet, an index sheet, and 16 consecutive sheets covering the river from Paducah, Ky., to Florence, Ala. The channel, mileage points from Paducah, and fields, wooded areas, settlements, roads, and names of residents in the area adjoining the river are shown. Reassigned to RG 77: T 123.

ALABAMA

2.15. Map of Blakely and Vicinity. Showing the disposition of the 2nd Division, 13th Army Corps, during the siege & in the Assault of April 9th, 1865. Copied in the Engineer Department, February 5th, 1866.

1 inch to 200 yards. 15 x 12. Manuscript. First, second, and third positions of the 2d Division are distinguished. Map also shows wooded areas, fields, Confederate defenses, and a few buildings. Relief is indicated by hachures. RG 77: J 34.

2.16. Line of Investment of Fort Gaines Dauphine I, by Maj. Genl. G. Granger's Expeditionary Corps, Aug. 1864. Capt. M. D. McAlester, U.S.E., Chief Engr., [and] Capt. J. C. Palfrey . . . 1st Lt. A. H. Burnham . . . [and] 1st Lt. C. J. Allen, U.S.E., Assistants. Drawn by Ch. Spangenberg, Asst. Engr.

Large scale. 25 x 36. Manuscript. Fort Gaines is outlined in red and General Granger's investments are shown in blue. A list of the armament at each battery along the line of investments is included. Map also shows building sites, swamp areas, wooded areas, roads, and the point where most of the artillery and materials were landed. Some relief is indicated by hachures. The lower left-hand corner of the map is missing. RG 77: Dr. 121-5.

2.17. Topographical Map of Huntsville, Ala., and Vicinity. Prepared under the direction of Col. Wm. E. Merrill, 1st U.S.V.V. Engineers, Chief Engineer, Dept. of the Cumberland, By Major James R. Willett, 1st U.S.V.V. Engineers, Chief Inspector, R.R. De-

fences, Dept. of the Cumberland. Surveyed by Jno. Willett & Chs. Peseux, 1864.

1 inch to 440 feet. 44 x 71 (3 sections). Manuscript. Relief is shown by contour lines in brown and contour intervals in red; drainage features are in blue, wooded areas in green, streets and roads in brown, and a probable fortified site outlined in red. Map also shows railroads, buildings, and names of some residents outside the city. RG 77: Z 63.

2.18. [Map of Mobile Bay showing defense works, soundings, and obstructions, with scattered notes about armament of defense works and navigability of the bay and the Tensas River.]

1 inch to ½ mile. 39 x 25. Manuscript. Drainage features in blue, defenses and city blocks of Mobile in red, and obstructions and roads in yellow. RG 77: Dr. 121-15-10.

2.19. Mobile and Vicinity. Prepared by Order of Maj. Gen. N. P. Banks; D. C. Houston, Major & Chief Engineer. July 1863. N. F. Hyer, C. E., F. D'Avignon, [and] B. von Reizenstein, Delrs. Photographed by Walter Ogilvie.

1 inch to 2 miles. 32 x 34. Annotated photocopy. Roads are emphasized in red. Map is annotated to show obstructions in the entrance to and at the head of Mobile Bay, fortifications in addition to those shown on base map, place names, railroads, bridges, ferries, and names of roads. The base map was issued as "Department of the Gulf Map No. 11." RG 77: J 26-2.

2.20. Map No. 1. Rebel Defences, Mobile, Ala., occupied by Union Forces under Maj. Gen. E. R. S. Canby, Comdg., April 12th, 1865. Drawn by order of Maj. McAlester, Chief Engineer, Army and Div. West Miss., Under Direction of Lt. S. E. McGregory, Comdg. Topographical Party.

1 inch to ⅛ mile. 35 x 51. Manuscript. Three lines of entrenchments are shown: the inner in red with redoubts numbered; the two outer lines in orange with redoubts on the middle line lettered and redans numbered. Batteries Buchanan and Missouri and the Water Battery are located by name. Noted, "Sent to Engineer Bureau with letter of June 17th, 1865. [Signed] M. D. McAlester, Bvt. Majr., Chief Engineer, Army & Div. West Miss." RG 77: Dr. 121-15.

2.21. No. 2. Siege Operations at Spanish Fort, Mobile Bay, by the U.S. Forces under Maj. Gen. Canby. Captured by the Army of West Miss. on the Night of April 8 & 9th, 1865. Drawn by order of Maj. McAlester, Chief Engineer, Army & Division West Miss., under direction of Lt. S. E. McGregory, Commanding Topographical Party.

1 inch to 200 yards. 31 x 41. Manuscript. Drainage features and bays in blue, Confederate defense works in red and Union siege lines and works in blue, and lines

showing limits of fire in red. Map also gives positions of Union troop commands and shows wooded areas, swamps, roads, and obstructions in the Blakely River. Some relief is indicated by hachures. Noted, "Sent to Engineer Bureau with letter of June 17th, 1865. [Signed] M. D. McAlester, Bvt. Majr., Chief Engineer, Army & Div. West Miss." RG 77: Dr. 121-16.

2.22. No. 4. Map of the Defences of the City of Mobile. Drawn under the direction of Lieut. Col. V. Sheliha, Chief Engr., Dpt. of the Gulf [Confederate].

1 inch to about ⅘ mile. 22 x 18. Annotated photoprocessed. Shows the three lines of entrenchments erected 1862-64 with letters and numbers of redoubts on the two inner lines added by hand. Noted and signed "Approved, Saml. H. Lockett, Col. & Chf. Engr., Dept. Ala., Miss. & E. La., For the Lieut. Gen'l. Comd'g. Dept." Also noted, "Captd. from the Rebels" and "Sent to Engineer Bureau with letter of June 17th, 1865. [Signed] M. D. McAlester, Bvt. Majr., Chief Engineer, Army & Div. West Miss." RG 77: Dr. 121-15-3.

2.23. Plan of Siege Operations Against Fort Morgan by the U.S. Forces, under Maj. Genl. Gordon Granger, Aug. 1864. Capt. John C. Palfrey, Corps of Engrs., Lt. A. H. Burnham, [and] Lt. Chs. J. Allen, Corps of Engrs., in charge of works. Surveyed and Drawn by Capt. W. H. Wheeler [and] Lt. S. E. McGregory, Co. A., 96 U.S.C.I. Engr. Troops. Litho. in the Office of the Chief Engineer, Dept. of the Gulf.

1 inch to 300 feet. 19 x 26. Published. Shows defense lines and works. The number and kinds of armament along the line of works are listed with letters keyed to positions on the map. Reassigned to RG 77: Dr. 82-53-5; Z 288.

2.24. Stevenson, Ala., Showing the Defenses of the Post erected after Plans of Col. Merrill, Chief Engr., D[epartment of the] C[umberland]. By Major P. V. Fox, 1st Mich. Engr's. Surveyed & Plotted by 1st Lieut. C. A. Ensign, 1st Mich. Engr's. September 1864.

Large scale. 29 x 37. Manuscript. Relief is suggested by red form lines; woods are indicated by green symbols and fallen timber by green and brown symbols; and drainage features are in blue. Map also gives heights above and below the railroad and includes survey notes. Scattered comments describe the terrain. Noted, "Engr. Department, Dec. 31, 1864. Recd. with Col. Merrill's letter of 19 Dec. 1864." RG 77: Dr. 121-7.

2.25. Map of that portion of the Tennessee River [in northern Alabama and Tennessee] between Savannah and Chattanooga together with the country adjacent. Taken from Map of Middle Tennessee. Being compiled [in 1865] under direction of Col. W. E. Merrill.

1 inch to 4 miles. 16 x 50. Published. State boundaries,

railroads, and drainage features are in color. Map also shows roads, place names, names of residents, factories, mills, salt wells, and foundries. Relief is indicated by hachures. The title given above appears on the back of the map with a label that reads: "Issued by command of Maj. Gen. Geo. H. Thomas. A. C. Wharton, Lt. Col. and Top'l. Eng'r., D. C." Reassigned to RG 77: J 32.

ARKANSAS

2.26. Map of the District [State] of Arkansas. Compiled from Surveys and Military Reconnoissances by order of Lieut. Col. H. T. Douglas, Chief, Engineer Dept., Richard M. Venable, Capt. and Chief of Topographical Engineers, Dist. West La. and Arks.

1 inch to 4 miles. 70 x 77 (2 sections). Manuscript. Roads shown in red were reconnoitered; roads shown in blue were taken from township maps and other sources. Double, dotted, and broken lines differentiate between public or main roads, settlement roads, and trails. County boundaries are in various colors. Prairies are outlined in green. Swamp or overflowed areas, drainage features, railroads, and names of some residents are also shown. Some relief is indicated by hachures. Noted, "Engineer Department, Washington, July 17, 1865. Received with Maj. McAlester's letter of July 5, 1865." Title is preceded by "Dep't. Trans. Miss., Topographical Bureau." The map also has the emblem of the "Topographical Bureau, Dist. Arks., Mar. 21st, 1864." RG 77: Dr. 123-15.

2.27. Map of Route [from Little Rock to Camden via Arkadelphia, and return] pursued by Army commanded by Maj. Gen. Fredk. Steele From March 24th till May 2nd, 1864. Drawn, May 1864 by Lt. Fred. Sommer, Engineer Staff of Maj. Gen. Steele.

1 inch to 4 miles. 28 x 20. Manuscript. The route is in brown. A partially torn note at lower right-hand corner is dated, "Eng. Dept., Oct. 7, 1864." RG 77: Dr. 123-5-2.

2.28. [Maps of Dallas, Desha, Drew, and Ouachita counties.]

1 inch to 1 mile. Dallas County: 31 x 52; Desha: 36 x 49; Drew: 46 x 36; Ouachita: 36 x 45. Manuscript. Roads, trails, fords, bridges, drainage features, prairies, properties, and names of residents are included. Notes relate to character of terrain and vegetation. Each map has the emblem of the "Topographical Bureau, Dist. Arks. . . . 1865." These are identified on the related filecard as captured Confederate maps turned in by Capt. McAlester of the Department of the Gulf in 1865. RG 77: Z 48.

2.29. Vicinity of Dooleys Ferry, Ark.

1 inch to about 2,000 feet. 20 x 25. Manuscript. Roads are in red and drainage features in blue; and wooded areas are shown by green symbols. Property lines and

names of property owners are included. Relief is indicated by hachures. Noted and signed, "Respectfully forwarded, J. Henry Sargent, Asst. Engr." RG 77: Z 280.

2.30. Map of Du Val's [sic] Bluff, Arkansas, and Vicinity, including Cavalry Depot and Remount Camp. Prepared under Direction of Capt. J. B. Wheeler, U.S. Engs., Chief Engr., Dept. Ark., by Capt. J. F. Sanders, 4 Ark. Cav. Vol.

1 inch to 440 feet. 2 sections, 20 x 46 each. Manuscript. Drainage features in blue, and defense works at the Bluff in red. Timber, roads, buildings, and the United States Military Railroad are also shown. Relief is indicated by form lines. Title is preceded by "Engineer's Office, Department of Arkansas." RG 77: Z 327.

2.31. [Map and inset ground] Plan of the Fortification [Fort Hindman] at Post, Arkansas, Surrendered to the U.S. Forces Jan. 11th, 1863. Destroyed after the evacuation. Surveyed & drawn by Julius Pitzman, Capt., & A.D.C. to Maj. Genl. Sherman.

Map: 1 inch to 1,000 feet. Ground plan: 1 inch to 100 feet. 23 x 19. Manuscript. Lines of march and final positions of Federal troops in red. Map is noted as a copy. RG 77: Z 189.

2.32. Map of Helena, Ark., and Vicinity, Showing the location of the Fort [Curtis] & Batteries. Wm. Hoelcke, Capt. & Addl. A. de. C., Chf. Eng., Army S.W.

1 inch to about 125 yards. 34 x 24. Manuscript. Defense works in red. Abatis, wooded areas, fields, and buildings are also shown. Relief is indicated by hachures. Noted, "Engineer Department, September 27, 1865. Received with Capt. Hoelcke's letter of 22d Sept. 1865." RG 77: Dr. 123-19-1.

2.33. Little Rock and Vicinity, Arkansas.

Large scale. 2 sections, 32 x 36 each. Manuscript. Defenses in red and main approach roads in brown. Buildings, city blocks, names of some residents, swamp areas, and timber are also shown. Notes read: "Respectfully Submitted with my Inspection Report of Dec. 22d, 1864. [Signed] Q. A. Gillmore, Maj. Genl., Insp. Genl. Fort., Div. West Miss." and "Eng. Dept Recd. Jany. 20/65." The map described in entry 2.34 is a continuation of this map. RG 77: Dr. 123-9-1.

2.34. North Side of Arkansas River opposite Little Rock.

Large scale. 20 x 36. Manuscript. Shows the Memphis and Little Rock Railroad and railroad station, machine shop, and engine house; the U.S. depots and military pontoon bridge; and a continuation of the defenses of Little Rock. Swamp areas, fields, timber lands, and roads are also included. Notes are the same as those on the map described in entry 2.33. RG 77: Dr. 123-9-2.

2.35. Map of the approaches to Little Rock made under instructions from Maj. Gen. Sterling Price, Comm'dg. Dist. Ark's., by Capt. T. J. Mackey, C. S. Eng'rs., August 1863. J. D. Hutton, C. E.

1 inch to ½ mile. 27 x 35. Manuscript. Roads in red. The street pattern of the city; defenses north of the Arkansas River; the Memphis and Little Rock Railroad and Depot; bridges; buildings with names of residents along the principal roads; headquarters of Generals Pagan, Parsons, and McRae; and drainage features and swamps are shown. Some relief is indicated by hachures. Noted, "Engineer Department, Washington, July 17, 1865. Received with Major McAlester's letter of 5 July 1865." RG 77: Dr. 123-9-3.

2.36. Map of the Battlefield of Pea Ridge, Ark.

Large scale. 15 x 16. Manuscript. Federal lines in red and Confederate in blue. Progressive positions are indicated. Roads, fields, wooded areas, and the site where McCulloch was killed are shown. Relief is indicated by hachures. Noted, "H.Q.A., Sept. 11, 1865. Respectfully forwarded to Engr. Dept. C. B. Comstock, Bvt. Bg. Gn., A.D.C." RG 77: Q 109.

2.37. Croquis of the Battlefield of Prairie Grove, Arkansas. December 7th, 1862. Drawn by T. W. Williams, 15 Ills. Infy.

1 inch to ½ mile. 16 x 21. Manuscript. Federal positions in blue and Confederate in red. Red numerals in-

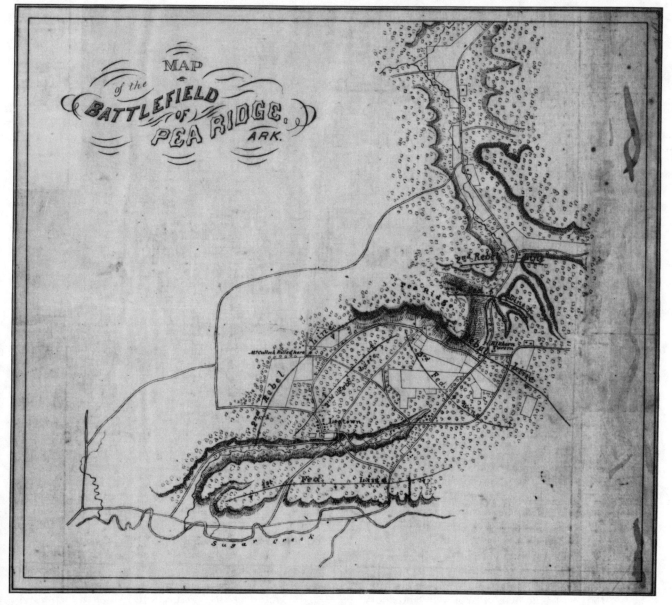

Union and Confederate lines on the battlefield of Pea Ridge, Ark. RG 77: Q 109. See entries 1.39 and 2.36.

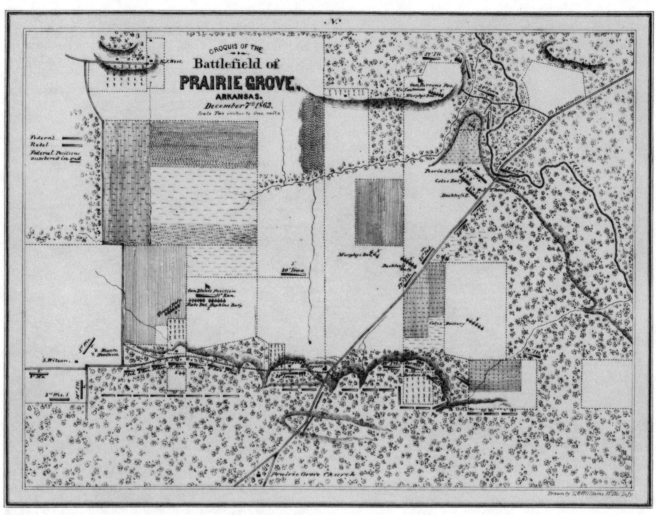

Battlefield of Prairie Grove, Ark., Dec. 7, 1862. RG 77: Q 463. See entries 1.39 and 2.37.

dicate successive Federal positions. Roads are in brown and drainage features in blue. Fields and wooded areas are also shown, and some relief is indicated by hachures. Signed: "Wm. Hoelcke, Captain & Addl. A. de. C., U.S.A., Chf. Engineer, Depart. of the Mo." and noted: "Engineer Department, September 27, 1865. Received with Capt. Hoelcke's letter of 22d Sept. 1865." RG 77: Q 463.

DISTRICT OF COLUMBIA

2.38. [Map of the District of Columbia and adjoining parts of Maryland and Virginia showing defense works and lines encircling the cities of Washington, D.C., and Alexandria, Va.]

1 inch to ¼ mile. 54 x 58. Printed with manuscript additions. A composite map made of part of a map of the District of Columbia compiled by A. Boschke and published in 1861 with adjoining parts of Maryland and Virginia added in manuscript and signed "Theo von Kamecke, March 1864." Defenses in red, drainage features

in blue, Government properties shaded green, and military roads orange. Wooded areas, property lines, and names of residents in the area outside the limits of Washington are shown on the base map by Boschke. Relief is indicated by contours but no interval is given. Noted, "Brig. Gen. E. R. S. Canby, A.A.G., War Department, April 4, 1864." RG 77: Z 445.

2.39. Sketch showing the triangulation of the principal Defenses of the District of Columbia executed under the general direction of Col. J. N. Macomb, U.S. Topl. Engrs., by Charles A. Schott, Asst., U.S. Coast Survey, January to May 1863.

1 inch to about ½ mile. 31 x 52. Manuscript. Triangulation stations in red. Title is preceded by "U.S. Coast Survey, A. D. Bache, Supdt., Section III." Map is signed "Chas. A. Schott . . . August 18, 1863." RG 77: F 118.

2.40. Defenses of Washington. [Maps 1 through 12 accompanying General Barnard's report.]

Map 1: An index map for sheets 2 through 12, overprinted on a published base entitled "Extract of Military Map of N. E. Virginia Showing Forts and Roads, Engineer Bureau, War Dept., 1865." Scale 1 inch to 1 mile. 25 x 18. Published, with colors added by hand. Roads in orange and defenses in red. Areas covered by sheets 2 through 12 are outlined and numbered in blue. Maps 2 through 12: Detailed maps of parts of the vicinity of Washington showing defense works and lines. Scale 1 inch to 450 feet. Maps 2 through 8, 10, and 12: 26 x 39; map 9: 26 x 23; map 11: 25 x 28. Manuscript. These maps cover the area from Hunting Creek, below Alexandria, Va., north through Virginia to the Potomac River at the southern tip of Montgomery County, Md., eastward along the northwestern and northeastern fringes of the District to Bennings Road. The southeastern and southwestern parts of the present District are not covered. Defense works and lines are shown in detail, and military and county roads, buildings, and names of residents are also given. Relief is indicated by form lines. RG 77: Dr. 171-91 through Dr. 171-102.

2.41. Environs of Washington Prepared from original Surveys in the Engineer Department. [ca. 1864-66.]

1 inch to ⅙ mile. One map in 10 sheets averaging 30 x 39, accompanied by an index map 17 x 17. Manuscript. The index indicates that this map was originally designed for 12 sheets, but the 2 sheets covering the southeastern part of the map apparently were never started. Three of the remaining 10 sheets are unfinished. Contour lines in red; the interval is added in pencil on some of the sheets. The street pattern and many buildings are shown in the cities of Washington, Georgetown, and Alexandria; forts, batteries, and rifle pits encircling the three cities are included; and wooded areas, swamp areas, roads, property lines, buildings, and names of residents outside the city limits are given. RG 77: F 99.

2.42. Old Capitol Prison and Carrol Branch Prison, Capitol Hill, 1st Street East, between A. Str. Sth. & A. Str. Nth., Washington, D.C. [Ground plan and cross sections.]

Ground plan: 1 inch to 30 feet. Sections: 1 inch to about 9 feet. 15 x 20. Manuscript. RG 92: Map 1, series 1-32.

2.43. Contraband Quarters, Mason's [Roosevelt] Island, Washington, D.C. [Ground plan; view and cross section of one of the buildings.]

Ground plan: 1 inch to 80 feet. Cross section: 1 inch to about 10 feet. 15 x 20. Manuscript. RG 92: Map 1, series 1-24.

2.44. Headquarters of Maj. Genl. Augur, Including Offices of Provost Marshal, Commissary of Musters, Chief of Ordnance and Printing. Washington, D.C., Sept. 1st, 1865. [Ground plan of the buildings located

at the corner of Pennsylvania Avenue and Fifteenth and a Half Street, North.]

1 inch to about 16 feet. 20 x 15. Manuscript. Buildings shaded red were built by the Quartermaster Department in the usual mode; others are shaded yellow. A note gives information about the construction of the principal building, which is also shaded yellow. Initialed "N. G. S." RG 92: Map 1, series 1-35.

2.45. Buildings at Washington Arsenal [now Fort Leslie J. McNair], Washington, D.C. [Ground plan and views.]

1 inch to 80 feet. 20 x 15. Manuscript. A note reads, "2 Barracks -Cost $2000." RG 92: Map 1, series 1-1.

FLORIDA

2.46. Northern Part of Florida. Compiled and Published at the United States Coast Survey Office, A. D. Bache, Superintendent. 1864. Drawn by H. Lindenkohl.

1 inch to 10 miles. 19 x 25. Published. Railroad lines and State boundary in red; drainage features in blue. Roads, swamps, lighthouses, forts, towns, and smaller settlements are shown, and scattered comments describe the vegetation. RG 23: Special Maps.

2.47. Map of the Channels, Shoals, &c. near Fort Jefferson, Tortugas. Reduced from Surveys made in 1845-46 by Major H. Bache, Topl. Engrs. Drawn under the direction of 1st Lieut. H. S. Putnam, Topl. Engrs., by H. G. Webber, C. E., May 1862.

1 inch to 330 yards. 27 x 38. Manuscript. Fort Jefferson is outlined in red. Shoals are buff; those with more than 5 but less than 20 feet of water were originally green with black dots. The green is now faded and cannot be easily distinguished from the buff. An inset view of the fort is included. Noted and signed: "Topographical Engineers Office, Fort Jefferson, June 14th, 1862. H. S. Putnam, 1st Lt., Topol. Engs. & Col. Vols." RG 77: L 98.

2.48. Fort Pickens, Fla., [and vicinity]. Showing the positions and strength of the Enemy's Batteries, so far as known by actual observation, and also of our own sand Batteries. [Signed] Lt. Walter McFarland, U.S. Corps Engineers, Fort Pickens, June 10, 1861.

1 inch to 250 yards. 20 x 24. Manuscript. Limits of fire from Fort Pickens to shore in red lines. Notes on the map give the observed or supposed armament of the Confederate forts and batteries and the armament of Fort Pickens and the Federal sand batteries on Santa Rosa Island. A note reads: "Sent to Bvt. Brig. Gen. Jos. G. Totten, Chief Engineer, U.S. Army, with letter of June 14th, 1861, by Bvt. Major Z. B. Tower, Engineer in Charge of Engineering operations at Fort Pickens, Fla." RG 77: Dr. 78-53.

2.49. Map of Jacksonville and vicinity, Florida, [showing defenses]. Surveyed April 1864. [Signed] Wm. H. Dennis, U.S. Coast Survey.

1 inch to about 275 yards. 21 x 22. Manuscript. Fields, buildings, roads, and vegetation are shown, and relief is indicated by hachures. Title is preceded by "U.S. Coast Survey, A. D. Bache, Supdt." RG 77: L 108-1.

2.50. Pensacola & Vicinity. Prepared by Order of Capt. P. C. Hains, Act. Chief Engineer, [Department of the Gulf], Under direction of Lt. H. C. Prevost, Adjt. Compiled from Maps & Information obtained by C. D. Elliot, Asst. C. E., Major D. C. Houston, Chief Engineer of Dept. Litho. by Lt. McGregory; transferred and printed by W. Probert, August 1864.

Large scale. 24 x 38. Published. Coastal areas and drainage features in blue. Roads and trails, ferries, some property lines and names of owners, swamp areas, and some topographic features are shown. Map is one of the numbered series of maps issued by the Department of the Gulf. Reassigned to RG 77: L 102.

2.51. Map of the City of St. Augustine and Vicinity, Florida. Surveyed and Drawn under the direction of Colonel J. R. Hawley, 7th Regt. Conn. Vol., May 1863. C. J. Lorigan, N.Y.V. Engineers, Surveyor. S. E. Washburne, N.Y.V. Engrs., Assistant.

1 inch to about 200 feet. 29 x 101 (2 sections). Manuscript. Drainage features in blue; red lines show distances and bearings from Fort Marion to specified locations. The street plan of the city, important buildings, the old fort and magazine, barracks, and swamp areas are shown. Noted, "The property of Mr. J. R. Hawley." RG 77: L 107.

2.52. Topl. Map of Warrington and Vicinity. Compiled & drawn by C. Spangenberg, Asst. Engr.

1 inch to about ¼ mile. 27 x 40. Manuscript. Defenses in blue. Street plan of the city, the navy yard, buildings, roads, swamps, beaches, fields, and vegetation are shown. Some relief is indicated by hachures. The map is unfinished. RG 77: Z 353.

GEORGIA

2.53. Part of Northern Georgia Compiled under the direction of Capt. Wm. E. Merrill, Chief, Top'l. Eng'r., D.C., From the Cherokee Land Maps, . . . Surveys of Top'l. Engineers, D.C., . . . State Map of Georgia, and information.

1 inch to 4 miles. 3 sheets, each 23 x 16. Printed on cloth. Roads, railroads, drainage features, and names of some residents are shown. Sheet 1 is noted, "Printed in the field, Chattanooga, Tenn., May 5th, 1864." Sheets 2 and 3 are noted, "Lithographed, Topo'l. Eng'r. Office, Head-Quarters, Dep't. of the Cumberland" and "Official

Issue, Wm. C. Margedant . . ." Reassigned to RG 77: N 42; N 45; N 46.

2.54. Atlanta. From Vincent's Subdivision Map, published by the City Council. Drawn and printed at Topl. Engr. Office, Hd.Qrs., A.C., in the field, July 25th, 1864.

1 inch to ¼ mile. 17 x 12. Printed. A street plan of the city in which important or key buildings are located by numbers that are listed and identified at the bottom of the map. Reassigned to RG 77: Dr. 129-21; duplicate filed as N 53.

2.55. Map of Atlanta and Rebel Defenses . . . Drawn at Top. Eng. Office, Head Quarters, Department of the Cumberland.

1 inch to ¼ mile. 18 x 19. Manuscript. Line of defenses, drainage features, and selected wooded areas shown in colors. Noted, "Engineer Dept., Washington, October 24, 1864. Received this day with Letter of Sept. 30, .64." RG 77: Dr. 129-18.

2.56. Map Illustrating The First Epoch of the Atlanta Campaign Embracing the region from the Tennessee River to the Oostanaula River, showing the positions held and lines of works erected by the enemy, also the lines of works erected by the United States forces, the lines of march traversed by them, and their relative location in line of battle when attacking the enemy. Commanding United States Forces, Major General W. T. Sherman. Commanding Rebel Forces, Lieut. General J. E. Johnston. Compiled by Edward Ruger.

1 inch to 1 mile. 48 x 27. Manuscript. Colors distinguish Confederate and Union defenses and lines of march of the Union armies of the Cumberland, the Ohio, and the Tennessee. Names of residents are shown; relief is indicated by hachures. This is one of a series of five maps of the Atlanta campaign by Ruger that was used in the compilation of the Atlanta campaign maps published by the Office of the Chief of Engineers, 1874-77. RG 77: N 80.

2.57. . . . The Second Epoch of the Atlanta Campaign Embracing the region from Resaca to the Etowah River . . .

1 inch to 1 mile. 44¼ x 30¾. Manuscript. RG 77: N 81.

2.58. . . . The Third Epoch of the Atlanta Campaign Enbracing the region from the Etowah River south to include Marietta and Dallas: Exhibiting the flanking of Allatoona Pass; the Battle Fields of Dallas and New Hope Church, with connecting lines of works; the advanced line of Pine, Lost, and Kennesaw Mountains; the intermediate line of Kennesaw and Lost Mountains; and the rear line of Kennesaw Mountain, encircling Marietta, together with the as-

sault upon, and flanking of the same . . .

1 inch to 1 mile. 32 x 44½. Manuscript. RG 77: N 82.

2.59. . . . The Fourth Epoch of the Atlanta Campaign Embracing the region from Pine, Lost, and Kennesaw Mountains south to include Atlanta and its environs; exhibiting the lines of operations at Pine, Lost, and Kennesaw Mountains, at Smyrna Camp Ground, along the Chattahoochee River, and in the investment of Atlanta; also the lines of marches . . .

1 inch to 1 mile. 46 x 37. Manuscript. Lines of march as indicated in title and description of entry 2.56 are not shown. RG 77: N 85.

2.60. . . . The Fifth Epoch of the Atlanta Campaign Embracing the region from the Chattahoochie [sic] river south to include Jonesboro and Lovejoys [sic] Station. Exhibiting, in connection, the passage of the Chattahoochie [sic] river, the Siege of Atlanta, and the operations at Jonesboro and Lovejoys [sic] Station, also the lines of works erected by the contending forces, and the lines of marches . . .

1 inch to 1 mile. 35 x 30. Manuscript. Lines of march as indicated in title and description of entry 2.56 are not shown. RG 77: N 86.

2.61. Map illustrating the siege of Atlanta, Georgia, by the United States Forces under Command of Maj. Genl. W. T. Sherman; from the passage of Peach Tree Creek, July 19th, 1864, to the Commencement of the movement upon the Enemy's lines of Communication South of Atlanta, August 26th, 1864. Surveyed & compiled under the direction of Capt. O. M. Poe, Corps of Engrs., Chief Engr., Mily. Divn. Miss. Drawn in June, July, August, & Sept., 1865, by Capt. H. A. Ulffers, A.A.G.

1 inch to ¼ mile. 52 x 64 (2 sections). Manuscript. Union lines and defenses in blue and Confederate in red. Sites of Battle of Peach Tree Creek, July 20, Battle of Atlanta, July 22, and Battle of Ezra Church, July 28, 1864, are shown. Drainage features, wooded areas, fields, buildings, and names of residents in the vicinity of Atlanta are also shown. Relief is indicated by hachures. Plans and sections of Union and Confederate defenses appear as insets. Noted in pencil, "Turned in to the Bureau, July 10th, 1866." RG 77: N 68-1.

2.62. Map Showing the March Routes of the Army of the Tennessee from Atlanta to Savannah During the Campaign in Georgia under the command of Maj. Gen. O. O. Howard. Compiled and Drawn under the Direction of Capt. C. B. Reese, Chf. Engr., D. & A. of the Tenn. Drawn & comp'l. by L. Helmle, Capt., 3d Mo. Vol. Inf'y. Authorities: Surveys of the Engrs., of the 15th and 17th A. Cs., [and] Bonner's State Map of Georgia.

1 inch to 4 miles. 30 x 51 (two irregularly joined sheets).

Manuscript. Routes of the 15th and 17th Army corps in pink, Confederate fortifications in red, and Union fortifications in blue. Noted, "Approved, C. B. Reese, Bvt. Col. & Capt. of Engrs." and "Engineer Department, June 2, 1865. Recd. with Col. Reese's letter of June 1, 1865." Also noted "Traced from the Original by Williams, Engr. Office, Army of the Tenn." RG 77: N 58.

2.63. [Sketch showing the route of march of the 14th Army Corps from Atlanta to Savannah, November 16 to December 9, 1864.]

1 inch to about 4 miles. 27 x 34. Manuscript. The route is shown with dates indicating the progress of the march. Roads, streams, wooded areas, towns, and names of residents along the route are indicated. RG 77: Z 28.

2.64. Maps showing the Campaign of the 20th Army Corps From Atlanta to Savannah with the dates [of march and] Union and Rebel Defenses. From Surveys of Topographical Engineers, 20th Army Corps, Left Wing, Army of Ga. Information & Positions by Lt. Col. C. W. Asmussen, A.I., Genl., 20th Corps, U.S. Army.

Scales vary from 1 inch to ½ mile to 1 inch to 3 miles. 8 x 10. Manuscript. Eleven bound maps with title and symbol explanations on cover and 14 pages of notes. Union and Confederate defenses are distinguished by colors; drainage features are in blue. Routes of march from November 15 to December 11 and operations in the vicinity of Savannah from December 12 to 19, 1864, are shown. The daily notes accompanying the maps describe the order of march, weather, roads, availability of supplies, and distances covered. Noted on back cover, "Headquarters, Military Div. Mississippi, 25 Jan. 1865 . . ." RG 77: N 59-1.

2.65. [Forty-three detailed maps of the daily route of march of the 17th Army Corps in the "Savannah Campaign" from Terry's Mill near Atlanta to the Ogeechee River near Sebastopol, Ga., from November 15 to 30, 1864.]

Large scale. Average 10 x 5. Manuscript. Maps are drawn on pink-lined section paper. Dates and headquarters camp symbols indicate the daily progress of march. Towns, villages, buildings, names of residents, timber, fields, and roads are indicated along the route. See also entry 2.62. RG 77: Z 14-1 through Z 14-43.

2.66. Map of 1st Distrt., Campbell Co., Georgia, South of the Cherokee Boundary Line. Compiled under direction of Capt. W. E. Merrill, Chief Topl. Engr., D.C., by Sergt. Finegan from the notes of a captured Rebel Engineer & State map (south of the Chattahoochee Riv.) . . . Autographed & printed in the field. Chattanooga, May 23d, 1864.

1 inch to ½ mile. 20 x 22. Printed. Shows roads, drainage features, and names of residents. Relief is indicated

by hachures. Map is imprinted, "Official Issue, Wm. C. Margedant, Capt. & Supt., Topl. Engr. Office, D.C." Reassigned to RG 77: Z 10.

2.67. Map of the Battlefield of Chickamauga, A. Hager [or Huger] Draft.

1 inch to 2 miles. 16 x 12. Manuscript. Roads in red and drainage features in blue. Map also shows names of residents and indicates relief by means of hachures. Troop positions are not shown. Noted, "Copied from a Map in possession of Lt. Col. Clarke. Apr. 22d, 1864. Savannah. [Initials illegible] draftsman." RG 77: N 66.

2.68. Sheet No. 1. Map of the Battle Field of Chickamauga, September 19th, 1863, Between the United States Forces commanded by Maj. Gen. W. S. Rosecrans and the Confederate Army under Gen. Braxton Bragg. Compiled under the direction of Col. W. E. Merrill, Chief Engr., Dept. of the Cumberland, by Edward Ruger... Published by authority of the Hon. Secretary of War in the Office of the Chief of Engineers, U.S. Army.

1 inch to about ⅓ mile. 30 x 40. Annotated printed. Troop positions are added in colors, blue for Union forces and red for Confederate. Cavalry and infantry positions are distinguished. Map is marked "(A)." A note reads, "The positions given by the various officers have been plotted on this sheet." RG 77: N 77-19.

2.69. Sheet No. 2. Map of the Battle Field of Chickamauga, September 20th, 1863 ...

1 inch to about ⅓ mile. 30 x 40. Annotated printed. Map is marked "(B)." See also entry 2.68 for title and other remarks. RG 77: N 77-20.

2.70. Topographical Map of Dalton, Georgia. Prepared under the direction of Col. Wm. E. Merrill, 1st U.S.V.V. Engrs., Chief Engineer, Department of the Cumbd., by Maj. Jas. R. Willett, 1st U.S.V.V. Engrs., Chief Inspector of Rail Road Defences, Dept. of Cumbd. Surveyed and drawn by P. M. Radford, February 1865.

1 inch to 440 feet. 2 sections, 26 x 40 each. Manuscript. Contour lines in brown and intervals in red, drainage features in blue, streets and roads in yellow, and lines of works and fortifications in red. Railroads, buildings, names of some residents, and remarks on the character of the terrain are included. RG 77: Z 72-2.

2.71. Map of Macon and Vicinity. Compiled from Information by Capt. E. Ruger under the Direction of Lt. Col. J. G. Wharton, Top. Engineer, Hd. Quarters, Department of the Cumberland. Drawn by Chas. Helmle, Draughtsman.

Large scale. 2 sheets, identified as sheets 1 and 3: sheet 1, 48 x 31; sheet 3, 33 x 25. Manuscript. Shows names of residents along the roads leading into Macon

industrial and business sites, a burial ground for Union prisoners, defenses, an arsenal, and fort. Drainage features in blue. Relief is indicated by red form lines. Sheet 3 includes the following inset map of the city: "Map of the City of Macon, Ga., shewing the Location of Buildings occupied by C. S. Gov., also the Location of Buildings which can be seen a long distance from the City and the location of buildings occupied by prominent Union or Secesh Citizens. Compiled by F. Bathschweiter [?], Draughtsman. Topographical Engineer Office, Department of the Cumberland." 1 inch to 400 feet. 12 x 15. Manuscript. Buildings described in the title are differentiated by colors; some of these and other buildings are identified by an index number or letter. RG 77: N 76-1; N 76-3.

2.72. Map showing Approximate Position and Entrenchments of the Army of Miss. [along the Chattahoochee and in the vicinities of Marietta and Dallas and Kennesaw and Lost Mountains] Together with the respective positions occupied by Hardee's & Hood's Corps, Army Tenn., From May 25th to the 9th July 1864. Engineers Office, Army of Miss. Walter J. Morris, Captain, actg. Chief Eng'r. Fred. G. Gutherz, Del.

1 inch to about ⅘ mile. 26 x 31. Manuscript. Flags of various colors or design denote the different Confederate troop positions as given in the title and also the Federal positions. Also shown are names of residents in the area. RG 77: N 220.

2.73. Information Map of Part of Georgia [in the vicinity of Pumpkin Vine Creek]. Printed at Engr. Office, Head-Q's. Dep't. of the Cumberland, in the field, May 30th, 1864.

1 inch to ½ mile. 11 x 16. Negative photocopy. Shows roads, wooded areas, and names of residents. Reassigned to RG 77: N 50.

2.74. Map of Savannah and Vicinity illustrating the Operations of the Army under Command of Maj. Gen. W. T. Sherman resulting in the Fall of that City, Dec. 21st, 1864. Compiled under the Direction of Bvt. Lieut. Col. O. M. Poe, Capt. Engrs., U.S.A., from captured Maps, Coast Survey Maps, and Surveys made during the Progress of the Siege. Drawn by Maj. E. F. Hoffmann, A.D.C., and Capt. H. A. Ulffers, A.A.G.

1 inch to ½ mile. 2 sections, 31 x 52. Manuscript. Union lines are in blue and Confederate in red. Plans and profiles of forts and batteries are included. Signed "O. M. Poe, Corps of Engrs., Bt. Brig. Gen., U.S.A., Sept. 25th, 1866." RG 77: N 70.

2.75. Reconnoissance of Wilmington River and St. Augustine Creek from Wassaw Sound to Savannah River, Georgia, By the Hyd Party under direction of

C. O. Boutelle, Asst., C.S., December 1864 [with inset plans of] Fort Thunderbolt . . . Battery on Turner's Rocks . . . [and the] Fort on Causten's Bluff . . . by Eugene Willenbucher, December 1864.

Map: 1 inch to about ⅝ mile. Plans: 1 inch to 55 yards. 36 x 25. Manuscript. Colors distinguish 12- and 18-foot curves in the mouths of the Tybee and Wilmington Rivers and show channels in each. Noted, "Engineer Department. Feb'y. 7, 1865. Recd. from Coast Survey Office with Mr. Hilgard's letter of 7th inst." RG 77: Dr. 129-23.

KENTUCKY

2.76. Camp Nelson and Its Defences, Jessamine Co., Ky. Surveys, made by order of Lt. Col. J. H. Simpson, Chief Eng., Dept. of the Ohio, during the winter of 1863 & 1864, under the direction J. R. Gilliss, Ast. U.S. Eng., by Messrs. R. Moore, F. T. Hampton, & C. Slayton.

1 inch to about 275 yards. 26 x 40. Manuscript. Best routes are in red, water pipes in blue, and defenses in red. Map also shows buildings, telegraph lines, forests, felled timber, cleared land, and heights above the low water of the Kentucky River. Relief is indicated by form lines and shading. Noted and signed, "Office U.S. Engineers, Cincinnati, O. Official: J. H. Simpson, Lt. Col., Eng'rs., U.S. Army." RG 77: Dr. 132-20.

2.77. Defences of Camp Nelson, Ky. Main Line across Neck of Land from Kentucky River to Hickman Creek. Constructed under direction of Lieut. Col. J. H. Simpson, Corps Eng's. Commenced by Capt. O. M. Poe, Corps Eng's; Finished by J. R. Gilliss, Asst., U.S. Eng; Surveyed and drawn by Geo. B. Nicholson. Aug. 1864.

1 inch to 200 feet. 30 x 52. Manuscript. Defenses in red and drainage features in blue. Map shows contours at intervals of 5 feet, buildings, names of a few residents, woods, fields, and roads. Noted and signed, "Office U.S. Engineers, Cincinnati, O., Sept. 27th, 1864. Official: J. H. Simpson, Lt. Col., Engrs., U.S. Army." Also noted, "Annual Report of Lt. Col. J. H. Simpson, Nov. 15th, 1864." RG 77: Dr. 132-21.

2.78. Topographical Map showing Defences [in Kentucky] of Cincinnati, [Ohio], Covington & Newport, [Ky.] . . . Compiled chiefly from surveys made under the direction of Lt. Col. J. H. Simpson by Messrs. W. H. Searles, G. A. Aschbach, O. P. Ransom, and

Camp Nelson, Ky., and its defenses. RG 77: Dr. 132-20. See entries 1.61 and 2.76.

J. R. Gilliss in 1862 & '63. Drawn by John R. Gilliss and Chas. E. Swann.

1 inch to ¼ mile. 50 x 55 (2 sections). Manuscript. Turnpikes are in yellow, common roads in orange, defenses in red, and drainage features in blue. Map also shows standing and felled timber, orchards, buildings, and names of some residents. Figures in red indicate heights above the Ohio River. Relief is indicated by gray shading. Noted and signed, "Office Utd. Sts. Engineers, Cincinnati, O., Septbr. 7th, 1864. Official: J. H. Simpson, Lieut. Col., Engrs., U.S. Army." RG 77: Dr. 132-13.

2.79. Map of the Kentucky Central Rail Road and Valley of Licking River from Benton Sta. to Lexington, Ky., 80 miles, Showing all the important Bridges and their Defensive Works. Surveyed under the direction of Maj. J. H. Simpson, Chief Engr., Department of the Ohio, by G. A. Aschbach, Asst. U.S. Engr. Sketched and Platted Under the direction of Capt. T. B. Brooks, Vol. Engrs., By A. B. Miller, Asst. U.S. Engr.

1 inch to 1.38 miles. 25 x 46. Manuscript. River is shown in blue and railroad line in red. Map also shows relief by hachures, roads and bridges, and names of residents in areas adjacent to the railroad. Noted and signed, "Office, Chief Engr's., Dep't. of the Ohio, Cincinnati, O., July 31, 1863. Official Copy: J. H. Simpson, Maj. Engrs." The following maps of bridge sites showing locations of defenses and plans of blockhouses are shown as insets: Vicinity of Demossville Bridge 25 Miles from Covington. Cruiz Creek Bridge 19 Miles from Covington. Falmouth Bridge 39 Miles from Covington. Robinson's Bridge 56 Miles from Covington. Keller's Bridge 63¼ Miles from Covington. Kimbrough's Bridge 66¼ Miles from Covington. Short Stoner and Paris Bridges 78¾ Miles from Covington. Long Stoner Bridge 74½ Miles from Covington. Townsend Bridge 71 Miles from Covington. Kiser and Cooper's Run Bridges 73½ & 74 Miles from Covington. Block Houses Designed and located by Capt. W. E. Merrill, U.S. Eng'rs, and mostly built under his direction. Bridge site insets 1 inch to 800 feet. Blockhouse ground plan, transverse section, and side and end views 1 inch to 10 feet. Sizes vary from 4 x 6 to 8 x 10. Parts of the Licking River and tributaries near each bridge site are in blue; railroad line is in red. Locations of blockhouses, buildings, and names of residents are also shown. RG 77: Dr. 132-8.

2.80. Louisville and Its Defences.

1 inch to 1,000 feet. 30 x 46. Manuscript. Roads and streets in brown, drainage in blue, defenses in red, and Government buildings in blue. These buildings include military hospitals, quartermaster depots, a refugee house, stables, corrals, and harness and wagon shops. A few buildings in Jeffersonville and New Albany, Ind., are shown. Wooded areas, fields, and plots of land with buildings and names of residents near Louisville are shown. Relief is indicated by hachures. Noted and signed, "Office U.S. Engineers, Cincinnati, O., June 1865. Official: J. H. Simpson, Lt. Col., Engrs. U.S. Army." RG 77: T 124-3.

2.81. [Map of Munfordville and vicinity showing the] Camp of Second Division [and] Action of December 17th, 1861, "Rowlett's Station," Between . . . 32d Indiana, under Lt. Col. von Trebra, & a column of the Enemy.

1 inch to 400 feet. 39 x 51 (2 sections). Manuscript. Roads in brown and the Louisville and Nashville Railroad in red. Union and Confederate defenses, buildings, industrial sites, and a cemetery for Union men killed in action are also shown. Relief is indicated by form lines. RG 77: Z 500.

2.82. Sketch of Paducah and Vicinity. [By] John Rziha, Captain, 19th Inf., U.S. Army.

1 inch to ⅙ mile. 35 x 19. Manuscript. Drainage features in blue. Map shows the street plan of Paducah, campsites within and outside the city, defenses, roads, farm lands, timber, and a floating battery in the Ohio River. Some relief is indicated by hachures. Part of the map is missing. Noted and signed, "[U.]S. Forces, [Pa]ducah, Keny., Dec. 9, 1861. Respectfully forwarded to the Hd. Qrs. of the Dept. of the Missouri. C. F. Smith, Brigr. Genl., Comdg." RG 77: Z 206.

2.83. [Sketch map of Smithland and vicinity] Drawn by U. G. Scheller [?] Engineer.

1 inch to about 400 yards. 17 x 23. Manuscript. The town of Smithland is colored ochre; blue is used to outline the shores of the Cumberland and Ohio Rivers. Defenses are in red, and dotted red lines show distances from defenses to selected sites. Wooded areas and roads are also shown, and some relief is indicated by hachures. Noted and signed, "Hd. Qrs., U.S. Forces, Paducah, Keny., Dec. 13, 1861. Respectfully forwarded to the H'. Qrs. of the Dept. of the Misso., C. F. Smith, Brigr. Genl., Comdg." RG 77: Z 175.

LOUISIANA

2.84. State of Louisiana showing Theatre of Operations of the Forces under command of Maj. Gen. Banks during the months of March, April, May, June, and July and ending with the Reduction of Port Hudson, July 8th, 1863. Prepared by Order of Maj. Gen. N. P. Banks; D. C. Houston, Major & Chief Engineer. August 1863. Drawn by B. von Reizenstein. Photographed by Walter Ogilvie.

1 inch to about 10 miles. 30 x 33. Photoprocessed. Roads, railroads, place names, and drainage features are shown. Reassigned to RG 77: Z 273.

2.85. [Map of part of northwestern Louisiana from Bayou Pierre Lake to an area slightly north of Soda Lake.]

1 inch to 1 mile. 2 sections, 35 x 44 each. Manuscript. Badly yellowed and stained. Drainage features in blue and roads in red. Township lines, property lines, and names of residents are shown. Noted on reverse, "West Louisiana (Rebel Surveys)." RG 77: Z 272.

2.86. Military Map of part of Louisiana [between New Orleans, Vermillion Bay, and Port Hudson]. Compiled at the U.S. Coast Survey Office . . . 1863.

1 inch to 6 miles. 18 x 29. Published. Drainage features in blue. Roads, railroads, and place names are also shown. RG 23: Special Maps.

2.87. Country around Alexandria from sketch made by order of Brig. Gen. R. Arnold, Chf. of Cavalry, by Lieut. E. C. Miles, 5th Engrs., Co. A.

1 inch to ½ mile. 18 x 29. Manuscript. Drainage features in blue. Wooded areas, fields, names of residents, buildings, roads, and existing and destroyed bridges are shown. RG 77: M 126-1.

2.88. Atchafalaya Basin. Prepared by order of Maj. Gen. N. P. Banks. Henry L. Abbot, Capt. & Chief Top. Eng'rs., Feb. 8th, 1863 [with annotations pertaining to the campaign in April and May 1863].

1 inch to 4½ miles. 29 x 23. Annotated photoprocessed. Annotations show route of march from Brashear City to Alexandria, points of skirmishes along the route, locations of 19th Army Corps headquarters, and additional information about terrain, cultural features, and names of residents along the route. Drainage features are in blue and roads in red; some of the annotations are in color. The base map was issued as "Department of the Gulf, Map No. 8." RG 77: M 99½.

2.89. Baton Rouge to Port Hudson. Showing Position of 19th Army Corps, Maj. Gen. N. P. Banks, Com'd'g., on the 14th March 1863.

1 inch to 1 mile. 31 x 26. Manuscript. Colors distinguish positions of the 1st, 2d, and 3d Divisions. Noted and signed, "Approved, F. Harwood, 1st Lt. & Chief Top. Eng., Dept. Gulf." RG 77: Z 218-2.

2.90. Topographical Plan of the City & Battle Field of Baton-Rouge, Fought on the 5th of August 1862, drawn by Joseph Gorlinski, Civil Engr.

1 inch to 600 feet. 23 x 26. Manuscript. Shows position of Confederate forces, camps and entrenchments of U.S. troops, successive troop positions during the battle, and positions of the U.S. gunboat *Essex* and other ships in the river. The street pattern of the city, roads in the vicinity, and wooded areas are shown, and some relief is indicated by hachures. RG 77: Z 275.

2.91. Diagram showing the Position of Our Works at and about Brashear City, from Surveys and Notes by Maj. A. Elfield and Capt. H. L. Wheeler with additions by B. Von Reizenstein, del.

1 inch to 1,200 feet. 17 x 22. Manuscript. Drainage features in blue and Union works in red. Former Confederate defenses, the street pattern of Brashear City, roads, a railroad, wooded areas, swamplands, and the site of a proposed entrenched camp for 10,000 men at Berwick City are also shown. RG 77: Z 276.

2.92. [Sketch of Forts Jackson and St. Philip, defenses of the mouth of the Mississippi River, showing numbers of guns, limits of fire of batteries and casemate guns, and crest of parapets above low water of the river.]

1 inch to 400 feet. 26 x 63. Manuscript. Limits of fire from batteries of Fort Jackson in red and limits of fire from Fort St. Philip and casemate guns at Fort Jackson in black. Noted: "(No 1) Sketch . . . furnished to Mr. Fox, Asst. Secy. Navy, with my memorandum of Jany. 28/62, To be returned to Engineer Departt., U.S., Washington (as also all copies which may be taken from it), when other use for it shall have ceased. [Signed] J. G. Barnard, Brig. Genl., Chief Engineer, Army of Potomac." Other notes signed by Barnard describe the defenses of the forts. Also noted, "Engineer Department, Aug. 21, 1863. Rec'd. from the Rear Admiral, W. Gulf Blockading Squadron, without letter." RG 77: Dr. 88-51.

2.93. Approaches to New Orleans. Prepared by order of Maj. Gen. N. P. Banks. Henry L. Abbot, Capt. & Chief, Top. Engrs., Feb. 14th, 1863.

1 inch to about ½ mile. 31 x 24. Photoprocessed. Fortifications in red. Street pattern of the city, buildings and names of some residents outside the city, swamp areas, wooded areas, roads, railroads, and canals are also shown. Reassigned to RG 393: Department of the Gulf, Map 2.

2.94. Camp Parapet [and vicinity], Defences of New Orleans. [Compiled] under direction of Major D. C. Houston, Chief Engineer. Surveyed by Maurice Hauke, drawn by M. Hauke and B. Von Reizenstein, November 1863. Copied November 1864 by F. H. Arlitt.

Large scale. 66 x 37. Manuscript. Drainage in blue, buildings in red with surrounding plots in green or brown, roads and streets in brown, and line of fortifications in blue, green, and brown. Facilities and general plan of the camp, wooded areas, swamp areas, property lines, and names of residents are also shown. Noted, "Recd. at Engr. Dept., Jany. 20, 1865." RG 77: Dr. 133-77.

2.95. Company Canal Defences Situated on the right bank of the Miss. River in the Parish of Jefferson, La., [near New Orleans] surveyed by Jos. Gorlinski, Civ. Eng.

1 inch to 200 feet. 23 x 36. Manuscript. Canal is colored blue. Positions of camps, drill grounds, buildings, the new military road, a section of the New Orleans and Opelousas Railroad crossing the canal, fields, cleared land, abatis, woods, and swamp areas are shown. RG 77: Z 279.

2.96. Battlefield of Pleasant Hill. Surveyed and Drawn by Lt. S. E. McGregory By Order of Maj. D. C. Houston, Chief Engineer, D.O.G. [Department of the Gulf].

1 inch to 200 yards. 14 x 17. Manuscript. Confederate troop positions in red, Union in blue. Names of Union commanders appear beside troop locations. Buildings, open fields, wooded areas, positions of Union ammunition and "Pioneer" trains, headquarters of Maj. Gen. N. P. Banks, roads, and some property lines are included, and relief is indicated by hachures. RG 77: M 125-1.

2.97. No. 1. Map of Road from Pleasant Hill towards Mansfield. Surveyed by Lieut. E. C. Miles, Ass't. Engr., April 7, 1864.

1 inch to ½ mile. 17 x 17. Manuscript on orange-lined section paper. Troop positions during the march along the route, site of the Battle of Wilson's Farm, April 7, 1864, and position of "enemy" at sundown are shown. Noted, "Schedule 'B' Referred to in Genl. Lee's Report of April 13, 1864." RG 77: M 125-2.

2.98. Map of Red River and the Country South [and east of Alexandria]. Surveyed under the direction of Capt. E. Gottheil, Chief Engineer, Dist. Wesn. La., Head Quarters, Engineer Department, Dist. Western Louisiana.

Large scale. 20 x 30. Manuscript. Roads in red. Swamps, prairies, lakes, bayous, place names, and Fort de Russy are shown. "No. 67" appears below the title. RG 77: Z 330-1.

2.99. Map Showing the Route of the Army During the Red River Campaign in the Spring of 1864. Surveys & Reconnoissances by Osw. Dietz, Civil Engineer, [and] Lieuts. Miles & McGregory.

1 inch to about 6 miles. 24 x 26. Annotated photoprocessed. Drainage features are in blue and campaign routes in orange; colored flags indicate sites of military engagements. Some additional place names are added to the base, which shows lines of public surveys, names of residents, and property lines along the major rivers. RG 77: M 114.

2.100. Topographical and Hydrographical Map of a Survey of a part of the Eastern Portion of the Parish of St. Bernard made by Order of Major General B. F. Butler, Commanding Department of the Gulf, New Orleans, Dec. 31, 1862. [Signed] By Wm. H. Wilder, C. of T.E.

1 inch to ¼ mile. 53 x 49 (2 sections). Manuscript. Drainage features in blue. Compass bearings in red numerals. Soundings in lakes, bayous, and lagoons given in feet. RG 77: Z 335.

MARYLAND

2.101. Camp of Instruction [and vicinity at Annapolis Junction] Surveyed by C. P. Manning, Civil Engr., under the direction of Col. T. J. Cram, Lt. Col., Corps Topl. Engrs.

1 inch to 400 feet. 47 x 66. Manuscript. Wooded areas shown in green, roads and railroads in brown, contour lines in red, drainage features in blue, and grasslands in light green. Brown lines show corn or plowed fields; light brown indicates other fields, some of which have penciled notations describing crops. Map also shows buildings and names of residents. A copy of this map, on tracing cloth, filed as F 75 is noted: "T. J. Cram, Col., aid-de-camp, Lt. Col., Corps T.E. This map with Annual Report, October 1, 1862." RG 77: F 82.

2.102. Map of the Battle of the Antietam fought on the 16th and 17th September 1862 between the United States Forces under the Command of Maj. Genl. Geo. B. McClellan and the Confederates under Genl. Robt. E. Lee. Prepared by Command of Maj. Genl. Geo. B. McClellan from Surveys under the direction of 1st Lt. Nicholas Bowen . . . [and] 1st Lt. A. H. Cushing, U.S. Corps Topl. Engrs., [and] Chas. Shoemacker, E. F. Bowke, Jos. McMakin, [and] C. A. Mallory, Assts., under the direction of 1st Lt. A. H. Cushing, Topl. Engs. October 1862.

1 inch to 1,000 feet. 35 x 46. 2 sections. Manuscript. Union troop positions are shown in four colors, which distinguish first, advance, and final positions and intermediate movements. Names of commanders are shown beside the positions, and numbers indicate successive movements. Confederate lines of battle on September 16 and 17, reserve positions, and line of retreat are shown in red. Map also shows roads, names of some residents, and Confederate and Union signal stations. Relief is indicated by hachures. RG 77: F 85.

2.103. Map of that portion of the Battle Field of Antietam occupied by the troops under Maj. Gen. Burnside, made by order of Maj. Gen. McClellan from surveys made under the supervision of Capt. R. S. Williamson, Top'l. Eng'r., on Staff of Maj. Gen. Burnside, by H. C. Fillebrown [and] E. S. Waters, Civ. Eng'rs.

1 inch to ⅙ mile. 25 x 19. Manuscript. Troop positions are located by name of commander. RG 77: F 79.

2.104. Map of the Battlefield of Antietam Published under the direction of Russell A. Alger, Secretary of War, by the Antietam Battlefield Board [composed of] Lieut. Col. Geo. W. Davis, U.S.A., President, General E. A. Carman, Late Union Army, [and] General H. Heth, Late Confederate Army. Surveyed by Col. E. B. Cope, Engineer, [and] H. W. Mattern, Assistant Engineer of the Gettysburg National Park. Drawn by Charles H. Ourand, 1899.

1 inch to 150 yards. 64 x 52. Manuscript. Contour lines are in brown, drainage features in blue, and wooded areas in green. Map also shows cornfields, stubble, grasslands, plowed fields, outcrops of rock, fences and the kinds of material used in their construction, haystacks, roads, and names of some of the residents. This base map was used for the series of 14 maps showing troop positions at Antietam at different periods between daybreak and 5:30 p.m., September 17, 1862, issued as an atlas by the Antietam Battlefield Board in 1904 and revised and reissued in 1908. Record copies of both editions of this atlas are among the Records of the Office of the Chief of Engineers, RG 77. RG 77: 6291, roll.

2.105. Military Map, Baltimore Co., Md., compiled from the best Authorities and corrected by actual survey under the direction of Col. W. F. Raynolds, A.D.C., Chief Eng., 8th Army Corps. Drawn and Lithographed in the Office of the Chief Eng., 8th Army Corps, by Geo. Kaiser, Pvt., 10th N.Y. Vols., 1863.

1 inch to 1 mile. 40 x 31. Published. Drainage features are hand-colored in blue. Map also shows forts, camps, roads and railroads, names of residents, and concentric circles at intervals of one mile from the center of Baltimore City to a distance of 12 miles. Reassigned to RG 77: Dr. 135-13; duplicate filed as F 87.

2.106. Batteries for Entrenchment on south side and Batteries on north side, Conowingo Bridge, Susquehannah [sic] River; Md. [Panel of plans and sections.]

Plans: 1 inch to 50 feet; sections: 1 inch to 25 feet. 15 x 8. Manuscript. The colors have no significance. The sheet is noted, "Engineer Department, Nov. 24. 1864. Recd. with Capt. Turnbull's letter of 23 Nov." RG 77: Dr. 145-13.

2.107. Map of Cumberland, Alleghany Co., Md.

1 inch to about 270 feet. 37 x 25. Manuscript. Drainage features in blue. Street names, buildings, industrial sites, and names of some property owners are included. Some relief outside the town is indicated by shading. RG 77: Z 140.

2.108. [Plan of Fort Sumner, Montgomery County, composed of Redoubts Cross, Davis, and Kirby and also showing nearby rifle pits and Batteries Alex-

ander and Benson, part of the defenses of Washington, D.C.]

1 inch to 130 feet. 21 x 35. Manuscript. Unexplained figures in red relate, probably, to angles of the redoubts. Penciled notations show changes in the construction of the redoubts and in armament. RG 77: Dr. 171-190–L-1.

2.109. Map of the Located Route of the Metropolitan Rail Road and the Adjacent Country. Comprising the District of Columbia and the Counties of Montgomery, Frederick, and Washington in the State of Maryland . . . Completed April 30, 1855, from Surveys made in 1853 and 1854.

1 inch to 2 miles. 25 x 36. Manuscript. Roads are in brown, railroads in use are in red, and the line of the Chesapeake and Ohio Canal is in blue. Different kinds of lines distinguish the located and experimental lines of the Metropolitan Railroad, lines surveyed by the Baltimore and Ohio Railroad Co., canal surveys, and the Washington Aqueduct. Some relief is indicated by shading. Noted, " 'Copy,' Bureau of Topogl. Engineers, September 8th, 1862, [initialed] D.C." RG 77: Rds. 169.

2.110. [Map of part of Montgomery County showing] Topographical Approaches on the Left Bank of the Potomac to Washington City from the North West. Surveyed by Parties of U.S. Coast Survey detailed by A. D. Bache, Supt., to act under the orders of Lieut. Col. J. N. Macomb, Chf. Topl. Engr. of the Army of the Potomac. Parts of Sept. & Oct. 1861. Field work by F. W. Dorr & C. Rockwell, U.S.C.S. . . . Drawn by E. Hergesheimer. Photographs by G. Mathiot and D. Hinkle.

1 inch to ½ mile. 22 x 23. Photocopy. Shows roads, wooded areas, and names of some residents. Noted, "Photograph No. 17 Furnished Lt. Col. J. N. Macomb, Chf. Topl. Engr., Army of Potomac, Coast Survey Office, Jan. 18th, 1862." Reassigned to RG 77: F 74-1.

2.111. Map of Montgomery County, Maryland. Compiled in the Bureau of Topographical Engineers from the latest and best authorities, Sept. 1862.

1 inch to 2 miles. 20 x 27. Manuscript. A small part of Prince Georges County is included. Roads, buildings, and names of some residents, particularly in the area immediately adjacent to the District of Columbia, are shown. Some relief is indicated by shading. RG 77: F 72.

2.112. [Point Lookout: a series of eight ground plans of military properties erected and used during the Civil War.] (1) U.S. General Hospital. (2) Government Wharf, Quarter Master & Commissary Store Houses, Lumber Shed &c. . . . September 17, 1865. (3) Third Section of Rebel Prison, Cook, Mess & Commissary Houses . . . September 18, 1865. (4) First Section of Rebel Prison, Mess House &c. . . . September 18, 1865. (5) Offices, Sales Room & Dwell-

ings, Stables, Barracks &c. &c. . . . September 17, 1865. (6) Office, Mechanics & Contraband Quarters, and Blacksmith Shop, Stables & Cabins . . . September 18, 1865. (7) Head Quarters, Dispensary & Ordnance Buildings, Stable, Cabins &c. . . . September 18, 1865. (8) Cattle Yard, Cow Stable and Cabins, Shop &c. . . . September 18, 1865.

Large scale. Each sheet is 20 x 15. Manuscript. Colors enhance the drawings. Except for No. 1, each is initialed "N. G. S." RG 92: Maps 57-1 through 57-8.

2.113. Plan of the Battle Field at Pleasant Mills near Cumberland, Md. August 1st, 1864.

1 inch to 1,000 feet. 10 x 14. Manuscript. Drainage features in blue, roads in yellow, Union positions in blue, and Confederate positions in red. Positions of cannons shown by symbols. Wooded areas, buildings, and names of residents are included, and relief is indicated by shading. RG 77: Z 160.

2.114. Part of the map of the Battlefield of South Mountains [sic], Sept. 14th, 1862. Shewing the Positions of the Forces under the Command of Maj. Genl. A. E. Burnside. Surveyed and Compiled by Arthur de Witzleben [and] Theodor [sic] von Kamecke.

1 inch to ⅕ mile. 23 x 27. Manuscript. Confederate troop positions in red, Union in blue, and contour lines in brown. Map also shows wooded areas, fields, and names of residents. RG 77: F 91-3.

2.115. Battle Fields of South Mountains [sic] shewing the Positions of the Forces of Major Genls. Burnside and Franklin and of the Enemy during the Battle fought by the Army of the Potomac under the Command of Major Genl. G. B. McClellan 14th Sept. 1862. Bureau of Topogl. Engineers.

1 inch to 1,000 feet. 52 x 33 (2 sections). Manuscript. Relief is shown by contour lines in red; contour interval 100 feet. Symbols differentiate morning and evening positions of the Union and Confederate forces. Fields, wooded areas, and names of residents are shown. RG 77: F 91-1; F 91-2.

2.116. Part of Washington County, Md. Bureau of Topographical Engineers, September 1862.

1 inch to ½ mile. 3 sheets, average size 22 x 17. Photoprocessed. Shows roads, property lines, and names of residents or property owners. Map covers areas south of a line drawn due east from Williamsport. RG 77: F 276-2.

2.117. [Map of area in the vicinity of Hagerstown, Funkstown, and Williamsport, Washington County, Md., and Falling Waters, W. Va.]

1 inch to ¼ mile. 44 x 61 (2 sections). Manuscript. Positions of the different corps of the Union forces, roads, and drainage features shown in color. Map also shows positions of the Confederate forces and works, wooded areas, and names of residents. Relief is indicated by hachures. Noted in pencil, "v. Kamecke & Witzleben." This is one of the manuscript versions of a map published in 1879 by the Office of the Chief of Engineers entitled, "Map of the vicinity of Hagerstown, Funkstown, Williamsport, and Falling Waters, . . . Accompanying the Report of Major General G. G. Meade on the Battle of Gettysburg, dated October 1st, 1863." RG 77: F 97-4.

2.118. Sketch of the position of C.S. Forces Around Williamsport, Md., under Com. of Maj. Gen. J. E. B. Stuart, Sep. 19th, 62. By Wm. W. Blackford, Capt., Corps Engrs. [Confederate].

1 inch to ½ mile. 12 x 8. Manuscript. The title is misleading since position of forces is not given. Map shows roads, topographic features, and names of residents. RG 77: US 253-13.

MISSISSIPPI

2.119. Map of Big Black River Rail Road Bridge and Vicinity Shewing Entrenchments (blue) Constructed, by Order of Brig. Genl. P. J. Osterhaus. Also Entrenchments (red) of the Enemy Carried, May 17th 1863. Surveyed, Entrenchments Constructed and Drawn, by F. Tunica, Engineers.

"150 Paces to the Inch." 34 x 37. Manuscript. Map also shows wooded areas, roads, Negro quarters and other buildings, and names of a few residents. Relief is indicated by hachures. Noted, "Engineer Department, March 23, 1864. Recd. with Lt. J. M. Wilson's letter of March 8, 1864." RG 77: S 15-5.

2.120. Map of the Battlefield of Champion's [sic] Hill, May 16th, 1863 . . . Engineers' Office, Dept. of the Tenn., Capt. C. B. Comstock, Chief Engr. From Surveys by F. Tunica, Asst. Engr., and Sketches by Brig. Genl. A. P. Hovey & Capt. A. Hickenloper [sic]. Drawn by H. A. Ulffers, Asst. Engr.

1 inch to ½ mile. 20 x 33. Manuscript. Union positions shown in blue and Confederate in red. The Union positions are also distinguished to show successive advances at 10:30 a.m., 11 a.m., and 2 p.m. Wooded areas, roads, and names of residents are also shown. Noted, "Engr. Department, Mar. 23, 1864. Rec'd with Lt. J. M. Wilson's letter of Mar. 8, 1864." RG 77: S 19-10-2.

2.121. Map of Corinth, Miss., and Vicinity.

Large scale. 82 x 72 (2 sections). Manuscript. Confederate entrenchments in red and Union entrenchments in blue. Batteries are identified by name or letter. Drainage features, roads and railroads, buildings, and names of some residents are also shown. Relief is indicated by hachures. RG 77: Dr. 138-11.

2.122. Plan of the Position at Iuka, Tishamingo Co., Miss. Surveyed & drawn by Ch. Spangenberg, Ass. Engr., Septbr. 8th, 1862.

1 inch to ¼ mile. 14 x 16. Manuscript. Crossed swords indicate the site of the battle of September 19th, 1862. Red crayon lines apparently indicate extension of roads to the east of Iuka and near the site of the battle of the 19th. A note beside these lines reads, "Sketched in by Gl. Rosecrans on the Battlefield." General Rosecran's Headquarters, roads, names of residents outside the city, fields, and wooded areas are also shown. Relief is indicated by hachures. Noted, "Engr. Dept., Mar. 23, 1864. Recd. with Lt. J. M. Wilson's letter of Mar. 8, 1864." RG 77: S 14-12.

2.123. Map of the Route [in Pontotoc and Lafayette Counties] Pursued by the Cavalry Expedition under Col. T. Lysle. Dickey, Chief of Cav., in the Raid upon the Mobile and Ohio R.R., Dec. 13th-19th, 1862. Surveyed and drawn under the direction of Lieut. J. H. Wilson, Chief of Top. Engrs., Dept. of the Miss., by Topping and Hartwell, Ass't. Top. Engrs.

1 inch to 1 mile. 20 x 63 (2 sections). Manuscript. The route is shown in red. Map also shows roads, buildings, names of residents, troop positions, and encampments in the area adjacent to the route. RG 77: S-8.

2.124. Map of Tishomingo County, Mississippi. Compiled under the Direction of Col. George Thom, A.D.C. & Chief of Topl. Engineers, Dept. of the Mississippi.

1 inch to 2 miles. 23 x 24. Manuscript. Map shows roads, railroads, drainage features, place names, and names of some residents. RG 77: Z 190.

2.125. Map of the Country Between Millikens Bend, La., and Jackson, Miss., shewing the Routes followed by the Army of the Tennessee Under the Command of Maj. Genl. U. S. Grant, U.S. Vls., in Their March from Millikens Bd. to Rear of Vicksburg in April and May 1863, compiled, surveyed, and drawn under the direction of Lt. Col. Js. H. Wilson, A.I. Gnl. & 1st Lt., Engrs.

1 inch to 2 miles. 27 x 36. Manuscript. Routes in orange, positions of Union forces in blue, Confederate troop positions and defenses in red, and drainage features in blue. Also shows sites of Battles of Port Gibson, Raymond, Jackson, Champion Hill, and Big Black River Bridge and defenses and siege lines in front of Vicksburg. A note below the title describes the terrain, soils, agricultural products, roads, streams, fords, and bayous. Levees, mills, fords, ferries, post offices, and names of a few residents are also shown. Relief is indicated by hachures. RG 77: S 19-1.

2.126. Map of the Siege of Vicksburg, Miss., By the U.S. Forces Under the Command of Maj. Genl. U. S. Grant, U.S. Vls., Maj. F. E. Prime, Chief Engr. Sur- veyed and constructed under direction of Capt. C. B. Comstock, U.S. Engrs., and Lt. Col. J. H. Wilson, A.I. Genl. 1st Lt., Engrs. . . . Drawn by Chs. Spangenberg, Asst. Engr.

1 inch to about ¼ mile. 33 x 30. Published. Union works in blue and Confederate in red. Street plan of Vicksburg, buildings in and outside the city, roads, railroads, drainage features, and wooded and swamp areas are shown. Relief is indicated by hachures. Topographic profiles, cross sections of some Union and Confederate batteries, and cross section of a Confederate rifle pit are included. Map was engraved on stone by J. Schedler, No. 120 Pearl St., New York City, and was issued by the "Head Qrs. of the Dept. of the Tenn., Vicksburg, Miss., Aug. 20th, 1863. C. B. Comstock, Capt. of Engrs." Reassigned to RG 77: Dr. 138-19.

2.127. Sheet[s] No. 1, 2, [and] 3. Surveys around Vicksburg Showing the Rebel Defences and the Federal Works During the Siege.

1 inch to 300 feet. Sheet 1 (No. 20), 37 x 52; sheet 2 (No. 21), 36 x 57; and sheet 3 (No. 22), 55 x 57. Manuscript. Federal works shown in blue and Confederate in red; contour lines also in red. Roads, railroads, and drainage features are also shown. The street pattern and buildings of Vicksburg are shown on sheet 2. Cross sections of batteries, scale 1 inch to 20 feet, are included on sheet 3. Each sheet is noted and signed: "Hd. Qts., Dept. of the Tenn., Sept. 7th, 1863. Forwarded to Engineer Department with letter of this date. (C 5312) John M. Wilson, Capt., Engrs., for Capt. C. B. Comstock, Corps of Engs.," and "Engineer Department, Recd. Sept. 23d, 1863." RG 77: Dr. 138-20 through Dr. 138-22.

2.128. Map of the New Line of Works for the Defence of Vicksburg. Copied from the Original by Augustus Koch, 2nd Lieut., 51st U.S. Cola. Inf'y. and Asst. Eng'r.

1 inch to 300 feet. 51 x 35. Manuscript. Contour lines in red. New line of works in blue with names of batteries included. A few defenses shown in red. Street pattern of Vicksburg and a few buildings are also shown. Noted and signed: "Submitted with my report of Dec. 26th, 1864. Q. A. Gillmore, Maj. Genl., Inspr. Genl. Forts., Divn. West Miss.," and "Recd. at Eng. Dept., Jany. 20, 1865." RG 77: Dr. 138-49.

2.129. Map of the Picket Line around Vicksburg, Miss.

1 inch to about ⅓ mile. 22 x 18. Manuscript. Old Confederate breastworks and batteries at time of capture in red; drainage features in blue. New line of defenses and approaches to the city also shown. Noted and signed: "Respectfully submitted to accompany my report already forwarded, Q. A. Gillmore, Maj. Genl., Inspr. Gnl. Forts., Divn. West Miss., New Orleans, La., Jany. 5th, 1865,"

and "Recd. at Engr. Dept., Jany. 20, 1865." RG 77: Dr. 138-50.

2.130. Map of the Country between Vicksburg and Meridian, Miss., Showing the Route Followed by the Seventeenth Army Corps Under the Command of Maj. Genl. J. B. McPherson in February 1864. Surveyed by Lt. H. M. Bush and Assistants S. Davis & S. W. Dunning under the Direction of Capt. A. H. Hickenlooper, Chf. Eng.

1 inch to 2 miles. 25 x 79. Manuscript. County boundaries are colored; routes of the 16th Army Corps in blue and those of the 17th in red; defense lines in red and drainage features in blue. Map also shows roads, wooded areas, and names of residents along the routes taken by the two corps. Noted, "Engr. Department, May 11, 1864. Rec'd. with Capt. Hickenlooper's report of Mar. 25th, 1864." RG 77: Dr. 138-35.

2.131. "Plate No. IV. Camp of the Right Wing, 13th Army Corps, on the Yocknapatafa [Yocona River], Decbr. 21st, 1862. Surveyed under the Direction of 1st Lieut. Js. H. Wilson, Chief Topl. Engr."

1 inch to ½ mile. 24 x 27. Manuscript. Colors used to show troop positions; headquarters of General McPherson and of divisional commanders are located and underlined in colors. Section corners are indicated by crossed brown lines. Roads, railroads, fields, wooded areas, and names of some residents are shown. Relief is indicated by hachures. Included is an inset cross section of the "Bridge across Yockna [sic] River, near Free Bridge, constructed and destroyed by the 3d Divn., R.W., 13th Army Corps," scale 1 inch to 24 feet. A note describes the character of the countryside and its passability. RG 77: S 4-2.

MISSOURI

2.132. Military Map of Cape Girardeau, Mo., and Vicinity, Showing the location of the Forts. Wm. Hoelcke, Captn. & Addl. A. de. C., U.S.A., Chief Eng., Departt. of the Mo.

1 inch to 800 feet. 20 x 28. Manuscript. Drainage features in blue. Roads and streets, buildings, fields, wooded areas, and swamp areas are shown. Relief is indicated by hachures. Noted, "Engineer Department, September 27, 1865. Received with Capt. Hoelcke's letter of 22d Sept. 1865." RG 77: Dr. 139-30.

2.133. Map of Jefferson City, Mo., and Vicinity, showing the line of defenses. Wm. Hoelcke, Captn. & Addl. A. de. C., U.S.A., Chief Eng., Departt. of the Mo.

1 inch to ⅓ mile. 13 x 17. Manuscript. Defenses in red and drainage features in blue. Street names are given and buildings in the city and vicinity are shown. Approach

roads, bridge sites, brick yards, and a mill are also shown, and names of a few residents outside the city are given. Noted, "Engineer Department, September 27, 1865. Received with Capt. Hoelcke's letter of 22d Sept. 1865." RG 77: Dr. 139-29.

2.134. Sketch Shewing the Relative Positions of the Enemy's Works & Our Batteries During the Attack [on New Madrid, Mo.,] on the 13th of March 1862, Maj. Genl. John Pope Commanding the Army of the Mississippi, by F. Tunica, Engr.

1 inch to about 1/19 mile. 25 x 38. Manuscript. Drainage features outlined in blue; roads, the street pattern of New Madrid, and defenses colored brown; and swamp areas in colored symbols. Federal troop positions are in colors that differentiate Engineer and Cavalry troops from other troops; companies are identified. Red lines indicate range of guns from Federal works to Confederate works and to gunboats stationed in the river. A list of the number of guns used by the Confederate and Union forces appears in tabular form. Noted, "Engr. Dept., July 18/64. Recd. with Gen. Cullum's letter of the 16th inst." RG 77: Dr. 139-12.

2.135. Map of New Madrid, Mo., and Vicinity, showing the position of the fortifications. Surveyed & drawn by Louis Boedicker, 1st Lieut., 2nd Mo. Arty., Ass. Eng.

1 inch to 1,000 feet. 25 x 17. Manuscript. Drainage features and swamp areas emphasized in blue. Wooded areas, fields, buildings, and roads are also shown. Some relief is indicated by hachures. Signed, "Wm. Hoelcke, Captain & Addl. A. de. C., USA, Chief Engnr., Departt. of the Mo." Noted, "Engineer Department, September 27, 1865. Received with Capt. Hoelcke's letter of 22d Sept. 1865." RG 77: Dr. 139-19.

2.136. Map of Pilot Knob, Mo., and Vicinity. Wm. Hoelcke, Captn. & Addl. A. de C.

1 inch to about 500 yards. 23 x 18. Manuscript. Defenses are in red; some are noted as abandoned. Spot elevations given in red figures. Drainage features in blue. Buildings, farms, fields, names of some residents, a stone quarry, iron furnaces, and roads are shown. Relief is indicated by hachures. Noted, "Engineer Department, September 27, 1865. Received with Capt. Hoelcke's letter of 22d Sept. 1865." RG 77: Dr. 139-31.

2.137. Topographical Sketch of the Routes from Little Piney Ford on Gasconade River to Rolla. By H. A. Ulffers.

1 inch to about ½ mile. 16 x 26. Manuscript. Shows campsites of the 1st, 3d, and 4th Divisions, fields, names of residents along the route, and the location of Fort Wyman. Relief is indicated by hachures. Signed, "Head Quarters, 4th Div: Camp Halleck near Rolla, Decr. 22nd, 1861. Asboth, Brig. Gl., Cg. 4th Divn." RG 77: Q 88-1.

2.138. Topographical Map of the Country around Rolla. By H. A. Ulffers, Asst. Top. Eng.

1 inch to ⅓ mile. 23 x 31. Manuscript. Campsites of 1st, 3d, and 4th Divisions located in different color. Fields, buildings, names of some residents, roads, and a railroad line are also shown. Relief is indicated by hachures. Signed, "[?]Asboth, Brig. Gl., Cg. 4th Divn. Headquarters, 4th Division, Camp Halleck near Rolla, Jany. 25th, 1862." RG 77: Z 187.

2.139. Military Map of the City of Saint Louis and Vicinity From Surveys Made Under the Direction of Col. Geo. Thom, Chief of Top'l. Eng'rs., Department of the Mississippi, by J. Pitzman. I. G. Kappner & J. D. Abry., Ass't. Top'l. Eng'rs., 1862.

1 inch to ⅙ mile. 48 x 72. Manuscript. Contour lines in red and drainage features in blue. Forts, batteries, the United States arsenal, Benton Barracks, and a "House of Refuge" are located, and some street names are given. RG 77: Q 93.

2.140. Map of the Picket-Roads, Springfield, Mo., 1862. Surveyed & Platted, October 1862, Springfield, Mo. Copied April 1863. C. F. Eichacker, Lieut. & Eng. in charge of Fortifications.

1 inch to ⅙ mile. 38 x 36. Manuscript. Forts are identified by numbers, and other military buildings are in red; roads and streets are in brown. RG 77: Q 90.

2.141. Map of the Battlefield of Wilson's Creek, Mo. Wm. Hoelcke, Captain & Addl. A. de. C., U.S.A., Chief Eng., Departt. of the Mo.[Dated] Hd. Qu., Departt. of the Mo., St. Louis, 1865.

1 inch to ¼ mile. 20 x 14. Manuscript. Confederate positions and campsites in red, Union positions and drainage features in blue. Fields, woods, a few buildings, and names of some residents are shown. Relief is indicated by hachures. Noted, "Recd. at Eng'r. Dept., Nov. 7, '65." RG 77: Q 462.

NORTH CAROLINA

2.142. Eastern Portion of the Military Department of North Carolina Compiled from the best and latest authorities in the Bureau of Topl. Engrs., War Department, May 1862.

1 inch to 5 miles. 43 x 32. Manuscript. Includes part of southeastern Virginia and shows coastline, shoals, lighthouses and lightships, swamp areas, forts, roads and railroads, windmills, fisheries, canals, and the site of a Revolutionary battlefield. Included is a table of soundings and tides from Coast Survey reports. Noted, "Photographed by L. E. Walker for the U.S. Engineer Bureau, June 1864." RG 77: H 85-1.

2.143. Campaign Maps, Exhibiting the Line of March of the 20th Corps From Savannah, Ga., to Goldsboro, N.C., with the Plans of the Battle Fields of Averysboro and Bentonsville From Surveys, Topographical Engineers, 20th Corps . . . 1865.

Scales and dimensions vary (see below). Manuscript. Ten maps, bound with title and symbol explanations on cover sheet. Nos. 1 through 8 and 10 show routes of march from January 17 to March 24, 1865. The scales of these maps are 1 inch to 5 miles, 1 inch to 5½ miles, and 1 inch to 6 miles. The dimensions are 10 x 8. Troop positions and Union and Confederate defenses are distinguished by colors. Drainage features in blue and county boundaries in different colors. Map No. 9 is as follows: Topographical Map showing the positions of the 14th & 20th Corps . . . in an engagement near Bentonsville, N.C., March 19th, 1865, [with an inset of the] Battlefield of Averysboro, N.C., March 16th, 1865. Map, 1 inch to ⅕ mile. 16 x 21. Inset, 1 inch to ½ mile. 7 x 5. Manuscript. RG 77: US 280.

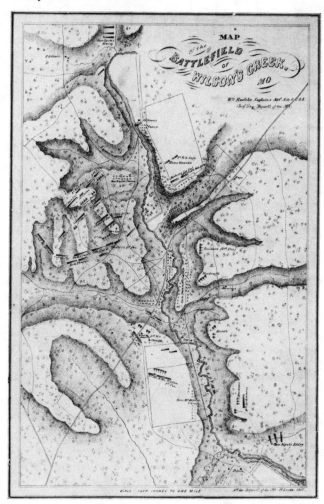

Manuscript map of the battlefield of Wilson's Creek, Mo. RG 77: Q 462. See entries 1.88 and 2.141.

2.144. Campaign Maps Exhibiting the . . . Line of March of The Army of Georgia From Goldsboro, N.C., to Avens Bridge, N.C., From Surveys, Topographical Engineers, Army of Georgia . . . 1865.

1 inch to 2 miles. 9 x 8. Manuscript. Six maps, bound with title and explanations of symbols on the cover sheet. Routes of march of the 14th and 20th Corps from April 10 to April 15, 1865, are shown. Troop positions and Union and Confederate defenses are distinguished by colors. Drainage features in blue and county boundaries in different colors. RG 77: H 96.

2.145. Map illustrating the Battle of Bentonsville, N.C., fought March 19th, 1865, between the United States Forces Commanded by Maj. Gen. H. W. Slocum and the Rebel Forces Commanded by Gen. Jos. E. Johnston, and the operations of March 20th & 21st under direction of Maj. Gen. W. T. Sherman resulting in the retreat of the rebels. Compiled under direction of O. M. Poe, Br. [Bvt.] Col., U.S.A., by Major E. [F.] Hoffmann.

1 inch to 1 mile. 21 x 29. Manuscript. Union forces and defense lines in blue and Confederate in red. Notations identify the different Union commands. Vegetation, fields, roads, and names of residents are also shown. RG 77: H 90.

2.146. [Map of Federal Point, N.C., showing radia from Fort Fisher and Mound or Battery Lamb at 1/4 mile intervals from 1/2 to 1 1/4 miles and positions of blockading fleet.] Dated "Engineer Department, March 1865."

1 inch to 1/4 mile. 12 x 21. Manuscript. RG 77: Dr. 143-33.

2.147. Plan [and cross sections] of Fort Fisher carried by assault by the U.S. Forces commanded by Maj. Gen. A. H. Terry, Jan. 15, 1865; surveyed under the Direction of Bvt. Brigadier General C. B. Comstock, Chief Engineer, by Otto Jul. Schultze, Private, 15th Rgt., N.Y.V. Engineers.

Scale of plan: 1 inch to 160 feet. Cross sections: 1 inch to 32 feet. 37 x 26. Manuscript. Plan shows number and disposition of armament and includes notes relating to changes in armament. The line of torpedos and "Place of Explosion" are also shown. Noted and signed: "Hd. Qrs., U.S. Forces, Fort Fisher, Jan. 27th, 1865. Forwarded to Engr. Dept. with letter of this date, C. B. Comstock, Lt. Col., ADC, Bvt. B. G., Chf. Engrg." RG 77: Dr. 143-28.

2.148. Map of Fort Anderson, N.C., Captured February 19th, 1865, By the 'Army of the Ohio, Maj. Gen'. J. M. Schofield, Comd'g. H. S. Hebard, Draftsman.

1 inch to about 210 feet. 20 x 40. Manuscript. Shows facilities of the fort, the line of defenses, fields, timber lands, and swamp areas. Included are profiles of the batteries and breastwork. Noted and signed, "OfficiaL Wm. J. Twining, Capt'. and Ch'f. Eng'r." RG 77: Dr. 143-41.

2.149. Map of Part of Hatteras Island. Made under the Direction of Capt. F. U. Farquhar, Chief Engineer, Dept. of Va. & N.C., by Solon M. Allis, Co. K., 27th Mass. Vols.

1 inch to about 1/5 mile. 25 x 38. Manuscript. Roads are in red. Wooded areas, swamp areas, dunes, defenses, a campsite, and names of residents are shown. Noted, "Engr. Dept., Mar 22, 1864. Rec'd. with Lt. Farquhar's letter of 19 Mar. 1864." RG 77: Dr. 143-23.

2.150. Sketch of the Defences of Newbern [sic] Made Under the Direction of Capt. R. S. Williamson, U.S. Top. Engrs. Assisted by H. C. Fillebrown, C. E., [and] E. S. Waters, C. E.

1 inch to 1 mile. 22 x 14. Manuscript. Railroad line is in red. Defenses are numbered and keyed to a "Recapitulation" list giving number of heavy guns and field pieces captured at each position. The place of landing, the street pattern of New Bern, and drainage features are also shown. RG 77: H 82-1.

2.151. Map of Plymouth and the Defences, Made by Order of Capt. F. U. Farquhar, U.S. Engineers, By Solon M. Allis, 27th Reg., Mass V. Militia, October 1863.

1 inch to 500 feet. 28 x 33. Manuscript. Defense lines and works, street pattern of the city, public buildings, roads, wooded and swamp areas, destroyed bridges, road barricades, and a picket station are shown. Noted, "Dec. 7, 1863, Engr. Dept. Rec'd. this day, Transmitted with Lt. Farquhar's letter of Dec. 3, 1863." RG 77: Dr. 143-10.

2.152. Survey of All the approaches to the City of Raleigh Showing the line of Intrenchments, made by order of His Excellency Z. B. Vance, Governor of the State of North Carolina. Oct. 26th, 1863. [Signed] H. T. Guion, Lt. Col., Arty. & Eng.

1 inch to 500 feet. 39 x 41 (2 sections). Manuscript. Map also shows the city street pattern, railroads, public buildings, tracts of land and names of residents outside the city, wooded areas, cleared lands, abatis, swamplands, and campsites. Relief is indicated by hachures. RG 77: H 95.

2.153. Map of the Rebel Lines at Raleigh, N.C., Evacuated April 13th, 1865, upon the approach of the Army commanded by Maj. Gen. W. T. Sherman, U.S.A. Reduced under the direction of Capt. O. M. Poe, Corps of Engineers, Bvt. Brig. Gen., U.S.A. &

Chief Engineer, Mil. Div. Miss. From captured Rebel map. B. Drayton, Draughtsman.

1 inch to ⅛ mile. 30 x 27. Manuscript. Defense works outlined in red. Map also shows the city street pattern, roads, railroads, wooded areas, fields, buildings, and names of some residents outside the city. Relief is indicated by hachures. Noted, "Eng. Dept., Dec. 5, 1865. Recd. with Gen. Poe's letter of 4 Dec. 1865." RG 77: Dr. 143-35.

2.154. [Sketch of the action at Roanoke Island, N.C., February 8, 1862, showing Confederate defenses, positions of Federal and Confederate gunboats and Federal transports, the landing place, and the site of the battleground.]

1 inch to about 1⅓ miles. 12 x 12. Manuscript. Coastal areas outlined in blue. Legend gives name changes of Confederate forts after they passed to Union control. Noted, "Gen. Totten with compliments of J. G. Foster. Eng. Dept., Rec'. Feb. 27/62." RG 77: H 81-2.

2.155. Plan of Fortifications around Wilmington, N.C., and Obstructions in Cape Fear River, from Sketches furnished by Lewis J. Shearman from August 1861 to August 1863.

1 inch to ½ mile. 87 x 36. Manuscript. Railroads are in red. Map also shows common roads, military roads, encampments, sites of shipwrecks, lighthouses, saltworks, rice fields, some topographic features, and names of some residents. RG 77: Z 94.

PENNSYLVANIA

2.156. Tracing Copy (Captured from Rebels). Portions of Penna. and Maryland [and West Virginia].

Large scale. 34 x 36. Manuscript. Area covered includes parts of Adams and Franklin Counties, Pa., all of Washington and Frederick Counties, Md., and all of Berkeley Co., W. Va. Roads, railroads, and names of residents in parts of Frederick Co., Md., and Franklin Co., Pa., are shown. RG 77: Z 265.

2.157. Map of Franklin County, Pennsylvania. Engineer Office, First Corps, A[rmy]. N[orthern]. V[irginia, Confederate]. Drawn by Paul Hoffmann.

Large scale. 20 x 17. Manuscript. Roads are in red. Railroads and names of some residents are also shown, and relief is indicated by hachures. RG 77: US 253-12.

2.158. Southern Portion[s] of Franklin & Adams Counties, Pa. Photographed for the Bureau of Topographical Engineers, Oct. 1862.

1 inch to ⅘ mile. Five overlapping sheets, each 23 x 18. Manuscript. Roads and names of residents are shown, and relief is indicated by hachures and shading. The phrase "Photographed for . . ." appearing in the title suggests that this manuscript copy was used for photographic reproduction. RG 77: E 66.

2.159. Battlefield of Gettysburg, Pa., 1st, 2nd, & 3rd of July 1863.

1 inch to about ¼ mile. 28 x 39. Annotated photoprocessed. A base map of the battlefield annotated in colors to show corrections or additional place names, names of residents, and Union and Confederate lines and defenses. Note on the reverse reads: ". . . This is a photograph from a map mainly made by Major (then Sergeant) E. B. Cope of my force (while the Chief Engineer of the Army of the Potomac) and under my direction. It is valuable as showing how a good topographer can represent a field after a personal reconnoissance. It was mostly made from horseback sketches based upon the map of Adams County, Pa., G. K. Warren." A further note on the reverse indicates that the map was later used in the preparation of the Civil War *Atlas*. A partially obliterated note on the face of the map reads: "Substituted for the Tracing of which this is a photograph, Engineer Bureau, War Dept., October 24/66. [Initialed] D.C." A manuscript map on tracing cloth (probably the tracing referred to and the map mentioned by Warren) is filed as E 72-1. RG 77: E 72-3.

2.160. Map of the Battle Field of Gettysburg . . . Surveyed and Drawn under the Direction of Bvt. Maj. Gen. G. K. Warren, Major of Engineers, By 1st Lieut. W. H. Chase, Corps of Engineers, assisted by 1st Lieut. Thomas Turtle, Corps of Engineers, [and] 2nd Lieut. F. A. Hinman, [Corps of Engineers], and Civil Assistants . . . Draughtsmen, Edwin A. Chase, W. A. Wansleben, John H. Dager, [and] C. F. Trill. [The survey was made during the fall of 1868 and the summer and fall of 1869, and the map was revised on the ground by P. M. Blake, Civil Engineer, in May and June 1873.]

1 inch to 200 feet. 154 x 152 (in 4 sheets, each sheet in 5 parts, making a total of 20 sections). Manuscript. Contour lines are red, wooded areas are green, drainage features are blue, names of residents at time of the battle are red, and names of residents in 1868-69 are black. Map also shows Union works and signal stations, fences by kind of construction, wooded areas by kind of trees, buildings and their construction material, and burned houses. This map is referred to as the base map used in compiling the three maps showing military activities at Gettysburg, July 1, 2, and 3, 1863, described in entry 2.161. Signed and noted, "Official, G. K. Warren, Maj., Engrs., Brevet Major General, U.S.A." RG 77: E 81.

2.161. Map[s] of the Battle Field of Gettysburg [showing troop positions on] July 1st, 2nd, [and] 3rd, 1863. Published by authority of the Hon. the Secretary of War, Office of the Chief of Engineers, U.S. Army, 1876.

1 inch to 1,000 feet. Set of 3 maps, each 39 x 32. Published. The base map is reduced from the map described in entry 2.160, which was compiled from surveys

under the direction of Gen. G. K. Warren. The troop positions on the three published maps (one for each of the three days of battle) are in colors, blue for the Army of the Potomac commanded by Maj. Gen. George G. Meade and red for the Army of Northern Virginia commanded by Gen. Robert E. Lee, and were compiled and added by John B. Bachelder from "Official Reports, consultations on the field, private letters, and oral explanations of the Officers of Both Armies." The three maps described here are noted and signed, "Approved, Geo. W. McCrary, Secretary of War, Sept. 26, 1877." The published record set of maps issued by the Office of the Chief of Engineers that is in the National Archives includes a set of the maps issued in 1876 without annotations and also the 1883 and 1912 editions. RG 77: E 119-1 through E 119-3.

2.162. Sketch of Defensive Works and Approaches at Harrisburg, Pa.
1 inch to 400 feet. 18 x 25. Manuscript. Form lines are in red and roads in brown. Signed, "John A. Wilson, Asst. Engineer," and noted, "Engineer Department, Sept. 2nd, 1863. Rec'd. with Capt. Wheeler's letter of Aug. 31/63." RG 77: Dr. 145-10.

2.163. Sketch showing Proposed defences of Harrisburg, Pa., and Conowingo Bridge, Md.
1 inch to ½ mile. 13 x 37. Manuscript. Relief is indicated by brown hachures and shading. Defenses and railroads in red. Noted, "Engineer Department, Nov. 24, 1864. Recd. with Capt. Turnbull's letter of 23 Nov." RG 77: Dr. 145-11.

2.164. Batteries for Entrenchment at Harrisburg, Susquehanna Riv. South side. [Panel of plans and sections.]
Plans: 1 inch to 50 feet. Sections: 1 inch to 25 feet. 14 x 8. Manuscript. The colors have no significance. Noted, "Engineer Department, Nov. 24, 1864. Recd. with Capt. Turnbull's letter of 23 Nov." RG 77: Dr. 145-12.

2.165. Rendezvous for Drafted Men, Philadelphia, Penna. Drawn & Executed by George S. Clark, Captain, 15th Regt., Penna. Volr. Cavalry and Superintendent of Barracks. Coloring & Lettering by Horatio J. Kurtz, Private, 203d Regt., Penna. Volrs. [Ground plan.]
1 inch to 16 feet. 51 x 95. Manuscript. A highly detailed, colorful plan. Numbered views of the buildings composing the camp border the ground plan. RG 77: Z 432.

2.166. Sketch of the Defenses of Pittsburg [sic] made by order of Captain Craighill, Corps of Engrs., USA, July 20th, 1863, By B. W. O'Grady.
1 inch to ⅔ mile. 20 x 17. Manuscript. Defenses in blue. Noted, "Engineer Department, July 23, 1863. Received with Capt. Craighill's letter of 21 July 1863." RG 77: Dr. 145-9.

SOUTH CAROLINA

2.167. Plan of the City of Beaufort, S. C., as allotted by U.S. Tax Commissioners for the District of South Carolina, February 1863.
1 inch to 200 feet. 18 x 29. Manuscript. Blocks are numbered and many are subdivided; figures, some in red ink, give dimensions of blocks and lots. RG 77: I 41-1.

2.168. Plan of Intrenchments & Vicinity west of & near Beaufort, S.C., Office of Topographical Corps, N.Y. Vol. Eng's., Feb. 1863.
1 inch to about 450 feet. 19 x 35. Manuscript. Drainage features in blue and locations of fords in red; notes in red ink, partly illegible, describe the passability of parts of the marsh area. Areas of high land, a few buildings, and roads are also shown. Some relief is indicated by contours. Area where "Houses, woods, hedges &c being removed" is also shown. RG 77: I 44.

2.169. Map of a part of Beaufort and Colleton Districts between Broad River and South Edisto River.
1 inch to 1 mile. 28 x 37. Manuscript. Defense works, some of which are named, shown in red, a railroad line also in red, and roads in brown; other colors probably distinguish low areas, wooded areas, and cultivated fields. Names of residents are also given. Signed "John Laibanke [?], Com. 54 NYV." Also noted and signed, "Approved, Chas. R. Suter, Capt. & Chf. Engr., D.S." RG 77: I 47.

2.170. Charleston Harbor and Its Approaches Showing the positions of the Rebel Batteries, 1863 [and annotated to show the status of the siege of the city, July 17, 1863].
1 inch to about ½ mile. 27 x 20. Manuscript. Defenses held by the Confederates shown in red; those captured by Union forces shown in blue. Colored flags and symbols show positions of the besieging army and the attacking fleet during action. The title is preceded by the statement, "U.S. Coast Survey, A. D. Bache, Supdt.," and the map is noted, "Engineers Department, July 29th, 1863. Received with Prof. Bache's letter of July 28th, 1863." RG 77: Dr. 64-51.

2.171. Map showing the location of the Batteries in Charleston Harbour and Vicinity. Traced by Henri Pechot [or Pichot], Co. G., 1st. N.Y. Vol. Engrs.
1 inch to about ½ mile. 16 x 21. Manuscript. Location of batteries shown in red and drainage features in blue. Notations, also in red, give the number of guns and/or mortars at some, but not all, of the batteries. RG 77: Dr. 64-52½.

2.172. Map of the Defences of Charleston City and Harbor showing also the Works Erected by the U.S. Forces. Drawn under the direction of Bvt. Maj. Chas. R. Suter, U.S. Engrs., Chief Engineer Dept. S.C.

1 inch to 2,500 feet. 39 x 49 (2 sections). Manuscript. Confederate defenses and railroad lines in red, works erected by or in the hands of Union forces in black, swamp areas in blue, wooded areas in green, roads in yellow, cities and towns in pink, some submerged areas also shaded pink, and drainage features and coastal waters in blue. Underwater form lines are indicated. The title has penciled alterations, adding after U.S. "forces in 1863 & 1864." The remainder of the title is crossed out, and "To Accompany the report of Major Genl. Q. A. Gillmore, U.S. Vols." appears underneath. RG 77: I 58-1.

2.173. Fort Sumter . . . Horizontal Projection. Survd. & drawn by A. H. A. Becker, 1865.

1 inch to 20 feet. 30 x 40. Manuscript. Noted: "To accompany report of Major General Q. A. Gillmore, Comdg. Dept. of South Carolina. Hilton Head, S.C., Novr. 1st, 1865," and "Approved [signed], Chas. R. Suter, Brvt. Major & Chief Engr., D.S." RG 77: I 58-2.

2.174. [Map of part of Hilton Head Island showing the street plan of Mitchelville, military installations, defenses, Government corrals and cattle yard, plantations, and fields.]

Large scale. 65 x 78 (4 sections). Manuscript. Buildings colored pink; cleared lands pale green; drainage features, coastal outlines, lowlands, and swamp areas blue; fields orange; wooded areas green with distinguishing symbols for thick woods; and roads yellow. RG 77: I 52.

2.175. Route of the Expedition, Oct. 22nd, 1862, with the Battle grounds of Pocotaligo & Coosawhatchie. Prepared from Sketches on the Ground by Captain Eaton, Lieut. Edwards & Lieut. Mehles, Corps of Vol. Engrs. Compiled from U.S. Coast Surveys.

1 inch to ⅔ mile. 18 x 15. Manuscript. Drainage features in blue, swamp and wooded areas in different shades of green with distinguishing symbols, main roads in brown, other roads in yellow, Union positions in blue, and Confederate positions in red. Route of the Savannah and Charleston Railroad, bridges, names of residents, defenses, the range of Confederate batteries at Frampton, and positions of dead trees also shown. Signed "A. Burkhardt." Also noted, "Approved, Chas. R. Suter, Lt. & Chf. Engr., D.S." RG 77: I 40.

2.176. Map of the Rebel Lines of the Pocotaligo, Combahee & Ashepoo [Rivers], South Carolina, To illustrate the operations of the Army under command of Maj. Gen. W. T. Sherman, comdng. Mill. Div. of the Miss. From captured Rebel maps and from surveys made under direction of Brvt. Col. O. M. Poe,

Capt. Engrs., Mill. Div. of the Miss., during the Savannah-Goldsboro Campaign. 1865.

1 inch to 1 mile. 41 x 48 (2 sections). Manuscript. Defenses are in red. Map also shows the Savannah and Charleston Railroad, roads, swamplands, wooded areas, fields, drainage features, names of residents, and the area near Beaufort. Signed, "O. M. Poe, Corps of Engrs., Bt. Brig. Gen., U.S.A., Sept. 25th, 1866." RG 77: I 53-1.

2.177. United States Direct Tax Commissioners' Plat of the City of Port Royal, South Carolina, October 20th, 1864.

1 inch to ⅛ mile. 47 x 21. Printed with manuscript additions. The printed base map shows blocks, lots, and lot numbers of Port Royal. The manuscript additions cover areas to the north and south of the city and show section lines and plantations. Areas reserved to the Government for military purposes are bounded by red lines. Signed, "Wm. Henry Brisbane, W. E. Wording, [and] D. N. Conley [?], U.S. Direct Tax Commissioners for South Carolina." RG 77: Dr. 146-22.

TENNESSEE

2.178. Map of East Tennessee. Prepared under the Direction of Captain O. M. Poe, Corps of Engineers & Chief Engr., Mily. Div. of the Mississippi, from data furnished principally by Capt. O. M. Poe and Prof. Jas. M. Safford. 1864.

1 inch to 4 miles. 48 x 56 (2 sections). Manuscript. Drainage features, roads and railroads, saltworks, forges, and furnaces are shown. Relief is indicated by hachures. Map also covers adjacent parts of Georgia, Kentucky, North Carolina, and Virginia. RG 77: T 87-1.

2.179. Map of East Tennessee from Knoxville to Rogersville. Compiled from authentic maps, from valuable information furnished by Wm. R. Palmer, Col., com'd'g. Anderson Cavalry, & from surveys & reconnoissances made in the winter of 1863 & 1864, under direction of Lt. Col. N. Bowen, Capt. of Eng's., U.S.A.

1 inch to 2½ miles. 22 x 31. Manuscript. Drainage features in blue and a railroad line in red. Roads are shown, and some relief is indicated by hachures. A list of distances appears in the margin. RG 77: Z 234.

2.180. Military Map of Middle Tennessee and parts of East Tennessee and of Adjoining States being part of the Department of the Cumberland commanded by Major General Geo. H. Thomas, U.S.A. Compiled and drawn under the direction of Colonel Wm. E. Merrill, 1st U.S.V.V. Engrs., Capt., Corps of Engrs., and Chief Engr. Dept. Cumberld., with the assistance of Prof. J. M. Safford, late State Geologist

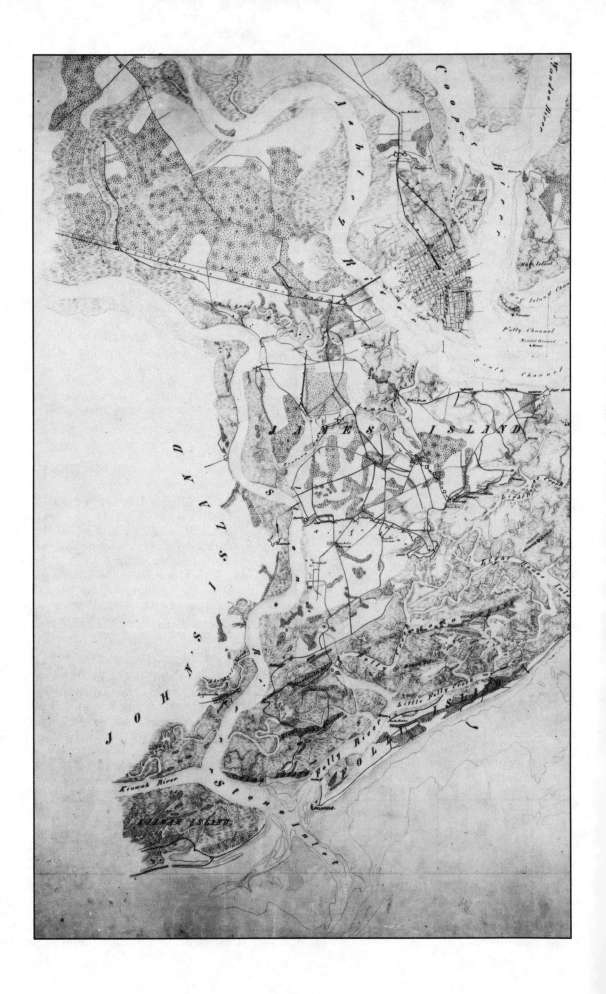

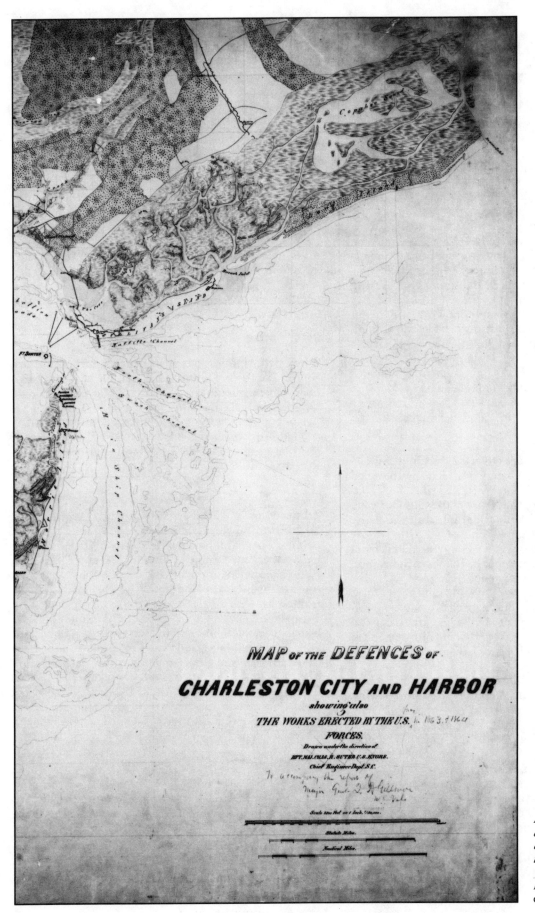

Manuscript map of the defenses of Charleston City and Harbor, showing also the works erected by Union forces in 1863 and 1864. RG 77: I 58-1. See entries 1.107 and 2.172.

of Tennessee, by C. S. Mergell, Asst. Engr., July 1865.

1 inch to 4 miles. 48 x 77 (4 sections). Manuscript. County names and boundaries in red. Map shows drainage features, place names, ironworks and saltworks, mills, furnaces, forges, foundaries, roads and railroads, and names of some residents. Relief is indicated by hachures. Parts of Alabama, Kentucky, Georgia, North Carolina, Mississippi, and Virginia are included. RG 77: T 84-2.

2.181. Map of Country in Vicinity of Brown's Ferry. Made to accompany report of Brigadier General Wm. F. Smith, Chief Engr., Department of the Cumberland. Drawn at Topl. Engineer Office, Head Qs., Army of the Cumberland, Chattanooga, Nov. 5th, 1863, by C. S. Mergell.

1 inch to 1 mile. 16 x 27. Manuscript. Position of troops and bridge equipage shown in red with numbers indicating successive troop positions. Roads also shown in red. A red dotted line shows an unfinished artillery road built by the Confederates. Drainage features in blue. A blue dotted line shows course of pontoon boats. Map also shows Confederate batteries and signal stations and names of some residents. Relief is indicated by hachures. RG 77: T 67.

2.182. [A set of eight maps covering the Chattanooga region in Tennessee, Alabama, and Georgia compiled under the direction of Capt. W. E. Merrill, Chief Topographical Engineer of the Army of the Cumberland. Some of these maps were lithographed at the army headquarters located at Winchester, Tenn.; others were done at Stevenson, Ala. They are dated from August 12 through September 8, 1863. An index map shows the area covered by each.]

1 inch to 1 mile. Average 21 x 14. Published. State boundaries, railroads, and drainage features are hand colored. Maps also show roads, buildings, and names of residents. Relief is indicated by hachures. Reassigned to RG 77: T 218 index and sheets 1 through 9.

2.183. Map Showing the Army Movements around Chattanooga, made to accompany the Report of Maj. Genl. U. S. Grant, by direction of Brig. Genl. Wm. F. Smith, Chief Engr., Mil. Div. Miss. [Surveyed] and drawn by H. Riemann, 44th Ills. Vols. [and dated] Topogr. Engr. Office, Hd. Qrs., Army of the Cumbd., Chattanooga, Jan. 4th, 1864.

1 inch to 2 miles. 31 x 45. Manuscript. No army movements are shown as title indicates. Map covers the region around Chattanooga in Tennessee, Alabama, and Georgia and shows roads and railroads, the site of the battlefield of Chickamauga, drainage features, fords and ferries, names of some residents, and gaps in the mountain regions. Relief is indicated by hachures. Noted, "Received May 4th, 1864, at the Engineer Bureau, from the U.S. Coast Survey Office, through Mr. J. C. Hilgard, Assistant." RG 77: T 73-1.

2.184. Map of the Battlefield of Chattanooga, Made to accompany Report of Major General U. S. Grant By Direction of Brigadier General W. F. Smith, Chief Engr., Mil. Div. Miss., Compiled and drawn by C. S. Mergell. Positions of Troops &c. drawn by E. Hergesheimer. [Dated] Topl. Engineer Office, Army of the Cumberland, Chattanooga, Ten., Jan. 23, 1864."

1 inch to about ⅓ mile. 39 x 36 (2 sections). Manuscript. Union troop positions and defenses in blue; names of commanders and successive positions of troops are given. Confederate positions, defenses, and line of retreat in red. Map also shows wooded areas, roads, railroads, General Sherman's concealed camp, and names of some residents. Relief is indicated by form lines and shading. A penciled note reads, "Mem. Redrawn on tracing cloth and hachure[d] and published by photolithography in the Off. Ch. of Engrs., 1875." RG 77: T 73-2.

2.185. Information Map [of area from Cottonport, Tenn., south to Dalton, Ga.]. Topographical Engineer Office, Head Qrs., Army of the Cumberland, Chattanooga, Nov. 26th, 1863.

1 inch to 1 mile. 56 x 27. Published. State boundary and railroads are hand colored. Map also shows names of residents and roads. Relief is indicated by hachures. Reassigned to RG 77: US 231.

2.186. Map of Cumberland-Gap and Vicinity laid down from Surveys, made by Capt. Sidney S. Lyon, acting Topographical Engineer, under Order of Genl. G. W. Morgan, commd'g. 7th Div., Army of the Ohio. Showing the location of the works constructed by the enemy and those erected by the forces of the United States.

1 inch to ½ mile. 35 x 27. Manuscript. Form lines are in orange and defenses in red. Map also shows campsites, mills, some buildings, and names of residents. Four inset landscape views of the Gap and vicinity made in April, May, and June 1862, are included. A note reads, "Mem. Contours not from the original plan. They have been laid down from memory . . ." Map is signed "Sidney S. Lyon, Capt., Co. F, 4th Ky. Cavalry, Acting Topog. Engineer, 23 Army Corps." RG 77: T 63-1.

2.187. [Map of Cumberland Gap and surrounding area in Tennessee, Virginia, and Kentucky showing defenses, military installations, and roads.]

"0,88 of a foot to one mile." 16 x 16. Manuscript. Defenses are in red. Contour intervals are indicated. Noted, "Position of roads &c by Capt. Lyon. Curves of ground by Lt. Craighill *from memory*, after three months' absence from the ground." and "Engineer Department, Dec. 16, 1862. Received with Lieut. Craighill's letter of 13 Dec. 1862." RG 77: Dr. 147-13.

2.188. [A panel of eight sketch maps.] Mountain Passes Practicable for Wagons from Cumberland Gap to Winters' Gap.

1 inch to 500 yards. Sketches vary from 7¼ x 9 to 7¼ x 10¼; panel: 22 x 28. Manuscript. Passes are Baptist Gap, Big Creek Gap, Children's Gap, Dunavan's Gap, Jacksboro Gap, Rogers' Gap, Wheeler's Gap, and Winters' Gap. Roads are in red. Relief is indicated by hachures. Buildings and names of some residents are shown. Map is signed "W. F. Foster, Capt., Engr. Corps," and noted on reverse "Rebel survey." RG 77: N 219-1.

2.189. Sketch [map] of Fort Donelson and Out Works ... by Lt. W. L. B. Jenney, V. Engrs., [and] Lt. W. Kossack ...

1 inch to 600 feet. 15 x 18. Manuscript. Shows roads, defense works, fallen timber, fields, campsites, barracks,

and the headquarters of Generals Grant and Smith during the siege. Relief is indicated by hachures. Notes relate to the number of Confederate guns that defended the fort and to actions during the siege. Signed "J. D. Webster, Col., Ch. Staff., Dist. W. Tenn." Noted: "Headquarters, Cairo, Ill., Feb. 28, 62. Approved and forwarded to the Chief Engineer, U.S. Army, Geo. W. Cullum, Brig. Gen., Chief of Staff of Engrs., Dept. of the Mo." and "Eng. Dept. Rec. March 5/62." RG 77: T 88-5.

2.190. Topographical Map of Fort Donelson, Tenn., and Vicinity. Prepared under the direction of Col. Wm. E. Merrill, 1st U.S.V.V. Eng'rs., Chief Engineer, Dept. of the Cumberland, By Maj. James R. Willett, 1st U.S.V.V. Eng'rs., Chief Insp. R.R. Defenses, Dept. of the Cumberland. Surveyed by John

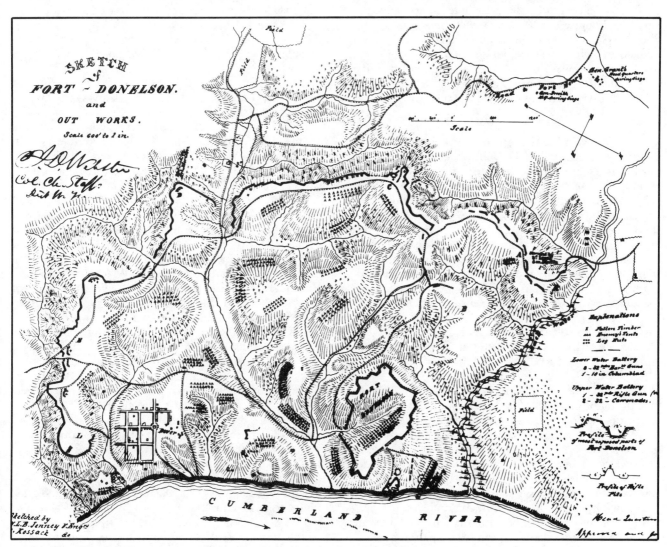

Sketch of Fort Donelson, Tenn. RG 77: T 88-5. See entries 1.117 and 2.189.

H. Willett, January 1865. Drawn by Serg't. Herrmann Nachtigall, Comp. K., 75th Regt., Pa. V.V.I.

1 inch to 440 feet. 45 x 35 (2 sections). Manuscript. Buildings, names of a few residents, and the sites of Fort Donelson and a deserted Confederate fort are shown. Relief is shown by brown contours with intervals given in red figures. Trees are shown by green symbols and the extent and character of timbered areas, cleared lands, and cultivated areas are noted. RG 77: Z 69.

2.191. Battlefield in front of Franklin, Tennessee, where the United States Forces commanded by Major General J. M. Schofield severely repulsed the Rebel Army under General J. B. Hood, November 30th, 1864. Compiled under the Direction of Col. W. E. Merrill, Chief Engr., D. Cd., by Edward Ruger, Supt., Topl. Engr. Office, Milty. Divn. Tenn. . . . Surveys made by Major James R. Willett, 1st U.S.V.V. Engrs., and Major I. J. S. Remington, 74st Illinois V.V. Infy.

1 inch to ⅙ mile. 40 x 27. Manuscript. Union troop positions in blue and Confederate in red. Successive positions of troops are shown and cavalry troops are distinguished. Some relief is indicated by hachures. Roads, a railroad, wooded areas, buildings, and names of some residents are shown. Attached is a printed legend giving an account of General Hood's movements in October and November 1864 and information about the battle at Franklin. RG 77: Z 77.

2.192. Topographical Map of the Approaches and Defenses of Knoxville, E. Tennessee, Shewing the Positions Occupied by the United States & Rebel Forces during the Siege. Surveyed by direction of Capt. O. M. Poe, Chf. Engr., Dept. of the Ohio, during Dec., Jan., and Feb., 1863-4, by [signed] Cleveland Rockwell, Sub. Asst., U.S. Coast Survey, [and] R. H. Talcott, Aid . . . Drawn by C. Rockwell.

1 inch to about 280 yards. 26 x 30. Manuscript. Contour lines in red, Union defenses in blue, and Confederate works in red. Map also shows wooded areas and roads. Noted: "This copy made for Lieut. Genl. U. S. Grant by order of Maj. Genl. J. G. Foster," and "Received May 4th, 1864, at the Engineer Bureau from Capt. O. M. Poe, with his letter dated at Nashville, Tenn., April 28th, 1864." RG 77: T 71-1.

2.193. Plan of Knoxville and Vicinity and of the Fortifications built by the Garrison under the direction and Supervision of Brig'. Gen'l. Davis Tillson, also showing the position of the Rebel works during the Siege, 1864.

1 inch to about ⅑ mile. 31 x 45. Manuscript. Confederate works and positions in red and Union positions in blue. Drainage features also in blue. Forts and batteries are shown by name. Roads, railroads, and sites of a military and pontoon bridge crossing the Holston River are also shown. A note reads: "Engineer Department, February 28th, 1865. Received with the letter of Brig. Gen.

D[avis Tillson]., Comdg., 4 Division, 23d Army Corps., Dist. of East [Tennessee], of 15 February 1865." RG 77: Dr. 147-61.

2.194. Plan of Lookout Mountain Showing (Approximate) Position of Hospitals, Sawmills, Lake, and Pumps.

Large scale. 21 x 39. Manuscript. Drainage features in blue, wooded areas in green, roads in red, and buildings in yellow. Noted in a somewhat undecipherable hand, "See Report of Mr. Leeds, 23 Aug. 1864 . . .[signed] M. C. Meigs, QMG." Map is also signed "Lewis W. Leeds." RG 92: Post and Reservation File, Map 83.

2.195. Topographical Map of Memphis and Vicinity. Surveyed & drawn by order of Maj. Genl. W. T. Sherman under the Direction of the Chief Topl. Engr., Dept. of the Tennessee, by Pitzman & Frick, Asst. Topl. Engineers.

1 inch to about ¾ mile. 27 x 19. Photoreproduction. Colors added by hand to emphasize wooded areas, drainage features, low areas, and a race track. Map also shows roads, railroads, bridges, names of residents, and fields. Reassigned to RG 77: Dr. 147-16; duplicate filed as T 125-2.

2.196. Sketch of Fortifications [Fort Pickering] at Memphis, Tennessee, 1864, drawn by C. Spangenberg, Asst. Engr.

1 inch to 300 feet. 19 x 31. Manuscript. Shows the arrangement of the facilities at Fort Pickering. Noted, "Engineer Department, October 1, 1864. Recd. with Capt. J. M. Wilson's Annual Report of 21 Sept. 1864." RG 77: Dr. 147-36.

2.197. Topographical Map of the Battle Field of Nashville, Tenn., 15th & 16th Dec. 1864. Prepared under the direction of Col. Wm. E. Merrill, 1st U.S.V.V. Engineers, Chief Engineer, Dept. of the Cumberland, By Major James R. Willett, 1st U.S.V.V. Engineers, Chief Inspector R.R. Defences, Dept. of the Cumberland. Surveyed by Chs. Peseux & John H. Willett, 1864-[186]5. Drawn by Chs. Peseux.

1 inch to 1,760 feet. 40 x 32. Manuscript. Confederate lines and defenses in yellow and Union lines and defenses in red. Other colors are used to enhance the map. Wooded areas, names of residents, roads and railroads, and cultivated lands are also shown. Relief is shown by contours with intervals given in red numerals. RG 77: Z 76½.

2.198. Topographical Sketch of the Country Adjacent to the Turnpike between Nolensville and Chapel Hill, Tenn. Compiled from Original Reconnaissances under the direction of Capt. N. Michler, Topographical Engr's., U.S.A., By Major J. E. Weyss, Capt. John Earhart, [and] Lieut. W. Greenwood. n.d.

1 inch to 1 mile. 27 x 16. Manuscript. Roads, mills, cotton presses, stables, buildings, and names of residents are shown. Relief is indicated by hachures. RG 77: T 36.

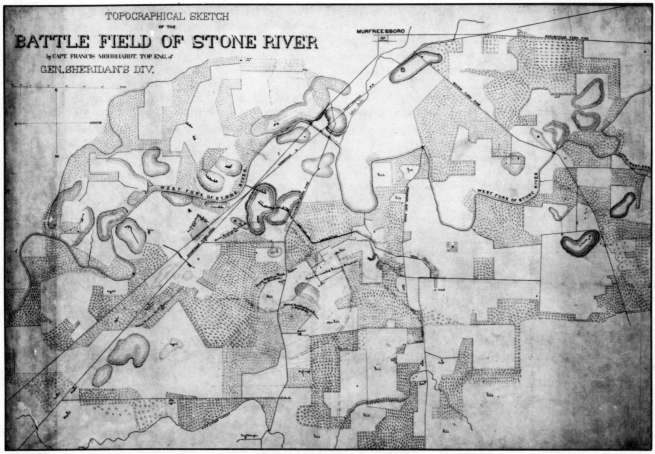

Manuscript topographic sketch of the battlefield of Stones River, Tenn. RG 77: Z 338-1. See entry 2.201.

2.199. Sketch of the Battle Field of Shiloh showing the disposition of the Troops under the command of Major General D. C. Buell on the 6th and 7th of April 1862.

1 inch to 1,000 feet. 22 x 21. Manuscript. Union positions in blue and Confederate in red. Names of Union troop commanders are given. Letters and numbers keyed to a legend denoting successive positions of forces. Noted and signed, "Headquarters, Army of the Ohio. In Camp, May 19th, 1862. Official, N. Michler, Capt., Topl. Engrs., U.S.A." Also noted, "For Col. Thom, Head Quarters of the Army, Washington City, D.C." RG 77: T 31-3.

2.200. Topographical Sketch of the Battle Field of Stones River near Murfreesboro, Tennessee, December 30th, 1862, to January 3d, 1863. Major General W. S. Rosecrans Commanding the Forces of the United States, General Braxton Bragg Commanding the Forces of the Enemy. Sheet No. II. Position of the U.S. Troops on the 31st of December 1862. Surveyed under the Direction of Capt. N. Michler, Corps of Topographical Engrs., U.S.A., by Major J. E. Weyss.

1 inch to ¼ mile. 22 x 28. Manuscript. Positions of the 14th Army Corps are shown in red, gray, and orange.

Map also shows Confederate line of works, a railroad, roads, wooded areas, fields, buildings, and names of a few residents. Some relief is indicated by hachures. Noted as official and signed "N. Michler, Capt., Top. Engrs., U.S.A." RG 77: T 28-4.

2.201. Topographical Sketch of the Battle Field of Stone [sic] River by Capt. Francis Mohrhardt, Top. Eng. of Gen. Sheridan's Div.

1 inch to about 950 feet. 27 x 40. Manuscript. Some troop positions in color and drainage features in blue. Map also shows a railroad, roads, defenses, wooded areas, fields, hospitals and other buildings, and names of a few residents. Faint penciled lines show "enemy" positions while Union positions are in ink. Some relief is indicated by hachures. RG 77: Z 338-1.

TEXAS

2.202. Eastern & Central Texas, Prepared by Order of Maj. Gen. N. P. Banks. Major D. C. Houston, Chief of Engineers, Feb. 1864 . . . F. D'Avignon, B. v. Reizenstein, Delns.

1 inch to about 25 miles. 32 x 24. Published. Major roads are hand colored in red. Map also shows forts,

drainage features, and railroads and includes comments about terrain, the passability of terrain from the coast to about 200 miles inland, vegetation, and agricultural supplies. Notes give information about crossings, navigability, and adjacent terrain of the principal rivers. Relief is indicated by hachures. This is one of the series of numbered maps issued by the Department of the Gulf. Reassigned to RG 393: Department of the Gulf, Map 6.

2.203. Topographical Map of the country between San Antonio & Colorado Rivers in the State of Texas. By Order of Captain Tipton Walker, Chief of Bureau, executed by Capt. W. Von Rosenberg, Assist.

Military Engineer, According to surveys made under his direction by the Assistant Military Engineers-Lieutenants H. R. Von Bieberstein, A. Giesecke, B. P. Hollingsworth, J. Von Rosenberg, and W. H. Brown. A.D. 1864.

1 inch to 1 mile. Map is in three sheets: I and II, 54 x 70; III, 53 x 75. Manuscript. Includes area between the two rivers from the gulf inland as far as Columbus in Colorado County and Panna Maria in Karnes County. County boundaries, towns and villages, roads, fields, prairies, wooded areas, and names of residents are shown. Comments are given on the type of country. Relief is indicated by hachures. The map was compiled under the

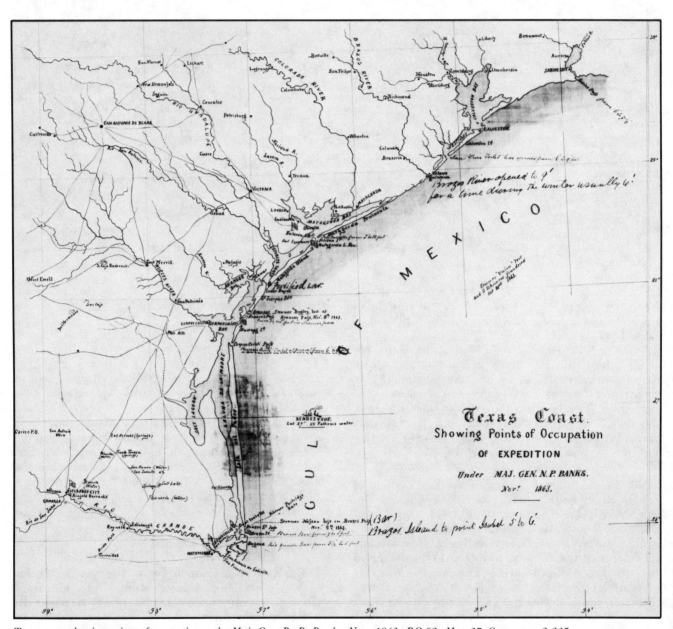

Texas coast showing points of occupation under Maj. Gen. R. P. Banks, Nov. 1863. RG 92: Map 37. See entry 2.205.

direction of the "Engineer Department, Topl. Bureau, District of Texas, New-Mexico & Arizona." RG 77: Z 49-1 through Z 49-3.

2.204. Coast of Texas and Its Defences. Capt. Tipton Walker, Chief of Topo-Bureau of Texas, New Mexico, and Arizona, drawn by P. Helferich, Asst. Engr., 1864.

1 inch to 8 miles. 28 x 53. Manuscript. Small-scale outlines of forts, drawn in red ink, appear as insets and are identified by names and numbers that correspond to numbered positions on the map. An inset map, scale 1:40,000, shows the line of defense works around the city of Galveston. Noted on reverse, "(Rebel Surveys)." RG 77: Z 298.

2.205. Texas Coast Showing Points of Occupation of Expedition Under Maj. Gen. N. P. Banks, Novr. 1863.

1 inch to about 25 miles. 16 x 17. Manuscript. Coastal waters outlined in blue and roads in red; U.S. flags, in color, indicate points of occupation. Notes relate to the events of the expedition and to the navigability of certain passes and channels. RG 92: Map 37.

2.206. Aransas Pass, Texas, Taken by the Union forces under Maj. Gen. Banks, Nov. 17th., 1863 . . . shows the position of the *bar*, also the Rebel batteries, each mounting 1-20 lb. Parrot gun. [By] Charles Hosmer, Sub-Asst., U.S. Coast Survey.

1 inch to about ⅓ mile. 13 x 10. Manuscript. Noted, "Copied from the Archives of the U.S. Coast Survey for the Engineer Department. [Signed] J. E. Hilgard, Assist., Coast Survey, In charge of Office . . . Washn., Jan. 4., 1864." Map also includes sailing directions for entering the pass. RG 77: Dr. 148-41.

2.207. Burr's Ferry [and vicinity, Sabine River, Louisiana and Texas.]

1 inch to about ⅙ mile. 19 x 27. Manuscript. Defenses, property owners, and wooded areas are shown. Noted: "Signed, C. G. Forshay, Chf. Con. Engr., Maj'r. Genl., Magruder's Staff, Houston, Texas, Aug. 20th, 1863. Topography by Col. Forshay & Capt. Deitz. Copied by H. A. E., Capt., Engs., Oct. 12th, 1863." RG 77: Z 54-5.

2.208. Map of Chambers County. Copied, for the use of the C.S. Army, in the Gl. Land Office of the State of Texas, January 2, 1863.

1 inch to about 2⅛ miles. 21 x 26. Manuscript. Property lines and names of property owners are shown in most of the county and in parts of some adjacent counties. A note on the related file card states that this is a captured Confederate map turned in by Capt. McAlester of the Department of the Gulf in 1865. RG 77: Z 51-10.

2.209. Galveston, Texas . . . Prepared by Order of Maj. Gen. N. P. Banks. Maj. D. C. Houston, Chief Engineer . . . Authorities, Coast Survey Charts [and] Reconoissances by W. S. Long, Asst. Engr., in Decr. 1862, Giving information furnished by refugees, Apr. 15th, 1864. Drawn by H. Holtz.

1 inch to about ⁴⁄₉ mile. 25 x 32. Manuscript. Shore lines of Galveston Island, adjacent islands, and mainland outlined in blue. Positions of forts and batteries are located by letters keyed to a list of remarks giving the armament of the major forts. This map is further identified in the title block as "Department of the Gulf Map No [-]." RG 77: Q 102.

2.210. Map of Galveston, Texas, Showing the Rebel Line of Works. Surveyed and Drawn by Order of G. L. Gillespie, Brevet Major and Chief Engr., Mil. Div. of the Gulf, Under the Direction of Lt. S. E. McGregory, Comdg. Topl. Party, by Pl. St. Vignes, Asst.

1 inch to about 425 feet. 25 x 38. Manuscript. Map also shows wharves, buildings, railroads and a railroad depot, street names or numbers, and lot lines and building sites in built-up part of the city. Fort Scurry and the South Battery are located by names. RG 77: Q 111-2.

2.211. Rebel Defenses of Galveston and Vicinity, Surveyed and Drawn by Order of G. L. Gillespie, Brevet Major & Chief Engineer, Military Division of the Gulf, Under the Direction of Lt. S. E. McGregory, Comdg. Topl. Party, Oct. 1865.

1 inch to about 1,700 feet. 25 x 37. Manuscript. Defenses and street names or numbers in red. Parts of the bay, harbor, and channel surveyed by McGregory in 1865 are tinted blue, and his soundings are shown in blue figures. Information copied from the Coast Survey chart of 1856, including soundings, is given in black. The location of Pelican Spit according to the Coast Survey chart of 1856, which differs from McGregory's survey, is indicated, and other differences in channels and bays between the chart of 1856 and McGregory's survey are shown. Explanatory notes describe McGregory's survey and the manner in which the information taken from the 1856 chart and from McGregory's survey is shown on this map. RG 77: Q 111-1.

2.212. Map of Pass Cavallo, Texas, Showing the position of the Rebel fortifications and rifle pits. Surveyed December 1st, 1863, by Charles Hosmer, Sub-Assistant, [U.S. Coast Survey].

1 inch to about ⅓ mile. 23 x 21. Manuscript. Includes a note on "The armament of Fort Esperanca [sic]." Noted: "Copied from the Archives of the U.S. Coast Survey for the War Department. [Signed] J. E. Hilgard, Assist., Coast Survey, in Charge of Office . . . Washgtn., Jan. 4, 1864." RG 77: Dr. 148-40.

2.213. Battle of Mouth of Sabine River, September 8th, 1863.

1 inch to ½ mile. 21 x 13. Manuscript. Shows positions of gunboats and transports at 3:30 p.m. and 5 p.m. and identifies them by letters and numbers keyed to a list of names. Positions of Confederate steamers and schooners are shown upstream. RG 77: Q 105.

VIRGINIA

2.214. Map of the State of Virginia [and Maryland, Delaware, West Virginia, and parts of adjoining States]. Compiled [by W. L. Nicholson] from the best authorities and printed at the Coast Survey Office. A. D. Bache, Supdt., 1862.

1 inch to about 14 miles. 26 x 39. Published. Railroads

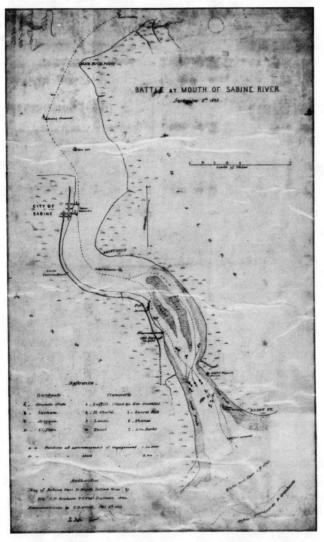

Positions of gunboats and transports at the mouth of the Sabine River at the beginning and close of the engagement on Sept. 8, 1863. RG 77: Q 105. See entries 1.129 and 2.213.

are in red. Roads and place names are also shown, and relief is indicated by hachures. Inset notes give information about area, population, railroad and canal mileages for Virginia, and railroad distances between points in Virginia and other States. Editions of August and December 1863 are also available. Reassigned to RG 77: G 145-1.

2.215. [Maps of part of Virginia covering the area from the Potomac River to the south boundary of the State and from Tappahannock and Wakefield in the east to beyond Lynchburg, Lexington, and Staunton in the west; prepared in the Engineer Department, Headquarters of the Army of the Potomac, 1864-65.]

1 inch to 1 mile. 35 maps, average 27 x 40. Manuscript, annotated published, and published. An index map prepared in the Office of the Chief of Engineers shows the coverage of 24 large and 2 small maps, but there are a few different versions, including annotated published copies and 2 maps on a larger scale showing fortifications southwest of Petersburg, making a total of 35 maps. Grid lines are in red. Roads, mills, furnaces, towns and smaller settlements, names of residents, railroads, and drainage features are shown, and relief is indicated by form lines. Many of the maps are signed "N. Michler, Capt. [or Major] of Engineers, U.S.A." RG 77: G 211.

2.216. Central Virginia showing Lieut. Gen'l. U. S. Grant's Campaign and Marches of the Armies under his Command in 1864-5. Engineer Bureau, War Dept. . . . Prepared by Order of the Secretary of War For the Officers of the U.S. Army under the command of Lieut. Gen. U. S. Grant.

1 inch to about 5½ miles. 32 x 33. Annotated published. Routes of the 2d, 5th, 6th, 9th, and 18th Corps and of the cavalry are overprinted in colors. Routes of General Sheridan's cavalry are distinguished from other cavalry routes by broken lines. The route of the 19th Corps is added by hand, and notes read, "Route of the 19th A. Corps delineated by Gen'l. Emory . . ." and "Recd. July 20, 1865, with Gen. Emory's letter of July 18, 1865." Relief is indicated by hachures. RG 77: G 165-4.

2.217. Central Virginia showing Maj. Gen'l. P. H. Sheridan's Campaigns and Marches of the Cavalry under his Command in 1864-65, drawn and lithographed under direction of Brvt. Maj. G. L. Gillespie, U.S.A., Chief Eng., Mil. Div of the Gulf, Oct. 1865. Authorities—Engineer Bureau, War Dept.

1 inch to about 5½ miles. 37 x 27. Annotated published. Routes of Sheridan's cavalry raids 1 through 7 are distinguished by different colors; General Lee's line of retreat is also shown in color. Attached to the map is a printed description of the seven raids. The map was published as "Engineers Office, Milit. Div. of the Gulf Map No. 6." RG 77: G 195-1.

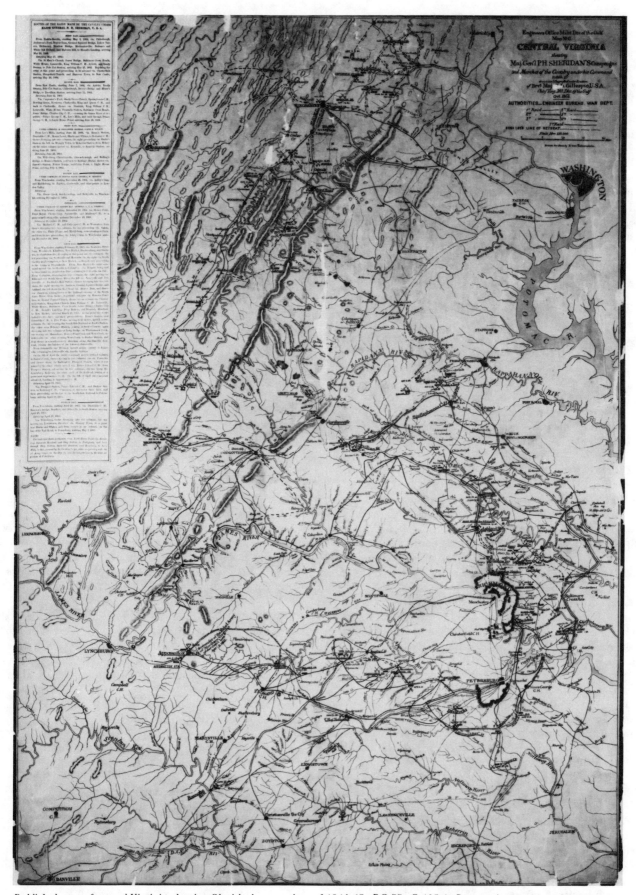

Published map of central Virginia showing Sheridan's campaigns of 1864-65. RG 77: G 195-1. See entries 1.138 and 2.217.

2.218. Map of N. Eastern Virginia and Vicinity of Washington compiled in Topographical Engineers Office at Division Head Quarters of General Irvin McDowell, Arlington, January lth, 1862. Corrected from recent Surveys and Reconnaissances under direction of the Bureau of Topographical Engineers, August 1st, 1862.

1 inch to 1 mile. 65 x 50 (2 sections). Published. The phrase "Surveys for Military Defences" precedes the title. Roads, names of residents, buildings, wooded areas, fields, railroads, the forts composing the defenses of Washington, other defenses, the site of the battlefield of Bull Run fought July 21, 1861, quarries, mills, and blacksmith shops are shown. Some relief is indicated by hachures. RG 77: Pub. 1862, No. 7.

2.219. Military Map of South-Eastern Virginia. Compiled at the U.S. Coast Survey Office . . . Drawn by A. Lindenkohl. H. Lindenkohl & Chs. G. Krebs, Lith. [Four editions, each without a date.]

1 inch to about 3¼ miles. 38 x 34. Published: two editions in color; two in black and white. The list of authorities on each of these maps is different. Two editions show drainage features in blue. Roads, buildings, settlements, railroads, and swamp areas are shown. RG 23: Coast and Geodetic Survey special maps.

2.220. [Map of part of southwestern Virginia between Lynchburg, Va., and Bristol, Tenn., along the route of the Virginia and Tennessee Railroad, n.d.]

1 inch to 1 mile. 35 x 197 (4 sections). Manuscript. Coal fields outlined in green and "copper fields" in orange, drainage features in blue, and county boundaries in red. Roads, mills, factories, furnaces, and mines are included. Relief is indicated by shading. RG 77: Z 418.

2.221. Map of Field of Occupation, Army of the Potomac, [from Dumfries south to Port Royal and west to Chancellorsville]. Prepared by order of Gen. Hooker from reconnoisances made under Capt. R. S. Williamson, Lt. N. Bowen, Gen. D. P. Woodbury, and others. Corrected April 10, 1863, [and signed] G. K. Warren, Brig. Genl., Vols.

1 inch to 1 mile. 31 x 36. Manuscript. Roads and railroads are in red. Drainage features, place names, and names of residents are included. Filed with this map is a similar map showing, in addition, wooded and swamp areas and noted, "Prepared in the beginning of 1863 at my Office, Hd. Qrs., A of P, [initialed] G. K. W." RG 77: Z 399-2.

2.222. Map to Show Lines of March of Second Army Corps and The Enemy, Oct. 14, 1863, [between Warrenton and Bristoe Station] . . . from reconnaissances after the movement . . . [signed] G. K. Warren, Maj. Genl., Vols.

1 inch to about 1 mile. 17 x 20. Annotated published.

Routes are added by hand in red ink to part of the map published by the Army of the Potomac. Identification on the reverse indicates that this map accompanied General Warren's report that was received and filed in the Adjutant General's Office in 1864. RG 94: Civil War *Atlas:* manuscript series. Map 6, Plate 45.

2.223. Map Showing the Topography of the Country and the Defences in front of Alexandria, Va.

1 inch to about 575 feet. 34 x 26. Manuscript. Drainage features in blue and spot heights in red figures. Roads, wooded areas, buildings, and names of a few residents are shown. Relief is indicated by contours. RG 77: Dr. 171-210-L-18.

2.224. Map of the U.S. Military Railroad Station at Alexandria, Va. Drawn at Office of Chief Engineer and Gen'l. Sup't., U.S. Military Railroads of Va., September 1865. From Actual Survey by Wm. M. Merrick.

1 inch to 50 feet. 34 x 59. Manuscript. The stockade is outlined in solid red except for parts removed, which are indicated by double red lines, one solid and one broken. Streets are shown by blue lines and railroad tracks by double red lines. Government buildings are distinguished by colors according to type of construction and occupancy. Forts, names of a few property owners, the site of Soldiers Rest, carpenters quarters, and the "slave pen" are also shown. RG 77: Rds. 194.

2.225. Map of the Washington and Alexandria Railroad and its Connections with the Baltimore and Ohio, Loudon and Hampshire, and Orange and Alexandria Railroads. Compiled and Drawn at the Office of Chief Engineer and General Superintendent, U.S. Mil. R. Rds. of Va., Alexandria, Va., May 1865, By W. M. Merrick, Draughtsman.

1 inch to 1,000 feet. 28 x 49. Manuscript. Railroad lines in red, defenses in orange, and Government properties in adjacent parts of Washington, D.C., in green. The Office of the Military Director, U.S. Government Railroads, is also located in Washington, D.C. RG 77: Rds. 195.

2.226. Soldiers Rest, Alexandria, Va. [Plans of buildings.]

1 inch to 10 feet. 35 x 45. Manuscript. Signed "George F. Kramer." RG 92: Map 111.

2.227. Freedmans Village near Arlington Hights, Va., July 10th, 1865. Genl. [ground] Plan No. 9.

Large scale. 15 x 20. Manuscript. RG 92: Map 110-5.

2.228. Reconnaissance of the Battle field at Bull Run, Va., fought July 21, 1861. Made on March 14, 1862, by Henry L. Abbot, 1st Lieut., Top. Engineers.

1 inch to 1,000 feet. 16 x 14. Manuscript. Roads, wooded

areas, remains of battery horses, and names of a few residents are shown. Estimated spot heights are given in figures, and relief is indicated by hachures. Filed with this map is a photoprocessed copy annotated to show troop movements during the battle. RG 77: G 73-2.

2.229. Battle Field of Young's Branch or Manassa Plains. Battle fought July 21, 1861.

1 inch to 15 chains. 22 x 20. Manuscript. Form lines and roads in red. A "Scale of Hills" gives heights of several named hills. Numbers, keyed to a list, locate the successive positions of the Confederate troops and sites where certain distinguished Confederates fell or lost their horses. Positions of Federal troops, houses, and names of residents are included. Oak and pine woods are distinguished by different types of symbols. RG 77: Z 396.

2.230. Map of the Battle Fields of Manassas and the Surrounding Region Showing the Various Actions of the 21st July 1861, Between the Armies of the Confederate States and the United States. Surveyed and Drawn by W. G. Atkinson, Acting 1st Lieu't., Engineers . . . Headquarters, 1st Corps, Army of Po-

tomac [Confederate], Manassas Junction, August 1861.

1 inch to 1,000 feet. 34 x 33. Manuscript. This copy on tracing cloth is noted "by order of Maj. Gen. N. P. Banks, comdg. Dept. of the Gulf [Union], Maj. D. C. Houston, Chief Engr., N. Orleans, June 3d, 1864, drawn by B. Von Reizenstein" and was prepared from a map inscribed "Presented to the city of New Orleans by General G. T. Beauregard, Genl., Comdg." Roads and drainage features are in colors. Fields with kinds of crops, pasture lands, wooded areas, buildings, names of residents, routes taken by "the Enemy," the site where the first shot was fired, and sites where certain distinguished Confederates were killed are shown. RG 77: G 136.

2.231. Map of the Battlefield of Bull Run, August 29th & 30th, 1862. Surveyed by order of Maj. Gen. Sigel and under direction of Maj. Kappner by G. Stengel and U. de Fonvielle . . . November 1862.

1 inch to ⅛ mile. 22 x 28. Manuscript. Wooded areas in green, roads in brown, and drainage features in blue. Relief is indicated by hachures and shading. Headquarters of Generals Sigel and Pope, an abandoned railroad, the position of Confederate artillery, and names of some

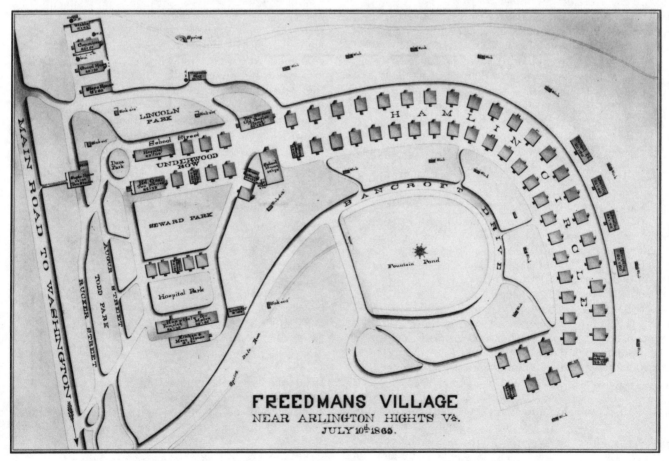

Freedman's Village near Arlington Heights, Va., July 10, 1865. RG 92: Map 110-5. See entries 1.158-x and 2.227.

residents are also shown. Noted, "Recd., Office of Surveys & Maps for the Army of the Potomac, Decr. 1862." RG 77: G 122½.

2.232. Map [and profile] of the City Point and Army Line and its Branches and Connections with the Weldon & Petersburg, Richmond & Petersburg, and Petersburg & Lynchburg R. Rds. Drawn at the Office of Chief Engineer and General Superintendent, U.S. Military Railroads of Va., Alexandria, Va. W. M. Merrick, Draughtsman.

Map: 1 inch to 2,000 feet. Profile: horizontal, 1 inch to 2,000 feet; vertical, 1 inch to 100 feet. 28 x 53. Manuscript. Defenses shown in red. Plank roads, other roads, and names of a few residents are shown. A small view of Petersburg as seen from "Shooting Hill" is included as an inset. RG 77: Rds. 196.

2.233. Military Railroad Map of City Point, Va., Principal Terminus of City Point and Army Railroad Line and Base of Armies Operating Against Richmond. Drawn at Office of Chief Engineer and General Superintendent, Military Railroads of Va., Alexandria, Va., June 1865, From Actual Survey by Wm. M. Merrick, Engineer and Draughtsman.

1 inch to 100 feet. 31 x 45. Manuscript. Colors distinguish new buildings erected by the Government, old brick and frame buildings, and frame buildings occupied by sutlers and by the "Christian Com[mission]" and stockade buildings, platforms, wharves, plank roads, and walks built by the Government. Contraband quarters, encampments, and headquarters of Generals Grant and Ingalls are also shown. RG 77: Rds. 197.

2.234. Lines of Entrenchment for defence of Camps at City Point, Va., as laid out and constructed October 1864 under direction of [signed] H. W. Benham, Lt. Col. of Engrs. & Brig. Genl. Comd'g. Defences of City Point. [Map and profiles.]

Map: 1 inch to 200 feet. Profiles: 1 inch to 10 feet. 19 x 60. Manuscript. Roads shown in red; redoubts and salients numbered in red. Descriptive notes relate to construction of entrenchments and their armament. A similar map in this file, apparently a copy, is inscribed, "For Major General Meade, Comg. Army of Potomac, Oct. 20, 1864." The following inset appears on both maps: [Map of City Point and vicinity showing line of entrenchments, wooded and open areas, roads, and names of residents.] 1 inch to ½ mile. 10 x 16. Manuscript. Entrenchments and the position of a pontoon bridge over the Appomattox River in red. RG 77: Z 407-2.

2.235. [Sketch of action near New Cold Harbor, Va.]

Large scale. 8 x 12. Manuscript. Confederate lines in blue and Union in red. Map shows site where Colonel Porter fell and includes remarks, probably by General Barnard, lettered A, B, and C and keyed to points on the map locating positions where he went, point where

companies of the 3d Batallion entrenched themselves, and the hollow where most of the regiment took shelter and remained the day of June 3. Noted, "Engineer Department, Received June 13, 1864. Private letter of Brig. Gen. Barnard, Corp of Engineers." RG 77: G 134.

2.236. Topography of the Battlefield of Cool-Harbor, [sic] Va. . . . constructed from Recgnocainces made under Direction of Maj. N. Michler, Corps of Engr., U.S.A., by Maj. J. E. Weyss, U.S.V., Princ. Ass., Engr. Dept., Army of P[otomac].

No scale given. 34 x 23. Manuscript. A penciled note next to the title block reads "made during the action from June 3d to 12th." Colored lines probably indicate troop positions; however, there is no key. Defense works are in colors. Roads, fields, wooded areas, buildings, names of residents, swamplands, and the site of the Army headquarters are shown. RG 77: Z 412-C.

2.237. [Rough sketch of the battlefield of Cross Keys, Va., June 8, 1862, compiled by Jed. Hotchkiss, 2d Army Corps, Confederate Army of Northern Virginia.]

Large scale. 9 x 12 (mounted on sheets 13 x 20). Manuscript. Confederate positions in red and Union in blue. A note reads "Yankees commenced moving to Top of Oak Ridge at 4 P.M." Lists of the Confederate troops are included with penciled corrections of the names of commanders. Pasted in the corner is a label with Hotchkiss' name and Staunton, Va., address with a statement that the map should be returned to him. This is the manuscript version of Map 2, Plate 111, Atlas to Accompany the Official Records of the Union and Confederate Armies. RG 94: Civil War *Atlas*, manuscript series. Plate 111, Map 2.

2.238. Survey of Culpepper [sic] and a Part of Madison Counties, Virginia, Made under the direction of A. H. Campbell, Capt., P.E. & Ch'f., Topl. Dept. . . . 1863.

1 inch to about 1⅓ miles. 24 x 27. Manuscript. Roads in red. Wooded areas and names of residents are shown, and relief is indicated by hachures. This map was compiled in the "Chief Engineers Office, D[epartment]. N[orthern]. V[irginia, Confederate]. Col. J. F. Gilmer, Chief Eng'r." It is noted and signed, "Approved May 5, 1863, Albert H. Campbell, Capt., R. Engrs. & Chf. Top. Dep., D. N. Va." RG 77: US 253-17.

2.239. Passages of the Rappahannock and Battle of Fredericksburg, December 10th to 16th, 1862. Sketch to accompany the report of Brigadier General Henry J. Hunt, Chief of Artillery, Army of the Potomac, compiled from the Surveys of the Topographical Dept., sketches made by Lieut. P. Haines [sic], T. E., and Col. C. S. Wainwright, 1st N.Y.A., Chief of Arty., 1st Corps, and a survey of the rebel position by Lt. Jed. Hotchkiss, T. E., to Lt. Gen. Jackson, C.S.A.,

by [signed] Alexander Doule, Major, 2d N.Y. Ay., Insp. of Arty.

1 inch to about 550 yards. 26 x 30. Manuscript. Confederate positions in brown and Federal in red and blue. Designations of commands are given and headquarters of commanding generals are located. Wooded areas in green, drainage features in blue, city blocks in orange, roads in brown, and swamp areas in pale blue with symbols. A penciled note dated March 20, 1863, and initialed "J. C. W." reads, "The property of Maj. Genl. Burnside & subject to his order." RG 77: G 117.

2.240. Sketch of the Battle of Fredericksburg, Saturday, Dec. 13th, 1862, [showing position of the] Right Wing, C.S.A., Lt. Gl. Jackson's Corps, By Jed. Hotchkiss, T. E., 2nd Corps, A[rmy]. N[orthern]. Va., [Confederate].

1 inch to about ⅝ mile. 22 x 13. Manuscript. RG 77: G 131.

2.241. Positions of Humphreys' Division, Battle of Fredericksburg, Decr. 13th . . . [and] Decr. 14th, 15th & 16th, 1862."

1 inch to 200 yards. 20 x 28. Manuscript. Positions of Allabach's and Tyler's brigades are distinguished by colors; numbers keyed to a legend indicate the successive movements of each brigade. Penciled note reads, "Accompanying Memoir or report of action by Genl. Humphreys, Dec. 20, 1862." RG 77: G 130-1.

2.242. Plan for defending Lexington, when there was only four hours to do it in, from an attack of infantry on the south, east, & west sides, the north side open for the retreat and the mill houses fortified to protect the bridge.

1 inch to 80 yards. 20 x 29. Manuscript. Buildings and fortifications in orange and drainage features in blue. Yellow hachures and shading indicate relief; red lines indicate lines of fire. Disposition of men and guns along the defense line is given in numbers. Sketches, with military figures, show cross sections of rifle pits, profiles of batteries, details of obstacles, and defense of a house open to attack on all sides. This plan was turned in to the Engineer Bureau from the files of Lieutenant Meigs, Chief Engineer of the Department of West Virginia. RG 77: Z 126.

2.243. [Map of the vicinity of Mine Run.]

Large scale. 16 x 10. Annotated photoprocessed. This map is marked in blue crayon "The Mine Run Campaign" but does not show actions of the campaign. Some roads are in red. Wooded areas, names of residents, stores, mills, and churches are shown. Penciled notations show name corrections. This map was used in the compilation of Map 6, Plate 47, *Atlas to Accompany the Official Records of the Union and Confederate Armies.* More names of residents are shown on this map than on the published ver-

sion appearing in the *Atlas*. RG 94: Civil War *Atlas*, manuscript series. Plate 47, Map 6.

2.244. Plan of the Town of Orange C.H. Showing Roads &c. constructed therein during the winter of 1863, '64. [Compiled] By order of Lt. Col. Wm. Proctor Smith, Chf. Engr., A[rmy]. N[orthern]. Va., [Confederate].

Large scale. 10 x 15. Manuscript. Colors are used to show new construction. Plank, macadam, and "rocked" roads are differentiated. Penciled notes probably give feet of lumber used for the platform at the railroad depot. The map is drawn on the reverse of a blank promotional form used in the United States Army and is signed "S. Howell Brown, 1st. Lt., Engr. Troops, In Chg. Topl. Dept., A.N.Va." RG 77: US 253-8.

2.245. Sketch of Mine in front of 2d Div., 9 Corps, near Petersburg, Va. Commenced June 25th, 1864. Finished July 23rd, 1864. Exploded July 30th, 1864. [Apparently drawn by Henry Pleasants, Lt. Col., 48th Regiment, Pennsylvania "Vet." Volunteers.]

Profile: horizontal, 1 inch to 50 feet; vertical, 1 inch to 10 feet. Underground plans: 1 inch to 10 feet and 1 inch to 50 feet. Section of crater: 1 inch to 10 feet. Section of main gallery at shaft: 1 inch to 2 feet. Sketches of magazines: 1 inch to 2 feet. 26 x 37. Manuscript. Noted: "Forwarded to Engr. Dept., U.S.A., with letter of Aug. 25, 1864. . . [signed] J. G. Barnard, Bvt. Maj. Genl., Chf. Engineer, Combined Armies." RG 77: Dr. 150-58.

2.246. [Maps of the area in the vicinity of Petersburg and Richmond compiled under the direction of Bvt. Brig. Gen. N. Michler, 1865-1867.]

1 inch to ⅛ mile. 28 maps, average 30 x 52. Manuscript. Two index maps prepared in the Office of the Chief of Engineers show the coverage of each map. Some of the maps are identified as being surveyed by Maj. J. E. Weyss and party and drawn by Weyss and others. Roads, railroads, defense works and entrenchments, wooded areas, cleared areas, fields, and names of residents are shown. Relief is indicated by hachures. The city blocks of Richmond and Petersburg are shown in detail. RG 77: G 204-33 through G 204-60.

2.247. Map of the Environs of Richmond and Petersburg Showing the Positions of the Entrenched Lines occupied by the Forces of the United States.

1 inch to about ⅔ mile. 48 x 31. Manuscript. Confederate defense lines in red and Union in blue. Roads, fields, wooded areas, buildings, names of some residents, railroads, and swamp areas are shown. Relief is indicated by hachures. Noted: "Head Qrs., Army of the James Engineer Department, March 24th, 1865. Official, [signed] Peter S. Michie, Bvt. Brig. Genl., U.S. Vols., Chief Engineer, Depmt. Va." RG 77: G 171.

2.248. Copy of Section of Photograph Map captured from the enemy Showing country adjacent to Richmond and Lines of Defensive Works surrounding the City. Headquarters, Army of the Potomac, Engineer Department, August 18th, 1864, [and one part dated] Dec. 20th, 1864.

1 inch to 1¼ miles. 29 x 23. Annotated printed. Some defenses are hand colored in red, and part of the James River is hand colored in blue. Map is a composite of four published sheets; the two lower sheets are identified as "Official" and signed "N. Michler, Major, Engineers, U.S.A." The title, which appears in the lower left-hand part only, is further annotated in pencil: "(found on the dead body of the Rebel Gen'l. Chambliss)." RG 77: G 151-1.

2.249. [Map of the Shenandoah Valley from Strasburg, Va., to Harpers Ferry and vicinity, W. Va., "captured in General Lomax's Quarter wagons" by General Custer on October 9, 1864.]

1 inch to 2 miles. 27 x 19. Manuscript. Roads in red. Railroads, drainage features, and names of residents (particularly in the area around Winchester, Va., and in Jefferson County, W. Va.) are shown. Relief is indicated by shading. Noted, "Eng. Office, 2nd Corps, A[rmy]. N[orthern]. Va. [Confederate], Sept. 12th, 1864." This map was redrawn and issued by the Engineer Bureau of the War Department in November 1864. The map described below is an annotated version of a photoprocessed copy. RG 77: G 154.

2.250. Topographical copy of a Map of the Valley of the Shenandoah River From Strasburg, [Va.], to Harper's Ferry, [W.] Va., with the adjacent counties west of it and south of the Potomac River, Captured in the rebel Gen'l. Lomax's Baggage Wagon by Brig. General Custer, U.S.A., of Major Gen'l. Sheridan's Command, October 9th, 1864, made in the Engineer Bureau of the War Department, November 1864. . . . Drawn by Denis Callahan. Photographed by L. E. Walker. [Annotated to show positions and routes of expeditions made into the valley in August 1864.]

1 inch to 2 miles. 35 x 21. Annotated photoprocessed. Annotations are in various colors that distinguish the routes and positions of the different commands of Wright, Emory, Crook, and Torbert. Routes of the commands of Wilson, Averell, Custer, and Lowell are also shown. Dates are given by each position, and crossed swords indicate sites of encounters with Confederate forces. RG 77: G 155-2.

2.251. Map of the Shenandoah & Upper Potomac Including Portions of Virginia, [West Virginia], and Maryland. Compiled from Surveys made under the Direction of 1st Lieut. John R. Meigs, U.S. Engrs., Chief Engineer Dept. West Virginia, and from other reliable authorities, 1864.

1 inch to 4 miles. 34 x 23. Published. Relief is indi-

cated by brown shading. Roads, railroads, place names, names of a few residents, and drainage features are shown. Reassigned to RG 77: G 150-1.

2.252. Map of the Battlefields of the Tolopotomoy and Bethesda Church Showing the Field of Operations of the Army of the Potomac Commanded by Maj. Gen. George G. Meade, U.S.A., From May 28th to June 2d, 1864. Surveyed under the orders of Bvt. Col. J. C. Duane, Major of Engineers, Chief Engineer, Army of the Potomac, By Bvt. Maj. C. W. Howell, 1st Lieut. of Engineers. Assisted by Mess'r's. L. C. Oswell, L. Bell, and R. B. Talfor, Topographical Engineers.

1 inch to ⅛ mile. 53 x 58 (2 sections). Manuscript. Union lines in blue and Confederate in red. Lines captured and turned are shown as a combination red and blue line. Three types of roads are distinguished by line symbols; wooded areas are distinguished by kinds of trees; railroads, buildings, and names of residents are shown; and some relief is indicated by form lines. RG 77: G 182.

2.253. [Sketch map of White Oak Swamp and vicinity southeast of Richmond.]

1 inch to about 2 miles. 10 x 16. Manuscript. Shows campsites of the 3d and 5th Excelsiors, roads, defenses, picket lines, forage facilities, houses, and names of some residents. Noted, "Lieut. Jas. W. Smith, 3rd Excelsior, June 12th, 1862," and initialed, "H. E. B." RG 77: G 113-12.

2.254. Topographical Sketch of the Battle Field of the Wilderness from Reconnoissances During the Actions of the 5th, 6th, and 7th of May 1864, made under the direction of Major N. Michler, Corps of Engineers, U.S.A., by Major John E. Weyss, U.S. Vols., Principal Assistant, Capt. W. H. Paine, Additional Aide de Camp & Assistant . . ."

1 inch to ¼ mile. 41 x 30. Manuscript. Shows defense works, buildings, names of residents, fields, wooded areas, and an unfinished railroad; turnpikes, plank roads, and local roads are distinguished and some are named. Relief is indicated by hachures. A penciled note reads: "found among Rolls of Office Maps turned in by Genl. Michler, does not belong to the regular series; replaced by Sheet No. 1 on the same scale." RG 77: G 204-17.

2.255. Map Showing the Position of Williamsburg From Surveys made by command of Maj. Genl. Geo. B. McClellan, Comd. the Army of the Potomac . . . Compiled and drawn By direction of Brig. Genl. Humphreys by Capt. J. Hope . . . May 30th, 1862.

1 inch to ½ mile. 23 x 18. Manuscript. Marshlands, forests, drainage features, "felled timbers," roads, and earthworks are in colors. Main and byroads are distinguished. Open fields, buildings, names of some residents, defenses, and the route taken and redoubt carried

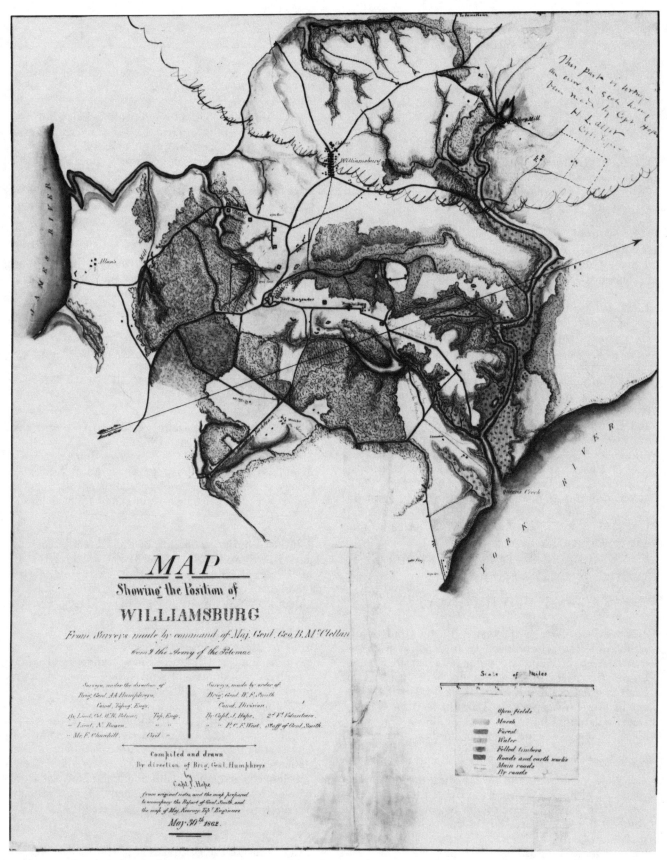

Position of Williamsburg, Va. RG 77: G 447. See entries 1.145 and 2.255.

by Hancock's brigade are shown. The upper right-hand part of the map is separated by a scratched line, and a note reads: "This part is wrong -an error in scale having been made by Capt. Hope. [Signed] H. L. Abbot, Capt., Engs." RG 77: G 447.

2.256. Sketch of the Second Battle of Winchester, June 13th, 14th, 15th, 1863, Topl. Office, A[rmy]. N[orthern]. V[irginia, Confederate]. Copied by J. Paul Hoffmann, Topog. Engr.

1 inch to ½ mile. 16 x 16. Manuscript. Confederate positions in red and Union in blue. Defenses in purple. Names of Confederate commands, wooded areas, and names of residents are shown. Relief is indicated by hachures. RG 77: US 253-5.

2.257. Reconnaissance of Secession Works and Plan of Seige of Yorktown made under orders of Gen'l. Barnard & Maj. Humphreys by Leiut. Abbot, Top. Eng'rs., Leiut. Comstock, Engrs., Leiut. Wagner, Top. Eng'rs., April & May 1862.

1 inch to about 210 yards. 31 x 36. Manuscript. Wooded areas in green and Union works in red. Notations indicate that Confederate forces and works are to be shown in red and Union in blue. A note reads, "Secession works as known to us before the evacuation." Map is also identified as: "Map No. 1, Siege Plan to accompany report to Chief Engr., U.S.A., of May 7th [6th], 1862. . . [signed] J. G. Barnard, B. Gen., U." Notations added in red ink: "Copied in the Engineer Bureau, War Department, for the Adjt. Genl's. Office. October 30th, 1865 [initialed] D. C.," and "W. R. O., Apl. 4, 1889. A true copy of the original [signed] C. D. Cowles, 1st Lieut., 23d. Inf." RG 94: Civil War *Atlas*, manuscript series. Map 1, Plate 14.

WEST VIRGINIA

2.258. Map of Part of West Virginia [and southwestern Virginia] compiled from original Surveys, the "nine sheet Map," and other reliable information, Under the Direction of Lieut. John R. Meigs, U.S. Engrs., chief engineer, Dept. West Virginia, 1864.

1 inch to 4 miles. 46 x 35. Published. Major drainage features in blue. Map also shows relief by shading, place names, names of some residents, roads, railroads, and trails. Reassigned to RG 77: G 203-1.

2.259. Map of a Part of [West Virginia and southwestern] Virginia Exhibiting the Routes of Genl. W. W. Averell in His Three Expeditions of August, November & December, 1863. Drawn under the Direction of Lieut. J. R. Meigs, Corps of Engrs., Chief Engr., Dept. W. Va.

1 inch to 4 miles. 45 x 33. Manuscript. Yellow, orange, and green lines distinguish the three expeditions. Roads in red and drainage features in blue. Map also shows

names of some residents and railroads. Relief is indicated by shading. RG 77: G 123-2.

2.260. [Map of area in the vicinity of Berkeley Springs.]

1 inch to about 2⅓ miles. 8 x 13. Manuscript. Roads in red and drainage features in blue. Map also shows some relief by shading and hachures, fords and ferries across the Potomac River, and names of a few residents. Notes give information about the trafficability of the area for troops and the loyalty and trustworthiness of the residents. Noted and signed, "Approved, James W. Abert, Capt., Top. Engrs." RG 77: G 463-16.

2.261. Map of Clarksburg and vicinity. Surveyed and drawn under the direction of 1st Lieut. John R. Meigs, U.S. Engrs., by Henry Topping, Asst. Engr., Septr. 1863.

1 inch to about ⅔ mile. "1:18,635 approx" added in pencil. 14 x 20. Published. Shows roads and railroads, coal banks, names of residents in the vicinity, wooded areas, orchards, fields, and grasslands. Government stables are located outside of the town. RG 77: WDMC 4-W. Va.

2.262. Sketch of the vicinity of Harpers Ferry, [W.] Va., by Wm. Luce, Oct. 1862.

1 inch to about 850 feet. 22 x 26. Manuscript. Roads in red. Map also shows defenses, a burnt bridge and rifleworks, railroads, buildings, and names of a few residents. Relief is shown by hachures and form lines. RG 77: F 78.

2.263. Preliminary Sketch of the Defences [of Harpers Ferry and vicinity] on Maryland Heights and of Adjacent Country. Surveyed from Aug. 28th to Octb. 6th, 1863, by Capt. N. Michler, Corps of Engineers, U.S.A., & John E. Weyss, Major, Ky. Vol. Drawn by Th. von Kamecke.

1 inch to ⅛ mile. 60 x 68. Manuscript. Drainage features in blue; defenses and triangulation lines in red. Relief is indicated by form lines, and some elevations are given. Buildings and names of some residents are included. RG 77: F 106.

2.264. Martinsburg [and vicinity].

1 inch to about 225 yards. 13 x 12. Manuscript. City blocks and outlying buildings in red, roads in brown, and drainage features in blue. Map also shows some relief by shading, character of the land, industrial sites, and names of a few residents. Noted and signed: "Approved, James W. Abert, Capt., US. Army, T. E., Dec. 1861." RG 77: G 463-11.

2.265. Plan of the Battlefield at New Creek, W. Va., August 4th, 1864.

1 inch to ¼ mile. 14 x 19. Manuscript. Roads in yellow, drainage features in blue, and relief in brown shading.

Red and blue lines probably indicate troop positions, but these are unidentified. Map also shows locations of Forts Fuller and Piano, buildings, and the railroad line. Initialed "F. M. K." RG 77: Z 125½.

2.266. Sketch of the Site of the O[pe]rations of the 10th, 11th, & 12th, July 1861, at *Rich Mountain* near Beverly, Randolph Co., [West] Virginia, between the U.S. Forces under Major Gen. Geo. McClellan and the Confederate troops, by Lieut. O. M. Poe, U.S. Topl. Engrs.

1 inch to 500 feet. 19 x 23. Manuscript. Shows defenses, the Confederate positions, proposed position for the Federal battery, and the place where the dead were buried. A penciled name, "Camp Garnett," appears near the defensive work. Noted, "Accompanying Memoir dated Augt. 18th, 1861, and a letter dated 3rd Septr. 1861." RG 77: G 63.

2.267. [Parts of Wood and Pleasants Counties and adjacent parts of Ohio.]

1 inch to about ½ mile. 42 x 61 (2 sections). Manuscript. Drainage features in blue. Map also shows roads, railroads, names of residents, a corral near Parkersburg, and islands in the Ohio River. Relief is indicated by shading. RG 77: Z 124.

INDEX

This is an index to proper names, places, and battles that appear in part I and part II. The numbers refer to entries, not pages.

A

Ashland, Ky., hospital plans, 1.158-f
Asmussen, C. W., 2.64
Atchafalaya Basin, La., route of campaign in spring of
    1863, 1.64, 2.88
Atkinson, W. G., 2.230
Atlanta, Ga., 1.190
    Battle and siege, 1.51, 2.60, 2.61
    Defenses, 1.18, 1.32, 1.51, 1.54, 1.55, 2.55
    March from to Savannah, 1.32, 1.52
    Street plan, 1.18, 2.54
Atlanta Campaign, 1.1, 1.12, 1.32, 1.51, 1.180
    Epochs, 1.50, 2.56 through 2.60
Atlantic coast, 1.165
    Extent of blockade, 1.174, 2.2
Atlas of *Military Maps illustrating the Operations of the Armies
    of the Potomac and James May 4th 1864 to April 9th 1865
    including Battlefields*, 1.137
Atlas of the Battlefield of Antietam, 1.72
*Atlas of the Battlefields of Chickamauga, Chattanooga, and
    Vicinity, An*, 1.4
*Atlas to Accompany the Official Records of the Union and
    Confederate Armies*, 1.8, 1.9
Augur, Major General, headquarters in Washington, D.C.,
    2.44
Augusta, Ga., 1.190
Augusta, Maine, 1.158-h
Augusta County, Va., 1.134
Austin, Tex., vicinity, 1.131
Averell, W. W., routes of expeditions, 1.28, 1.154, 2.250,
    2.259
Averysboro, N.C., battlefield, 1.32, 1.96, 2.143

B

Babcock, O. E., 1.60
Bache, A. D., 2.1, 2.2, 2.39, 2.46, 2.110, 2.170, 2.214
Bache, Hartman, 1.95, 1.107
Bache, J., 2.47
Bachelder, John B., 1.2, 1.102, 2.161
Bailey's Dam, Red River, La., 1.19, 1.65, 1.69
Baker, Fort, D.C., defense of Washington, 1.45
Baker's Creek, Miss., 1.193
Baltimore, Md.
    Defenses, 1.22, 1.71, 1.75
    Quartermaster installations, 1.158-i
Baltimore and Ohio-Railroad, 1.29, 1.71
Baltimore and Washington Railroad, 1.71
Baltimore County, Md., 1.22, 1.71, 1.75, 2.105
Bamberger, Solomon, 1.143
Bankhead, Fort, Tex., 1.130, 1.133
Banks, N. P., 1.46, 2.19, 2.230
    In Louisiana and Mississippi, 1.64 through 1.66, 1.68,
        1.181, 2.84, 2.88, 2.93, 2.96
    In Texas, 1.132, 1.159, 2.202, 2.205, 2.206, 2.209
Banks, Fort, La., 1.69
Baptist Gap, Tenn., 2.188
Barnard, J. G., 1.44, 1.45, 1.145, 1.149 through 1.151,
    2.40, 2.92, 2.235, 2.245, 2.257
Barnard, Fort, Va., defense of Washington, 1.151

Barnwell's report, 1.196
Barrancas, Fort, Fla., 1.47
Bates, Battery, Ky., 1.61
Bathschweiter, F., 2.71
Baton Rouge, La.
    Battlefield and city, 1.66, 2.90
    Defenses, 1.19, 1.66, 1.69
    State House, 1.66
Baton Rouge to Port Hudson, La., Union positions, 1.66,
    2.89
Bay Point, S.C.
    Coal depot, 1.108
    Fortifications, 1.110, 1.183
Bayard, Fort, D.C., defense of Washington, 1.45
Bayley, G. W. R., 1.62
Bayou Goula, La., 1.68
Bayou Lafourche, La., 1.67
Bayou St. John, fortifications, 1.69
Bayou Teche, La.
    Expedition, 1.64, 2.88
    Field of operation, 1.19
Beaufort, S.C., 1.7, 1.108, 2.167
    Defenses and entrenchments, 1.108, 1.110, 2.168
    Operations inland, 1.109
Beaufort District, S.C., 1.108, 2.169
Beaufort Harbor, N.C., 1.95, 1.159, 1.171
Beaufort River, S.C., mouth of, 1.172
Beauregard, G. T., 1.20, 1.143, 2.230
Beauregard, Battery and Fort, Charleston Harbor, S.C.,
    1.107, 1.110, 1.196
Beauregard, Fort, Bay Point, S.C., 1.183
Becker, A. H. A., 2.173
Belfast, Maine, 1.70
Bell, L., 2.252
Belmont, Mo., battlefield, 1.88, 1.194
Benham, H. W., 1.75, 2.234
Bennett, Fort, Va., defense of Washington, 1.151
Benton Barracks, St. Louis, Mo., 1.89, 1.158-m, 2.139
Bentonsville, N.C., battlefield, 1.32, 1.96, 2.143, 2.145
Berkeley County, W. Va., 1.25, 1.101, 1.140, 1.153,
    2.156
Berkeley Springs, W. Va., vicinity, 1.153, 2.260
Bermuda Hundred, Va., 1.137, 1.152
    Fortifications and signal tower, 1.151
    Union and Confederate lines, 1.149, 1.150
Berry, Camp, Maine, 1.158-h
Berry, Fort, Va., defense of Washington, 1.151
Berwick Bay, La., fort at, 1.69
Berwick City, La., 1.64; site of proposed camp, 2.91
Bethesda Church, Va., battlefield, 1.149, 2.252
Bienvenue Battery, La., 1.69
Big Black River Bridge, Miss.
    Entrenchments in vicinity, 2.119
    Site of battle, 1.84, 2.125
Big Creek Gap, Tenn., 2.188
Big River, Mo., railroad bridge, 1.90
Bird Key, Fla., fortifications, 1.47
Bishop, Fort, Ky., 1.61
Bisland, Fort, La., battlefield, 1.19, 1.64

Mitchelville, Hilton Head Island, S.C., 1.108, 2.174
Mobile, Ala., defenses and occupation, 1.36, 1.37, 2.19, 2.20, 2.22
Mobile and Ohio Railroad, 1.112
    Cavalry raid on in northern Mississippi, 1.83, 2.123
Mobile Bay, Ala., 1.166, 1.188
    Defenses, 1.36, 1.37, 1.161, 2.18, 2.19
    Siege operations at Spanish Fort, 1.3, 1.37, 2.21
Mobile River, Ala., obstructions at mouth, 1.36
Molitor, Edw., 2.13
Monett's Bluff, La., engagement, 1.65
Monroe, Fort, Va., 1.151
Montauk, steamer, 1.180
Monterey, Tenn., country south to Corinth, Miss., 1.31
Montgomery, Ala., 1.158-a
Montgomery, Fort, N.Y., 1.94
Montgomery County, Md., 1.25, 1.71, 1.75, 2.110, 2.111
Montpelier, Vt., hospital, 1.158-w
Moore, R., 2.76
Moore, Fort, Tex., 1.133
Morehead City, N.C., defenses, 1.98, 1.159
Morgan, G. W., 1.119, 2.186
Morgan, Fort, Ala., 1.37
    Siege operations against, 1.19, 2.23
Morgan County, Ala., 1.34
Morganton, Tenn., 1.114
Morganzia, La.
    Defenses, 1.69
    Road from to Semmsport, 1.65
Morhardt, Francis, 1.120, 2.201
Morris, Walter J., 2.72
Morris, Battery, D.C., defense of Washington, 1.45
Morton, Camp, Ind., 1.158-d
Morton, Fort, Tenn., 1.126
Morton, Fort, Va., defense of Washington, 1.151
Moscow, Tenn., vicinity, 1.113
Moultrie, Fort, S.C., 1.107, 1.110
Mount Sterling, Ky., defenses, 1.61
Mouton, Fort, Ala., 1.37
Muldraugh's Hill, Ky., 1.61
Munfordville and vicinity, Ky.
    Action at Rowlett's Station, 1.59, 2.81
    Defenses of railroad bridge, 1.61
    Quartermaster installations, 1.158-f
Murfreesboro and vicinity, Tenn., 1.17, 1.114, 1.126, 1.197
    Battle, 1.120.
    See also Stones River, Tenn.
Murray County, Ga., 1.18
Myer, Fort, Va., 1.151

N

Nachtigall, Herrmann, 2.190
Napoleonville, La., Quartermaster installations, 1.158-g
Narrows, The, New York Harbor, 1.94
Nashville, Tenn., 1.197
    Battlefields, 1.3, 1.17, 1.125, 2.197
    Defenses and fortifications, 1.126

Quartermaster installations, 1.158-v
    Vicinity, 1.17, 1.114
Nashville and Decatur Railroad, 1.112
Nat. Lyon, Fort, Va., 1.151
Natchez and vicinity, Miss., defenses, 1.85, 1.86
Natchitoches, La., vicinity, 1.63, 1.65
Neches and Sabine Rivers, Tex., country between, 1.128
Negley, Fort, Tenn., 1.126
Nelson, Camp, Ky.
    Defenses and plans, 1.60, 1.61, 2.76, 2.77
    Quartermaster installations, 1.61, 1.158-f
Nelson, Fort, Ky., 1.61
Nelson, Fort, Tex., 1.133
Nelson County, Va., 1.134
New Albany, Ind., Quartermaster installations, 1.158-d
New Bedford Harbor, Mass., defenses and Quartermaster installations, 1.77, 1.158-j
New Bern, N.C., defenses, 1.97, 1.98, 2.150
New Creek, W. Va., battlefield, 1.154, 2.265
New Creek Station, W. Va., 1.158-y
New Hampshire, Quartermaster installations, 1.158-n
New Haven and vicinity, Conn., 1.41, 1.158-b
New Hope, Ga., and vicinity, 1.190
New Hope Church, Ga., battlefield, 2.58
New Jersey
    Coast charts, 1.165
    Quartermaster installations, 1.158-o
New Madrid and vicinity, Mo.
    Fortifications, 1.88, 1.89, 1.91, 2.135
    Military operations, 1.88, 2.134
New Mexico, Military Department of, 1.30
New Mexico Territory, general information and operations near Fort Craig, 1.93
New Orleans, La.
    Approaches and defenses, 1.19, 1.69, 2.93 through 2.95
    Quartermaster installations, 1.158-g
    Vicinity, 1.68
New Orleans, Jackson, and Great Southern Railway, Miss. and La., 1.79
New River, S.C., 1.196
New York
    Defenses and fortifications, 1.94
    Quartermaster installations, 1.158-p
New York Bay and Harbor, N.Y., defenses, 1.94
New York City, N.Y., Quartermaster installations, 1.158-p
Newark, N.J., hospital, 1.158-o
Newburyport and vicinity, Mass., 1.77
Newnan, Ga., 1.190
Newport, Camp, Md., 1.158-i
Newport, Ky., defenses, 1.60, 1.61, 1.158-f, 2.78
Niagara, Fort, N.Y., 1.94
Nicholson, George B., 2.77
Nicholson, W. L., 2.12, 2.214
Noble, Camp, Ind., 1.158-d
Nolensville-Chapel Hill Turnpike, Tenn., country adjacent, 1.114, 2.198
Nolichucky River, Tenn., 1.115
Norfolk and vicinity, Va., defenses, 1.151

S

T